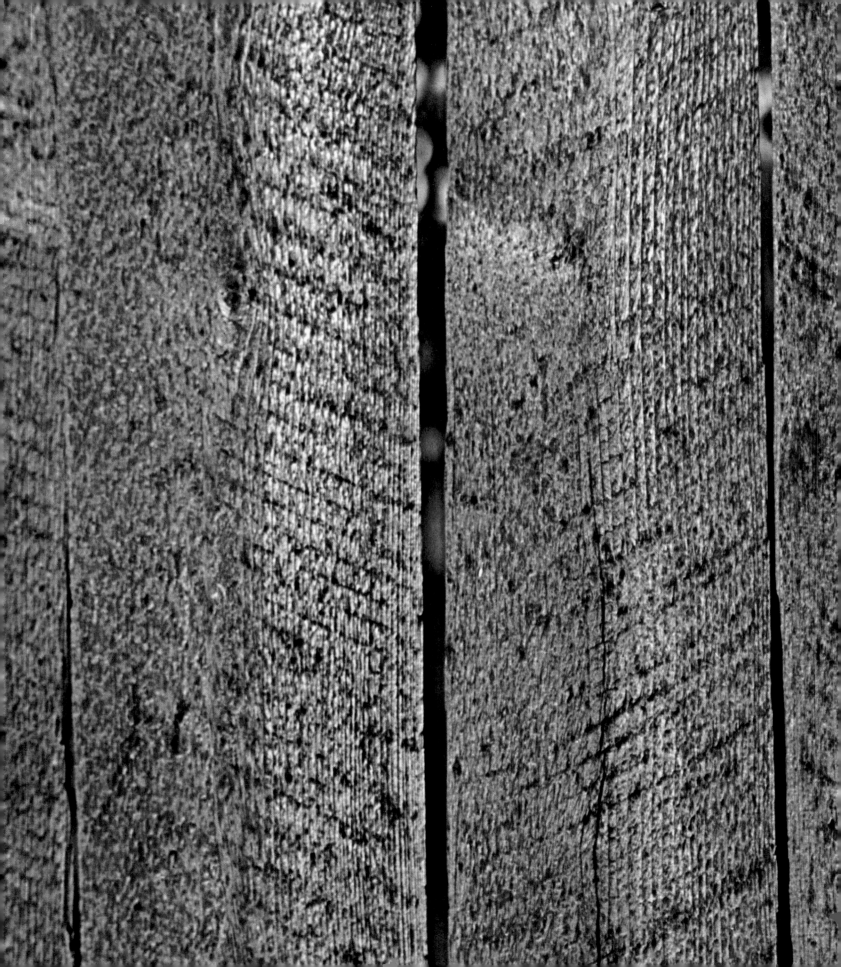

THE FAMILY CREATIVE WORKSHOP

9

Lamps and Shades, Lapidary
Leaded Glass, Leather Working
Lighted Indoor Gardens
Linoleum and Woodcuts
Machine Stitchery, Macramé, Magic
Maps and Pathfinding

Plenary Publications International, Inc.
New York and Amsterdam

Published by Plenary Publications International Incorporated 300 East 40 Street, New York, N.Y. 10016, for the Blue Mountain Crafts Council.

Library of Congress Catalog Card Number: 73-89331. Complete set International Standard Book Number: 0-88459-021-6. Volume 9 International Standard Book Number: 0-88459-008-9 Second Printing

Manufactured in the United States of America. Printed and bound by the W. A. Krueger Company, Brookfield, Wisconsin.

Composition by David E. Seham Associates, Inc., New York, N.Y.

Printing preparation by Lanman Lithoplate Company.

Publishers:
Plenary Publications International, Incorporated 300 East 40 Street New York, New York 10016

Steven Schepp
EDITOR

Bonnie Schiffer
Peggy Streep
ADMINISTRATIVE ASSISTANTS

Jerry Curcio
PRODUCTION MANAGER

Originating editor of the series:
Allen Davenport Bragdon

Editorial preparation:
Tree Communications, Inc. 250 Park Avenue South New York, New York 10003

Rodney Friedman
EDITORIAL DIRECTOR

Ronald Gross
DESIGN DIRECTOR

Paul Levin
DIRECTOR OF PHOTOGRAPHY

Donal Dinwiddie
CONSULTING EDITOR

Jill Munves
TEXT EDITOR

Sonja Douglas
ART DIRECTOR

Rochelle Lapidus
ASSOCIATE DESIGNER

Betty Friedman
ADMINISTRATIVE MANAGER

Barnet Friedman
COPYREADER

Lucille O'Brien
EDITORIAL PRODUCTION

Editors for this volume:
Donal Dinwiddie
LAPIDARY

Michael Donner
MAPS AND PATHFINDING

Linda Hetzer
LINOLEUM AND WOODCUTS

Nancy Bruning Levine
LEADED GLASS
LEATHER WORKING

Jill Munves
LIGHTED INDOOR GARDENS

Marilyn Nierenberg
LAMPS AND SHADES

Marilyn Ratner
MACHINE STITCHERY
MAGIC

Mary Grace Skurka
MACRAMÉ

Contributing illustrators:
Debi Bracken
Marina Givotovsky
Patricia Lee
Lynn Matus
Sally Shimizu

Photo and illustration credits:
LIGHTED INDOOR GARDENS: Charts on fluorescent and incandescent lighting, page 1082, courtesy of Lamp Business Division, General Electric Company. MACHINE STITCHERY: Photograph, page 1104, courtesy of the Museum of the American Indian. MAPS AND PATHFINDING: Perspective view and topographic map of imaginary landscape, page 1142, courtesy of U.S. Geological Survey.

The Project-Evaluation Symbols appearing in the title heading at the beginning of each project have these meanings:

Range of approximate cost:

¢ Low: under $5 or free and found natural materials

$ Medium: about $10

$$ High: above $15

Estimated time to completion for an unskilled adult:

Hours

Days

Weeks

Suggested level of experience:
Child alone

Supervised child or family project

Unskilled adult

Specialized prior training

Tools and equipment:
Small hand tools

Large hand and household tools

Specialized or powered equipment

On the cover:
Natural-color linen belt (center) is a combination of three macramé knots; sash (left and right) of linen rug warp and pearl cotton matches a dress yoke. See Macramé entry, beginning on page 1116. Photograph by Paul Levin.

Contents and craftspeople for Volume 9

William Brauer studied and taught printmaking in New York City. He lives in Waitsfield, Vermont, painting and doing etchings. He has shown his etchings in the "New Talent in Printmaking" show at the Associated American Artists Gallery in New York, and his work is in the collection of the Brooklyn Museum. He and his wife, a weaver, raise sheep and are remodeling their farm buildings with found objects.

LAMPS AND SHADES
Light Up Your Life

Ancient Greeks hung illuminating oil pots from ceilings and mounted torches on walls to light their households. These primitive artificial light sources enabled them to continue the day's activities into the evening. Given that beginning, it was logical that designers of early gas and electric fixtures made them look like candles and torches in their holders. But in the last century, art and science have joined to develop imaginative lamps, both fixed and portable, that do not look anything like candles and can be used to illuminate a small area, as for reading or sewing, to spotlight a piece of art or a theatrical scene and even to brighten an entire room.

If decorative lighting effects intrigue you, make a hanging lantern from a punctured tin can (opposite), thus creating fascinating patterns of light on your walls and ceilings. Early American tinkers pierced their wares in this fashion, and in Mexico, such punched tinware is still being made by native craftsmen using traditional designs handed down for centuries. Unusual lamp bases can be made from collectors' items like the Superior Tartar tin on page 1035. Or they can be handcrafted from a wide variety of materials including the glass cylinder lined with decoupage on page 1036. Shades, too, have great importance in a decorating scheme. If you would like to make a fashionable suede shade for a portable lamp, instructions appear on page 1038, or, if you want to salvage an old shade, you can do so with the stretchable fabric cover described on page 1039. Craftnotes on pages 1033 and 1034 will help you assemble a lamp in a safe and approved manner.

Jewelry, Lapidary and Metalwork
Tin lantern

In our Vermont farmhouse, we needed a lighting fixture over the kitchen table, our family gathering place. In one afternoon we made a pierced metal shade (opposite) from a large tin can that had been discarded at a local restaurant. We soaked the label off and used a razor blade to remove remaining glue. When the can was dry, we punched the images and patterns on the sides and top (originally the bottom) of the can. When the lamp is turned on, light floods from the open bottom onto the table, while soft rays of light filter out of the sides and top, casting intriguing patterns on the walls and ceiling.

Tin cans for such lamps can be found in your own cast-offs or obtained from a nearby restaurant. We used a size No. 12 can that had held pickles to make the hanging lantern pictured; the can measured 6 3/16 by 8¾ inches. A 6 3/16-by-7-inch, No. 10 can (like a 3-pound coffee can) will do as well. After removing labels, you may find that some cans are silver-colored, others bronze. The printing on some cans can be obliterated with the punched design, or it can be incorporated into your design for its pop-art value. The surface of the can selected also affects the end-product. Cans with ridged sides lend themselves to geometric designs worked in the direction of the ridges, while smooth-sided cans are better for pictures.

Most of the tools needed to make perforations can be found around the house. Soda-can openers form pie-wedge shapes around the top edge. A cold chisel leaves small slits or large slashes, depending on how hard it is hammered. Rectangular punctures can be made with an old screwdriver. Metal punches, reamers, nails and spikes make round holes. Tapping lightly on a nail or punch with a hammer can produce tiny decorative indentations without puncturing the can.

As you become adept at such tin crafting, you will want a pair of tin snips for cutting more elaborate designs. They come in a wide assortment of styles. Tin snips with straight or curved blades range from a 9-inch lightweight model to a 14-inch heavy-duty tool. Heavy-duty snips require less effort but cost more.

Before piercing the design you will need to wedge wood 2-by-4s into the can or fill it with sand. Either will keep the can from being crushed as you hammer on the

A free-form design of simple motifs was punched in a recycled tin can to make this lantern. Alternate designs you might try are shown in Figure A and photograph 3, page 1032.

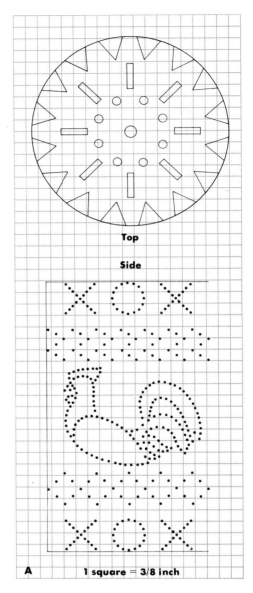

Top

Side

A   1 square = 3/8 inch

Figure A: To duplicate the round pattern for the lantern top, pierce the tin with a can opener, screwdriver and nails. Make a ⅜-inch hole in the exact center with a metal punch; the lantern will be suspended from this point. The rectangular pattern for a side of the lantern combines dotted borders of X's and O's with zigzag bands enclosing a rooster design. To enlarge the top pattern to a diameter of 6 3/16 inches and the side pattern to a height of 8¾ inches, transfer the patterns onto a grid of ⅜-inch squares. Prick holes in the enlarged pattern, tape the patterns on your tin can, and transfer the designs with a marker or a grease pencil worked through holes. Move and retape the side pattern each quarter turn around the can.

piercing tools. If you use sand for support, however, you will need to place the can with the open end facing up and work the side designs upside down. Then you will need to cover the open end of the can before upending it so that you can pierce the top. I prefer the wood-block method (photograph 1). After I have forced as many lengths of 2-by-4s into the can as will possibly fit, I pierce the can top. Then I use a hammer to flatten the can sides to facilitate piercing them. Then, when the design is completed, I can bend the can back into a reasonably round shape with a small rubber mallet, tapping from the inside.

You can copy your design from books illustrating Early American or Mexican crafts, use the designs shown in Figure A, or create your own free-hand designs as I did. If you create your own, before punching any holes, use a grease pencil or a felt-tip pen to sketch the design on the can so you can see how you like it. If you use wood blocks for support, you should pierce the top of the can first (photograph 2). Enlarge the pattern for the top, Figure A, onto tracing paper and prick the tracing wherever you want to pierce the tin. Attach the tracing to the can with masking tape and press the felt-tip pen's marker onto the holes to leave guide dots on the metal surface. When all the dots have been transferred, remove the tracing. Use the can opener for the triangular holes around the edge. For the ring of openings around the center, use either a screwdriver (if you want squared-off edges, Figure A) or a cold chisel (if you want slashes, photographs 2 and 3). Use a center punch or reamer to make the ⅜-inch hole in the center of the top (photograph 2). A threaded tubing ⅜ inch in diameter and 1¼ inches long will go through this hole. This hole must be centered or the lantern will not hang straight.

1: To keep a tin from being crushed as holes are punched, wedge scraps of wood inside.

2: Use a can opener to make triangular holes around the edge, and a cold chisel for slashes.

3: Remove wood blocks and hold the can up to the light to make sure that holes are large enough.

4: Reinsert the wood blocks inside the can, then hammer sides of the container flat.

As your work progresses hold the can up to the light from time to time to see if the holes are large enough to create an interesting pattern on walls and ceiling (photograph 3). If you are using wood blocks, flatten sides with a hammer (photograph 4). Then sketch your own penciled designs on the sides or enlarge the rooster, zigzag and XOX patterns (Figure A) onto tracing paper. Transfer the pricked pattern onto the sides as you did on the top and puncture the dots. Reshape the sides of the can with a rubber mallet. Any pencil or pen marks that remain can be removed with a tissue or be washed off with a damp cloth. For information on installing a light fixture inside the lantern, see Craftnotes opposite.

CRAFTNOTES: WIRING AN OVERHEAD ELECTRICAL FIXTURE

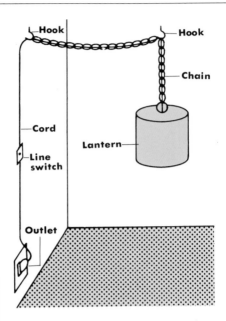

Hook
Hook
Chain
Cord
Lantern
Line switch
Outlet

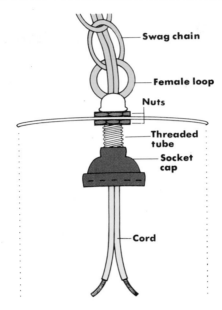

Swag chain
Female loop
Nuts
Threaded tube
Socket cap
Cord

To assemble the electric unit in the hanging lantern on page 1031, start by measuring the length of 18 SPT thermoplastic lamp cord with molded plug attached and the length of swag chain that you need (above). Allow enough cord length so you can thread the cord through the draped swag chain that will hold the lantern and run it down the wall to an outlet. (Installing a ceiling outlet and attaching the lamp to it is a job for an electrician.) The swag chain (with an end link that opens) is usually metallic, but electrical cord comes in a variety of colors to blend with your ceiling and walls. Or you can get the translucent kind that is quite inconspicuous. Other necessities are: a socket without a switch; ⅜-inch threaded tubing, 1¼ inches long; one ⅜-inch loop to connect tube and chain; two nuts and washers; knife; wire stripper; small screwdriver; two decorative hooks 2 inches in length; pliers; 75-watt bulb; and line switch.

Screw the loop onto one end of the threaded tube, then twist one nut and washer up from the opposite end until it meets the loop. Insert the tube through the hole in the center of the lantern top; work the lantern up against the nut. Hold the lantern from the inside by tightening the second nut and washer against the lantern. Disassemble the switchless light

bulb socket and screw only the socket cap (it twists off the main part) onto the tube; tighten cap's holding screw. Use a knife to separate the two wires in the end of the lamp cord for a distance of 2 inches. Use a wire stripper to remove ½ inch of plastic coating from each split cord end. Twist exposed wire strands tightly. Open a link at one end of the swag chain and close it over the loop. Weave the lamp cord through the chain, and pass the stripped ends through the tube and out of the socket cap.

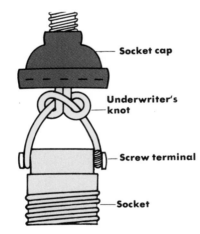

Socket cap
Underwriter's knot
Screw terminal
Socket

Before connecting the wires to the screw terminals in the socket, make what is called an Underwriters' knot. This knot reduces tension at the screw connections if the cord is accidentally pulled. To make the knot pass each end of wire through a loop in the other wire, with one end pas-

sing in front of the main cord and the other in back as illustrated. The knot will keep the wires well separated. Slip the socket core out of its metal housing. Bend each exposed end of twisted wire into a hook shape. Fit each hook around a terminal screw in the direction that the screw will turn, and tighten the screw. Then slip the socket core with connected wires back into the socket housing. Snap the socket cap and assembled socket together until you hear a click. Gently pull any slack in the cord up through the hole in the top of the loop.

Screw a decorative hook in the ceiling directly above the place where you want the lantern to be, as shown at far left. Attach the chain to this hook so the lantern is at the right height, then screw another hook into the ceiling near where it meets the wall above an outlet. Drape the balance of the chain and attach it to this second hook. Let the remaining electrical cord hang loosely down the wall. Making sure the lantern is not plugged in, pick a place on the cord at a convenient height and attach a line switch.

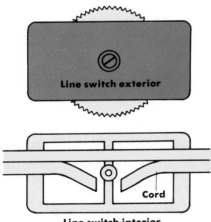

Line switch exterior

Cord

Line switch interior

To open a line switch, remove the holding screw and small nut. Use a knife to make a 2-inch slit in the middle of the cord. Leave one side of the cord intact but cut the other wire in the middle of the slit. Run the uncut wire through the open track in the switch, and wedge the cut ends into the divided channel. Replace the top of the unit that contains the switch and sharp metal points that will pierce the plastic coating of the cut ends of cord and make contact with the copper wire inside. Tighten bolt and nut. Screw a bulb into the socket, plug the cord into an outlet, and flick the line switch on and off to make sure everything works.

CRAFTNOTES: WIRING A TABLE LAMP

A table lamp is constructed by assembling three essential parts: the lamp base, the mounting post that holds the socket, and the socket itself. The base should be heavy enough to insure the stability of the lamp. It can be made from many materials, so it may be the most interesting part of the design. The cord that carries electricity is attached to the socket and runs down through the mounting post and out the back of the lamp base near its bottom. The cord will not be seen from the front.

Other materials and tools needed are: electric drill with ⅛-, ⅜-, and ¾-inch bits long enough to drill any hole your lamp requires; a ⅜-inch threaded tube the right length for your lamp base; 6 to 15 feet of No. 18 SPT thermoplastic lamp cord with a molded plug attached; wire stripper; knife; screwdriver; two nuts and washers that fit the threaded pipe. Depending upon your design, you may also need these stock parts, from hardware or electrical supply stores: harp locked into a saddle to hold the shade; neck piece to serve as a spacer below the saddle; vase cap (available in many diameters to cover the top of a wide-mouthed container used as a base); pre-drilled wooden or metal mounting blocks for the bottom of the lamp base; and a socket. A standard size socket for a three-way bulb with a push button or key switch is recommended for a lamp large enough to be used for reading.

Start by drilling a ⅜-inch hole from top to bottom through the center of the lamp base (or through top vase cap and bottom mount if the lamp base is hollow). (This step is not necessary for the hollow glass-tube base used for the decoupage lamp on page 1036.) If the bottom mounting block is not pre-drilled, drill another ⅜-inch hole through its center, use a ¾-inch bit to widen the mouth of the hole from the bottom to make a small recess for the holding nut. Then drill a ⅛-inch hole into the back edge of this block for wire to intersect with the ⅜-inch hole (see side view of mount at top right). Screw one end of the threaded tube into the block and secure it from underneath with a washer and nut. If the base is hollow, you can relieve pressure of the base on the mounting block with a nut and washer on the threaded tube just beneath the hole in the top of the lamp base as indicated in sketch at right above. With the front of the base facing you and the ⅛-inch hole in the mounting block away from you, lower the base over the threaded tube and rest it on the mounting block.

Install the neck (bottom right) or a vase cap (see Figure B, page 1037) next on the threaded tube, then a neck spacer. Fit the saddle over the threaded tubing to receive the harp. Separate the socket into its four parts. Squeeze the socket at the point marked "press" to release the socket shell from the cap. Screw the socket cap—which will be at the bottom of the socket—onto the threaded tube on top of the saddle. Now you are ready to thread the SPT cord through the ⅛-inch hole in the mounting block and up the ⅜-inch threaded tube through the socket cap. Follow the Craftnotes on page 1033 to wire and reassemble the socket. Screw in a light bulb, plug in the cord and test the switch. If all is in order, lock prongs of the harp into the saddle. Place the shade frame on the harp and hold it either with a finial nut and washer or a decorative finial. You can make a finial that will be a part of your lamp design, or you can buy a manufactured one at any electrical supply shop. After years of use, socket switches, contacts and cords may become worn. When any lamp flickers or refuses to light and the bulb is good, it is a signal that the wiring may be frayed or the switch faulty.

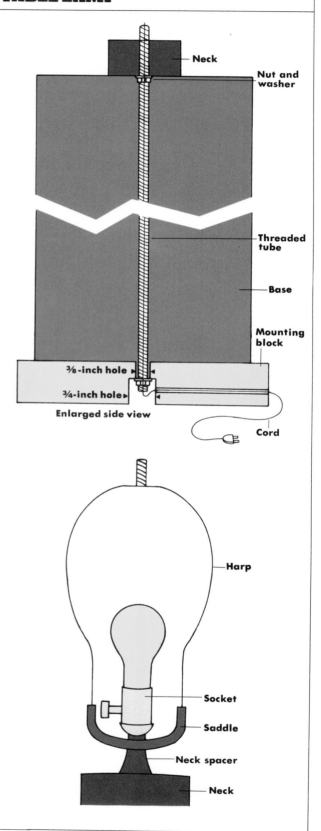

Neck

Nut and washer

Threaded tube

Base

Mounting block

⅜-inch hole

¾-inch hole

Enlarged side view

Cord

Harp

Socket

Saddle

Neck spacer

Neck

Jewelry, Lapidary and Metalwork
Canister lamp   ¢ ▣ ☺ ✈

A handsome canister lamp can be made from an antique tin (the Superior Tartar can pictured at right, below was made about 1890) or from a new, brightly decorated container. I bought the Superior Tartar tin at a country auction but if you enjoy browsing through antique shops you will be surprised by the number of similar canisters you can locate. If your taste leans toward pop art, you may find that your grocer stocks nuts, imported cooking oils, olives, tobacco, coffee or candies in tins fancy enough to make interesting lamps.

Once you find the canister, you are well on your way to having a new lamp. Necessary tools are: wood saw; drill with ⅛-, ⅜-, and ¾-inch bits; and a vise. For a lamp like that shown at right below, use a 2-inch-thick piece of poplar, walnut or mahogany for the base; a 1-by-2-inch block of the same wooden material and a ⅛-by-3½-by-5½-inch piece of black plastic for the neck (or a metal lamp neck can be used); and a 1-inch cube of wood for a finial. Other supplies needed are: 1 pint of spray lacquer in a color that harmonizes with the canister base; a standard 3-way socket; harp with saddle bracket; two nuts and washers; and a threaded metal tube about 3½ inches longer than the canister is deep. The Superior Tartar canister is 10½ inches tall, the base is 2 inches high and the neck is 1 inch high. These dimensions required threaded tubing 14 inches long.

Drill ⅜-inch holes through the top and bottom of the canister at center points. Center the canister on top of the 2-inch-thick wood block, and mark the shape of the canister bottom on the wood with a pencil. Mark and cut the wood base to allow a ½-inch projection on all sides. The lamp in the photograph has a 2-by-5-by-7-inch wood base. Drill and assemble the lamp as described in the Craftnotes on page 1034.

If you do not use a ready-made part for the lamp neck beneath the socket, you can make your own from a 1-by-2-inch wood block. Beneath this block, I put a shiny piece of black plastic, since I felt it harmonized with the metal container. Both the wood block and plastic have a ⅜-inch hole drilled in their centers for the threaded tube to pass through (photograph 5). Also drill a ⅜-inch hole one-third of the way into the center of the finial cube. Photograph 6 shows a vase cap with a ⅜-inch hole.

It is essential to the success of the lamp design that the shape, color and texture of the mounting block, the neck piece and the finial on top complement the lamp base. Choose spray lacquer, paint or wood stain that will do this. Give the wooden pieces two coats of finish before assembling the lamp. I have found black lacquer to work well with most designs.

A tin may buckle if there is too much weight on top of it. The washer and nut beneath the top hole and the plastic cap are positioned to ease that pressure. Instructions for making the red suede shade are on page 1038.

John Nowlin majored in the performing arts when he attended the University of Texas. A part-time job with a lamp company led to his present vocation. In New York and San Francisco, John and his associates design one-of-a-kind lamps, often using found objects such as ceramics and the old canister below.

This antique tin once containing creme of tartar makes an attractive canister lamp. To harmonize with the colors of the deer motif, the mount neck and finial were painted black and a red suede shade was trimmed with black velvet.

5: A piece of black plastic and the painted wood neck with ⅜-inch center holes are fitted over the threaded tube until they rest on the canister top.

6: A vase cap and neck were lowered over a threaded tube to support the socket and harp of the lamp in the color photograph on page 1036.

1035

Glass and Plastics
Potichomania lamp

*Several years ago a demonstration of de-
coupage under glass in a New York department store started Virginia Graef, an aspir-
ing painter, on a new career. She began to
read books about decoupage on glass which
aroused her interest in antique prints. Then
she asked John Nowlin, a professional lamp
designer, to assemble a lamp using a base
she had made. They were so pleased with the
results that they are now partners in Nowlin
and Associates, makers of custom lamps in
New York and San Francisco.*

7: The glass lamp chimney shown at left or the
wide-mouthed jar at right can be turned into lamp
bases with interior decorations.

Potichomania—the art of imitating painted porcelain ware—can itself be imitated
with decoupage in reverse, mounted inside a clear glass or plastic cylinder or
wide-mouthed jar. Where the decoupeur carefully cuts and glues prints on top of a
smooth surface, here the prints are facing out from within the lamp base.

For this project you need a transparent lamp base with an opening large enough
to admit your hand. The smallest glass that I ever used was 3 inches wide and 6
inches tall. A glass lamp chimney, clear plastic cylinder or wide-mouthed jar can be
used (photograph 7). If you use a jar you must drill (or have drilled) a ⅜-inch hole at

Animal prints pasted against the inside of a glass cylinder form this potichomania lamp base. The
wooden mount, brass vase cap and neck as well as the porcelain finial were custom-made. To make a
colorful silk shade cover for the lamp, follow instructions on page 1039.

the center of the bottom so the threaded pipe can pass through and be attached to the mounting base. As sources of suitable prints try gift wrap, wallpaper, postcards, menus, match covers, greeting cards, old books and print shops. Thick postcards can have the back peeled off to facilitate gluing. Other essentials that you can find at an art supply or hardware store are: 8 ounces of water-soluble white glue or clear acrylic medium; small spray can of glass sealer; small can of clear varnish; 4 ounces of turpentine to clean brushes; 4 ounces of colored acrylic paint; 1-inch natural-bristle brush, and 1-inch sponge brush (choose short-handled brushes so you can manipulate them easily inside the jar); curved manicure scissors; box of plastic food wrap; tacky stick; detergent; sponges and lint-free cloth.

8: Plan your design by attaching cut prints to the outside of the glass with a tacky stick. Then glue the prints, one at a time, inside the glass wall.

9: To eliminate air bubbles and the crinkling of glued prints, press the print firmly against the glass with your fingertips.

10: Use acrylic paint and a small brush to paint the inside of the glass after the prints are in place. At least three coats of paint are needed.

Before you begin to work make sure that the glass shape is sparkling clean inside and out. Do not use any glass cleaner that leaves a film of wax. I find that detergent and warm water work the best for cleaning the inside of the glass. Dry the glass with a lint-free cloth. Once you have cut out your prints, you are ready to begin designing the lamp base.

To see how the design will look, use the tacky stick to arrange prints on the outside of the glass (photograph 8). Since the inside of the glass is slightly smaller than the outside you will have a somewhat fuller design when these prints are later fixed in place inside the glass. When you have arranged the prints to your liking, cover the outside of the glass with plastic wrap that clings to the glass, thus keeping the prints in place and clean as you work.

Put white glue inside the glass behind one of the prints, then move the print so it is inside facing out against the glue. Press the print against the glass (photograph 9). Squeeze out the excess glue with your fingers until the print adheres evenly and no air bubbles remain. Glue the entire design in place in this way. When you have finished gluing down the prints, clean the inside of the glass with a sponge dampened with warm water. Be careful not to lift the edges of any print as you clean. If that should happen, reglue the edge immediately and continue cleaning.

When the glue is dry make sure all prints are on tight. Wipe the glass with the lint-free cloth. Spray the inside with one coat of clear glass sealer and let the sealer dry. Then you are ready to paint the background color. Use a 1-inch natural-bristle brush or a small sponge brush to apply acrylic paint behind the prints (photograph 10). The first coat will not be totally opaque; traces of brush strokes will show. But they should disappear with the second coat of paint. Let each coat of paint dry overnight, continuing applications until the background is totally opaque and no brush marks are visible. When the final coat is dry, give the entire interior of the lamp two coats of clear varnish to protect the paint. A mounting disk to place beneath the glass tube and a vase cap to fit on the top can be purchased at an electrical supplier or lamp shop. (In the lamp pictured, the wooden mounting disk, brass vase cap and porcelain finial were handcrafted to my specifications.) To wire the lamp, follow the Craftnotes on pages 1033 and 1034 and refer to Figure B at right. Turn to page 1039 for instructions on how to make the fabric shade cover.

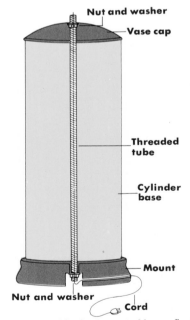

Nut and washer

Vase cap

Threaded tube

Cylinder base

Mount

Nut and washer

Cord

B

Figure B: To assemble the decorated lamp, first secure the threaded tube in the mount bottom with a nut and washer. Run electrical cord through the piping. Lower the hollow cylinder onto the mount. Thread wire through the opening in the center of the vase cap. Place the vase cap over the top rim of the cylinder. Next attach neck, saddle, harp and socket cap following Craftnotes: Wiring a Table Lamp on page 1034.

Suede was glued on to cover an inexpensive paper shade. Black velvet ribbon trims the edges.

Leathercrafts
Suede shade

Any plain paper shade can be covered with fabric and trim to add a decorator's touch to a lamp if the amount of light that comes through the shade for general illumination is not important. The bright, glossy surface and the columnar look of the tin canister pictured on page 1035 suggested the selection of smooth suede, dyed red, and black velvet ribbon to cover an A-shaped angular frame. Shade and lamp base should share a common texture, color or contour (so each goes well with the other) but you should vary one dimension of the shade, even if it is round, so its height does not equal the visual height of the lamp base. The lamp harp holding the shade should be long enough so you do not see the bulb when sitting or standing. The visual line where the lamp base meets the shade should be sharply defined.

Start with an inexpensive paper shade; it can be bought at any variety store. Shop with a list of the dimensions of the lamp base so you can visualize the proportions involved. I covered the shade pictured at left with less than 1 yard of red suede, but any leather thin enough to be folded could be used. Or you might prefer simulated suede, plastic, or fabric woven tightly enough so glue won't seep through. To be sure you buy enough material, take the shade with you as you shop. Shades that are smaller on the top than on the bottom require a diagonal cut across the material. Place the shade on an open bolt and roll it across, draping as you wrap. Buy more than enough material to cover the entire shade, even though you will notice that some draped yardage must be wasted. Any narrow ribbon, braiding or lacing can be used to trim shade edges. I find that ¼-inch black velvet ribbon adheres well to the suede and gives me a handsome combination. In addition you will need: mat knife; 36-inch metal ruler; tape measure; piece of tailor's chalk; heavy-duty shears; manicure scissors; 8 ounces of white glue; 1-inch-wide nylon bristle brush; an empty 4-ounce jar; and one dozen straight pins or clothespins.

Use tailor's chalk to trace a pattern on the reverse side of a piece of material a bit longer than the length of the larger perimeter or circumference of the shade. Cut a straight edge on one end of the material with a mat knife and metal ruler. Roll the shade over the fabric to establish the rough pattern, leaving a 2-inch margin along the top and bottom. Cut out the one-piece pattern. The only seam will be located at the back of a round shade or at a back corner of a rectangular shade. For gluing the material to the paper shade, mix one part water with two parts white glue in a jar to a consistency that can be painted on with a brush. Then apply the glue along the seam line of the paper shade with the brush. Place the shade on its side, seam up,

11: Apply white glue along the paper-shade seam. Line up the straight edge of the suede material with the seam, making sure that it overlaps the shade rims equally at top and bottom.

12: Cut off the extra material that extends beyond the shade rims. Then cut off an extra ⅛ inch of material just inside the shade rims. Trim will hide any ragged edge.

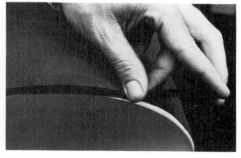

13: Cover edges of the shade with velvet ribbon. If any vertical trim is used on corners, put that on first, before the horizontal trim. Hold the trim in place with pins until the glue is dry.

and position the material on the shade, matching fabric edge to seam with excess margins extending evenly over shade rims (photograph 11). Paint on additional glue, a few inches at a time, and press the material against it. Use clothespins to hold the material in place while the glue dries. Since glue dries quickly, you will need to work your way around the shade, a bit at a time. As you return to the seam line, do not glue the last few inches and the seam overlap. Instead, first cut off the extra material even with the top and bottom of the shade. Then trim off an extra ⅛-inch at both top and bottom. The trim will cover any ragged edges (photograph 12). But before applying trim, return to the seam to complete your last cut. Allowing a ¼-inch seam overlap, cut away excess fabric on a straight line and glue.

Determine the length of trim needed for each edge of the shade and cut trim strips. If you are covering corners on a square or rectangular shade as I did, put trim on the vertical edges first, so the ribbon running horizontally will make neater borders (photograph 13). Use a toothpick instead of a brush to spread glue along the back of the ribbon. Pin strips along shade edges until glue dries.

Needlecrafts
Shade cover

¢ ▯ ⚐ ⚙

You can dress up any old or inexpensive shade with a fabric slipcover. Shade covers are practical because they can be popped on and off for easy laundering, and you can make shades from fabric that matches your upholstery for a custom look.

When you have the shade you want to cover, your local sewing center can supply you with the following materials and notions: a lightweight fabric with enough body to hold a pleat; matching thread; ¼-inch elastic seam binding; straight pins; ruler; pinking shears; and a needle or sewing machine. Multiply the circumference or perimeter of the bottom of the shade by three to determine the length of the fabric needed to allow for pleats. To determine the width needed for top and bottom openings add 5 inches to the depth of the shade. To piece strips together in a linear pattern of your own design, use these dimensions as a guide as you cut and sew.

Sew or machine stitch a ½-inch open hem along the bottom of the back side of the fabric. You will thread the elastic binding through this open hem. Cut a piece of elastic 2 inches shorter than the bottom circumference or perimeter of the shade. Feed the elastic through the open hem by gathering the hem and pushing the elastic through the open tunnel. Knot the ends of elastic together (photograph 14).

You can cover any worn or outmoded shade with a fabric cover like this. I simply ran open hems in the top and bottom of a piece of colorful silk. Elastic binding in the hems makes it easy to slip the cover on and off.

14: Thread ¼-inch-wide elastic binding through the open hem on the back side of fabric. A safety pin at the leading end may help you work it through. Knot the two ends of elastic as shown.

15: After you have sewed the side seam ⅔ of the way closed and placed the cover over the shade, gather excess fabric at top with one hand and trim. Leave enough fabric for a ½-inch top hem.

16: This is a view of the covered shade from the bottom. This effect was achieved by making the elastic band in the top seam much shorter so the top opening is relatively small.

Sew the ends of the cover together ⅔ of the way up, working from the inside of the fabric so stitches are not visible. Then slip the cover over the shade and draw the loose top together. Hold in place with one hand (photograph 15) and cut away excess fabric if necessary.

If you should have to cut off some fabric, be sure to cut on a straight line. Allow an extra ½-inch for the open hem at the top. Cut a piece of elastic 2 inches shorter than the top circumference to line up the top with bottom (photograph 16). You can also cut it shorter if you want the top to be more tightly closed. The smaller the opening the less heat and light that will escape. Hem the top edge as you did the bottom, insert elastic and tie. Finish the cover by sewing the remaining ⅓ of the back seam from the inside. Turn the cover right side out and slip it over the shade. Straighten and adjust the pleats so they are equally spaced around the shade.

For related entries see "Beachcombing," "Bottle Cutting" and "Leaded Glass."

LAPIDARY

From Drab Rocks, Radiant Gemstones

Ed Danaczko's fascination with stones and the wonders that can be worked on them began at the age of five. It has continued through his work as a field assistant for the Smithsonian Institution to his present position as a civil engineer specializing in engineering geology in New York City. At his home in Armonk, New York, Ed and his wife Eileen (a skilled craftswoman in her own right) instruct students in lapidary techniques and fashion original jewelry. The raw materials they use are the gemstone minerals they have collected on their wide-ranging prospecting trips.

Gem minerals of all sizes, patterns and colors are candidates for tumbling. Note the light green turquoises, lavender pink amethysts, patterned agates, and brown-black stones of smoky quartz (which is also called cairngorm).

The cutting and polishing of gemstones—called lapidary from the Latin *lapidarius* meaning "of stone"—was an established craft long before the Romans found a name for it. As early as 4000 B.C., Mesopotamians were engraving cylindrically shaped stones to be used as seals. At first they used hand tools to work such relatively soft materials as marble. By 3000 B.C., however, they were using wheels to help them shape and polish such hard materials as quartz and other semiprecious gemstones. Their technique paralleled that used today—the actual cutting and polishing of the stone was done by abrasives applied to the rotating tool.

Early craftsmen in Greece, Persia and Egypt were just as fascinated by the beauty of gem minerals—their brilliance, clarity, pattern and color—as the Mesopotamians had been. Indeed, they began to attribute to gemstones special powers to protect those who wore them. Thus the diamond came to mean protection against anger, the sapphire against poverty and snakebites, the ruby against unhappiness and bad dreams, and the turquoise against accidents. The practice of wearing birthstones today is a holdover from such old superstitions.

Like the Mesopotamians, other ancient lapidarists engraved stones with symbols, animal figures, and scenes from mythology. A favorite theme was the scarab —carved in a beetle shape. From this shape evolved the modern cabochon (from an old French word meaning "head"). A cabochon-cut stone is usually oval or circular in outline, and flat on the bottom with a curved top (see photograph opposite). This is the shape most popular with amateur lapidarists today.

It was not until the late Middle Ages that faceting gemstones—cutting their surfaces in a sequence of flat faces at different angles designed to catch and, like a prism, refract light—became widely practiced. These facets are what put the brilliant sparkle into diamond rings. As explained on page 1054, cutting them is a fine art. It requires knowledge of the stone's crystal structure, complex equipment and much patience (a brilliant cut has 56 cut and polished facets).

A beginner doesn't have to tackle the difficult art of faceting to enjoy the lapidary craft. He can shape and polish colorful stones by hand (page 1046), or in a relatively inexpensive tumbling machine (page 1042). With the aid of a diamond saw and a grinder/polisher (page 1045), he can cut, shape and polish a gemstone egg (page 1045) or a cabochon for a ring or brooch (page 1048) in a matter of hours. If he can't prospect for mineral specimens, he can buy inexpensive gem materials from rock and mineral shops. Some are already sliced into slabs. The slabs may be polished without sawing to make tabletop inlays, or even a set of wind chimes (page 1053). Or they may be formed into gems that fit into commercial jewelry findings or homemade settings (page 1051). The equipment used for each lapidary technique will vary, and is therefore listed with the projects that follow.

The Gem Minerals

Of 2000 or so minerals that have been identified, only a few dozen qualify as well-known gem materials. Of these, the most precious, such as diamond, emerald, ruby and sapphire, are too costly for most amateur lapidarists to work with. That still leaves a wealth of richly colored and dramatically patterned minerals—agates, jaspers, carnelians, malachites, turquoises, jades, quartzes (including amethyst and citrine) and the like—that can be fashioned into beautiful gemstones. Some are shown in the accompanying color photographs.

A good way to become familiar with the characteristics of such minerals is to study them at local natural history museums, or to attend meetings of local mineral clubs or societies. There you will find rock collectors and lapidarists who will be delighted to show you their collections. A list of these organizations is published annually in the April Rockhound Buyer's Guide issue of the *Lapidary Journal*, available at your local library. While you are there, look for some of the excellent books on minerals and lapidary techniques listed on page 1055.

The most important characteristic of any lapidary mineral is its beauty, not its reputation. As an example, one doesn't think of flint as a gemstone, but the strikingly patterned Ohio flint shown below and on page 1048 makes stunning jewelry. And, being flint, it is hard enough to wear well. So are the agate, quartz, carnelian, garnet, jade and tourmaline minerals. Softer minerals such as opal, malachite, turquoise and lapis lazuli do not wear as well. But their beauty is such that amateur lapidarists cannot resist cutting and polishing them.

Almost any mineral hard enough to resist scratching by a copper penny can be cut and polished into a wearable gemstone. That unusual-looking rock you picked up on your last outing might even be a candidate. Scrub the dirt off it and try scratching it with a penny. If it won't scratch, wet it with water and look for interesting colors or patterns. If you find them, try shaping and polishing the stone, using one of the methods described in the projects that follow.

These oval cabochons, gemstone eggs of clear quartz and blue and white lazulite, and the polished flat piece of agate are a small sample of what lapidarists can create from minerals like the large chunk of lace agate on which the stones are resting. The blue and white cabochons are lapis; the red and white, Ohio flint; the gold, tiger's eye; the dark green, malachite; the light green, amazonite; the darker reds, agate and carnelian, the largest cabochon, jasper. Note small opal at top and lace agate cabochon, far right.

Polished stones cemented to a triangular piece of driftwood suggest another way to use tumbled gems.

Jewelry, Lapidary and Metalwork
Tumbling gemstones

1: This large hexagonal tumbler barrel, mounted on the rubber rollers that turn it, will take 25 pounds of stones. Small round barrels can be used for smaller batches of stones. Both do an effective job of tumbling.

This is a way to get into lapidary work with a minimum of labor and expense. In the process you will learn some characteristics of different minerals, and discover the wonders that polishing a drab rock can accomplish. You will need a tumbling machine, photograph 1. They come in many shapes, sizes, and prices (from about $10 to $150), but all work on the same principle. A barrel holds the stones, abrasives and water. A motor rotates the barrel slowly, carrying the stones and abrasive mix up one side until the stones reach a height where they slide back down over the remaining stones, abrading and polishing as they go. A rubber or plastic barrel liner helps move and cushion the stones, and reduces the noise of tumbling.

Tumbler barrels range from about 6 to 12 inches in diameter, and will tumble loads ranging from 3 to 25 pounds of rock. A beginner with few stones to tumble should select a small barrel. Small units also tend to be quieter, an important factor if you live in an apartment.

In addition to the tumbler, you will need abrasive and polishing compounds. I use 80- and 220-grit silicon carbide powder for the first two grinds, and 400- and 600-grit for the two succeeding finer grinds. Cerium oxide is a good polishing powder and it costs less than tin oxide, another good polishing agent. Chromium oxide may be slightly better with such soft stones as lapis, lazulite and serpentine. But you will find cerium oxide works quite well with most minerals.

The size of your tumbling barrel and how high you fill it with rocks will determine how much abrasive and polishing compound you will need. How you match the amount of compound to a specific load is explained in the discussions on loading the barrel (opposite) and polishing the tumbled stones (page 1044). Adding certain buffer materials to the polishing mix will improve the polishing action and minimize the chipping that occurs when stones strike each other constantly. It is also a good way to bring the tumbler up to proper fill level if you are short of stones. Some favorite buffer materials are small chunks of wood, cork or corncobs, leather scraps, and sawdust. I prefer scraps of Pellon, a woven plastic material used to line and stiffen clothing, because it absorbs less of the polishing agent. Pellon comes in disc form for lapidary work or you can buy it at yard good stores. Plan to add a handful or two of cut-up Pellon scraps to each batch of tumbled stones you polish. In addition, have handy a small quantity of household detergent, a small scrub brush, and several plastic buckets (the size determined by the capacity of your tumbler) for measuring water and abrasives and mixing polishing compounds. An old kitchen colander can hold the stones while they are being rinsed off between each grinding stage.

The tumbler and grinding and polishing agents can be obtained from rock and mineral shops, or by mail from Allcraft Tool & Supply Co., Inc., 215 Park Avenue, Hicksville, N.Y. 11801, or Star Diamond Industries, 1421 West 240th Street, Harbor City, Calif. 90710. Rock shops can also provide the minerals for tumbling. When you order the tumbler, ask for an additional barrel liner for each separate grit and polishing agent you will use. They cost little, save time changing from one stage to the next, and minimize the danger of scratching polished stones.

Selecting the Material

Some lapidarists insist that you must never mix sizes, shapes and types of minerals to be tumbled in one batch; others don't follow such a rigid rule. Both get good results. Mixing very hard and very soft minerals in the same batch will wear down the soft ones rapidly, and putting many large chunks in with small ones won't do the small ones any good. But mixing a *few* larger stones in with a batch of smaller ones won't damage either appreciably; it is better than using an entire batch of only large stones, whose weight makes them more likely to chip or fracture as they roll together. If your stones are larger than 1½ inches in diameter (for a larger barrel) or 1 inch (for a small barrel), saw into smaller chunks (page 1045) for tumbling.

Cull out any material that is soft enough for a copper penny to scratch, or that has deep pits, cracks, or inclusions of other material much softer than the basic rock. (A pocket knife blade will readily scratch soft minerals like fluorite and calcite but not hard minerals like agate and quartz). Softer material may work out during tumbling, leaving deep depressions. Like the pits and cracks, these depressions won't polish out, and only serve to trap rough grit that will contaminate the fine grinding and polishing stages. If the rock has only a few deep pits, grind these out on a grinding wheel (see page 1049) before tumbling.

When you start, it is important to have enough stones to rough-grind two loads before you do any fine grinding. The chipped or pitted stones you cull from the first batch can be added to the second batch. The good stones from the second batch can be added to the first batch to be fine ground to make up for flawed stones culled from the first batch. This helps keep the barrel filled with enough stones to give a good tumbling action.

Loading the Barrel

First fill the barrel liner one quarter full of stones you want to tumble. Then pour in water up to the level of the stones. Next pour the water off into a plastic bucket. Use a second bucket to match the poured-off water with an equal volume of 80-grit silicon carbide. Then fill the barrel 40 percent full of water, and mix in the abrasive from the second bucket. Add stones until the tumbling barrel is 60 to 70 percent full. Then add 1 tablespoon (for small barrels) or 2 tablespoons (for large barrels) of household detergent. Tighten the barrel lid securely. Place the barrel on its rollers and start the tumbler (photograph 1).

Check the sound that the tumbler makes. You should hear a steady but subdued whooshing surflike noise as the barrel rotates. If the sound is intermittent, the tumbler is going too slow, allowing the stones to move back and forth without sliding over each other. Too much clattering means that the tumbler is rotating too fast, and the stones are battering each other. No sound of motion within the tumbler means it is rotating *much* too fast; the charge is being held against the barrel wall and you are getting little or no abrading action. These problems are rare with commercial tumblers, whose speeds are or should be matched to the capacity of the barrel used. But if you encounter them you can increase the speed by using a larger diameter pulley on the motor or a smaller diameter pulley on the tumbler. Or decrease speeds by using a smaller diameter pulley on the motor or a larger diameter pulley on the tumbling machine.

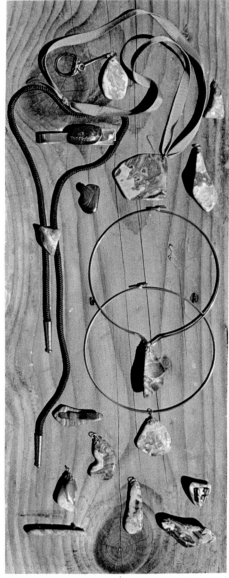

2: To make attractive jewelry from tumbled stones, glue one of various types of jewelry findings to the stone with epoxy cement, and attach wires, rings or clips as shown.

3: For polishing, the cerium oxide and water mixture should have the consistency of light cream. After pouring it over the finely ground stones in the tumbler, add detergent and pieces of Pellon cloth to the tumbler.

4: During the long polishing stage, check each day to see how the stones are doing. Clean off a few stones and inspect them. Polishing takes from 5 days to 2 weeks, depending on the type of minerals and how well they have been ground.

Venting the Tumbler

After the tumbler has been running for 15 minutes, stop it, up-end it and remove the lid. Silicon carbide sometimes reacts with the calcium in minerals to form a gas. Hence this precautionary measure to release gases that may be building up pressure in the tumbler, much as one would burp a baby who swallows air with his food. After venting the tumbler, refasten its lid and let it run for 24 hours. Then open it, pour off the water and spent abrasive, and add more 80-grit silicon carbide. If your tumbler barrel is small, add an ounce or two; if large (like the one in photograph 1), add 2 or 3 ounces of silicon carbide. Add water to slightly below the level of the stones. Then add a teaspoon or two of detergent, fasten the lid, and start tumbling again. Repeat the procedure of opening the tumbler and adding abrasive, water and detergent once every 24 hours until the tumbler has run for four days (for soft stones) or five days (for hard stones).

At the end of the four- or five-day period, pour the abrasive mix into a bucket, hose down the stones in a colander, and scrub each one individually with water and detergent to make sure all the 80-grit abrasive has been removed. Then rinse them. Tumble a second batch of stones with the 80-grit abrasive as you did the first batch. Clean them and examine carefully all the stones you have rough ground. Remove any cracked or pitted ones that might carry the 80-grit abrasive into the next grinding stage. Combine the good stones in one container.

Replace the good stones culled from the first two batches in a clean barrel liner up to the 60 to 70 percent level. (If you are far shy of this level, add wood or cork chips to bring the level up to at least 55 percent.) Add abrasive and detergent as you did for the first step, and fill with water to about 1 inch below the level of the stones. This time, of course, you will use 220-grit silicon carbide, a finer abrasive. Tumble this mixture for two to four days (the shorter time for soft minerals, the longer time for hard ones). Remember to vent the tumbler and add fresh abrasive, water and detergent every 24 hours as before.

At the end of the second grinding, the stones should be ready for fine grinding. The diameter of each stone and the rounding of its edges should be close to what you will have when the stone has been polished. The purpose of the fine grinding is to remove surface scratches the final polishing will not hide. Scrub the stones and barrel liner carefully and remove any pitted or cracked stones. Fill the tumbler with stones, 400-grit silicon carbide, water and detergent as before and let it run for 3 to 4 days, remembering to vent it and add fresh abrasive, water and detergent every 24 hours. Then clean all rocks and the barrel liner thoroughly and repeat the grinding procedure using 600-grit silicon carbide. Let this mixture run for 3 to 4 more days, again adding fresh grit, water and detergent at daily intervals.

When the 3 or 4 days are up, give the stones a final cleaning and a very close inspection. The stones should have a finely grained, frosted look and should begin to show shine when you rub them on a cloth. But no surface scratches should show. If they do, replace the stones in the 600-grit mix and let them tumble for several more days, or until the scratches can't be seen.

Polishing the Gemstones

For polishing, load a new or thoroughly cleaned tumbler barrel liner at least 55 percent (preferably 60 to 70 percent) full of the finely ground stones. Add water to 1 inch below the level of the rocks. Pour off the water into a separate container and mix cerium oxide polishing compound with it until the mixture has the consistency of light cream (photograph 3). Pour this mixture over the stones. Use scissors to cut about 1 square foot of Pellon cloth into ½-by-3-inch size pieces for a large barrel (half that for a small barrel) and add these pieces to the tumbler. Then add 1 tablespoon of detergent for a large barrel (or 1 teaspoon for a small one). Close the tumbler, run it for about 15 minutes and then open it to vent it. Then close it again and start your polishing run. It will take from five days to two weeks, depending on the softness of the stones and the ease with which they accept a polish. Check each day to see how they are progressing, taking out and cleaning a few stones for inspection each time (photograph 4). When you are satisfied with the polish, clean the stones with hot water and detergent. Then rinse, let dry, and plan how you will use them. The photographs, pages 1042 and 1043, may give you some ideas.

Gemstone eggs

$ ▨ ♚ ⚒

Although it is traditional to introduce beginners to the shaping of gemstones by having them make a cabochon, I have found that it helps my students to start with a decorative gemstone egg, like those shown in the color photographs at right and on page 1046. Making an egg teaches the basics of sawing, grinding and polishing mineral specimens. Because the egg is larger than most cabochons, working with it requires less precision, and the beginner can relax more as he or she learns to grind material to the curvature wanted. The egg is also a forgiving shape. As hens know, no two eggs are exactly alike, and the beginner can adjust the shape of the egg as he or she works, to compensate for flaws, flat spots, or curves that don't match.

Materials and Equipment
You will need a trim or slab saw (Figure A) with diamond blades, a grinder/polisher unit (Figure B) with grinding wheels, a sanding drum, and a leather-covered polishing wheel. (The saw blades are smooth metal discs; diamond fragments embedded in their rims do the cutting.) The saw and grinder/polisher may be bought as a combination unit for as little as $120, or separately for quite a bit more, from rock shops or the mail order sources given on page 1043. Since this is the same equipment you use for making cabochons (page 1048), buying it will give you a basic lapidary workshop. But don't buy hastily. Get to know local mineral club members if you can, and find out what they prefer; they may even show you how to rig home-assembled equipment that costs a lot less. The quality of commercial equipment varies widely and it rarely pays to buy the cheapest if you are serious about doing good lapidary work. Do make sure that there is no side play or wobble in the rotating shaft of any unit you are considering buying.

In addition, you will need cerium oxide to polish the egg, just as you needed it for the tumbled stones. You will also need liquid coolants for sawing, sanding and grinding. I use plain water for sawing small specimens with a 6-inch blade and a mixture of 50 percent flushing oil, 50 percent deodorized white kerosene for sawing larger specimens with a 10-inch blade. Oil depots carry the flushing oil and kerosene or you may order them through your local service station.

For grinding and sanding, use water. Commercial lapidary units come with fittings above the level of the grinding wheel to which you attach a small hose going to the water supply, as in Figure B. The water supply can be a large old coffee urn or picnic cooler with a spigot mounted at the bottom; place it on a shelf above

Shaping an egg like this from relatively soft marble is a good project for a beginner. The small stands for eggs can be found in gift or craft shops. You can make one by sawing a slice of copper pipe or cutting a section of mailing tube and covering it with decorative paper.

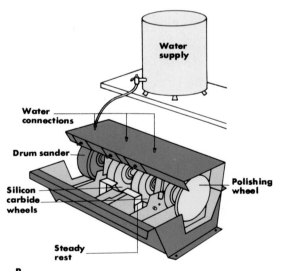

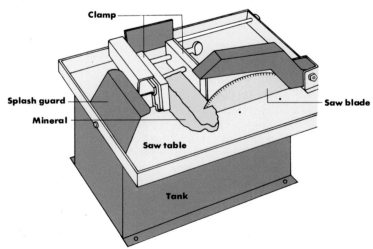

A

Figure A: For sawing, the mineral is fixed firmly in the clamp of a trim of slab saw, then is fed slowly at right angles into the diamond saw blade. For small specimens, use a 6-inch diameter continuous-rim diamond blade, .015 or .036 inch thick. For larger specimens, use a 10-inch diameter notched rim blade, .055 or .065 inch thick.

B

Figure B: A good grinder/polisher unit should have two 1½-inch wide, 8- or 10-inch diameter silicon carbide wheels, one of 100 grit, the other of 220 grit. It should also include a 3- or 4-inch wide, 8- or 10-inch diameter drum sander with circular belts of 400 and 600 grit wet sanding cloth, and an 8- or 10-inch diameter leather-covered polishing wheel with ¼-inch convex curvature. Such combination units either permit interchanging the various wheels or have separate mounting shafts for each. You can rig your own water supply using an old coffee urn, mounted on a shelf above the grinder and connected by a hose to the water fitting on the grinder.

CRAFTNOTES: HAND FORMING GEMSTONES

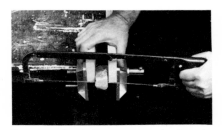

To cut and polish gemstones by hand you need a tungsten carbide blade that fits in a hacksaw frame (above); small metal file; nylon brush; 4 small panes of glass; small quantities of 100-, 220-, 400- and 600-grit silicon carbide abrasive powders and cerium oxide polishing agent; and a square of plywood and pieces of sponge rubber and leather to cover it.

Saw the mineral to the shape you want, as above, and file off any projections. Sprinkle 100-grit abrasive onto a pane of glass and add water to form a

slurry. Work the mineral over this slurry in a V motion, as above. When the worst scratches and pits are gone, clean the stone with warm water and detergent. Move to a new pane of glass and the 220-grit abrasive and repeat the grinding process. Follow this with the 400-grit and 600-grit abrasive, cleaning between each step, until all scratches and pits have been removed. Then glue sponge rubber to the plywood square and tack the leather over the sponge rubber tautly. Apply a watery mixture of cerium oxide and water to the leather with a small brush, and polish the stone.

For a curved surface such as a round pebble, smooth and polish with dampened, abrasive-loaded cloths and leather scraps held in one hand while you work the stone against the cloth or leather with the other hand.

5: Three stages in shaping a gemstone egg of pink rhodochrosite include: left, the roughly sawed mineral block; center, the egg with ends partially shaped; and right, the finished egg.

the grinder with a hose running from its spigot to the hose connection on the grinder. Or you can have your plumber make a special connection, involving a saddle valve and small gate valves from the household water supply to the grinder.

For sawing, grinding, sanding and polishing, wear a shop apron and safety goggles. The work is wet and often messy, and chips of mineral can crack and fly off, particularly during grinding. From a rock shop get an aluminum pencil used for marking minerals (graphite marks wash off too easily). Also have handy a small nylon brush and an old coffee can for mixing and applying the polishing compound, and a magnifying glass for inspecting the egg's surface.

For an egg the size shown in photograph 5, you will need a chunk of mineral about 2½ by 2½ by 3½ inches (photograph 5), if you have 10-inch grinding wheels; reduce the size of the egg if your grinder's wheels are smaller. Neither the shape nor the dimensions of the egg need be precise; uneven or rounded eggs won't matter if they are part of the material that will be ground away later. But any sharp protrusions should be ground off before you start. It's best to start with a soft material like marble, serpentine or rhodochrosite. Rock shops can supply the material and, for an extra charge, they may even saw it roughly to the shape suitable for working an egg. Many of these shops, as well as more advanced lapidarists, have large 20-inch slab saws, but you don't need a saw that large unless you plan to cut very large mineral specimens. (You could actually saw the material for the egg by hand, using a tungsten carbide blade in a hacksaw frame, as at left. But this is very tedious work unless the mineral is small and very soft, such as marble, azurite, serpentine, fluorite or rhodochrosite)

Sawing

Assuming you have obtained a 10-inch trim or slab saw and want to rough out a rectangular shape for your own egg, draw lines for the cuts you need to make with the aluminum pencil. Then clamp the mineral *firmly* in the saw clamp, as in Figure A, so that it will feed into the blade at a right angle, along one of the lines you have marked. Working in a well ventilated area, put enough flushing oil/white kerosene coolant in the tank below the saw to cover about ½ inch of the blade. Wear your goggles. Start the saw and feed the mineral at right angles to the blade very slowly until a starting notch or groove has been established (Figure D, page 1049). Once you have this notch, adjust the mineral in its clamp to feed along the line you have marked. Where rounded edges create problems, use small wood blocks or shims to help you clamp the mineral firmly. Then continue to feed at a rate no faster than ¼ inch per minute for hard materials like agate, or ½ inch per minute for soft materials like serpentine and rhodochrosite. After the first side has been sawed, reclamp and saw any other sides that need sawing to achieve the roughly rectangular shape. Always make sure the mineral is firmly clamped and feeds into the blade at right angles without bending or binding on the saw blade. If the blade starts to clog or glaze, hold a piece of brick against it briefly; this clears away the glaze and exposes the diamond chips in the rim that do the cutting.

Grinding the Shape

With the rectangular shape roughed out, scrub the mineral carefully with warm water and detergent. You are now ready to shape the egg on the 100-grit grinding wheel, following the sequence of steps shown in photograph 5 and Figure C. Don your safety goggles and turn the wheel on before turning on its water supply. Adjust the water so that it comes off the front of the wheel in a fine, misty spray. Hold the mineral firmly in both hands. Have your forearms firmly supported and keep your elbows in close. Move the mineral against the wheel just below the center line of the wheel.

Grind a shallow 45-degree bevel along all the sharp edges left by the sawing, working from each side up to the sharp edge to flatten the edge (1 in Figure C). With all sharp edges beveled, draw pencil lines around the circumference of the egg to divide its length roughly into thirds. Grind a cylindrical band around the first third of the egg (2 in Figure C), leaving the end of the egg untouched; then grind a section of the egg (3 in Figure C). Keep the shape of the egg balanced by checking it against an imaginary horizontal axis line running through the unworked ends of the egg.

In grinding, don't apply too much pressure. Use a wiping action that keeps the egg moving across the face of the wheel and avoids gouging or flattening the stone. Keep the wheel's grinding surface wet; dry whitish mineral dust on it signals it is too dry and the stone may be heating up to the point of cracking.

To blend the bands you have already ground and to shape the curvature of the egg along its length, use a rocking motion from front to back (4 in Figure C). Keep rotating the egg as you rock it to avoid creating flat bands running along the length of the egg. Check frequently as you grind to make sure that the curvature matches on opposing sides of the egg, when viewed from both sides and the ends. But don't try to shape either end of the egg at this stage.

When you are satisfied with the general outlines of the egg, move to the 220-grit wheel to shape the ends. Holding the egg at about a 45-degree angle to the wheel, work up to and around the ends with short, arc-like wiping strokes that round each end (5 in Figure C). Note that the arc around the front (actually the top of the egg) will usually be sharper than the arc around the bottom of the egg.

Egg-rolling Test

When you have the final shape you want, test the egg by rolling it on a table. If it rolls in a smooth arc without wobbling, you have a shape any hen could be proud of. If not, check for high or flat spots or uneven curves that need more shaping. Then grind some more until the egg passes the rolling test.

Scrub the egg carefully with warm water and detergent to clean off any rough grit. Then grind it lightly on the 220-grit wheel to remove any deep scratches or pits left by rough grinding. Use a gentle wiping action—you don't want to alter the shape you have already achieved. When you see only fine, shallow scratches or pits remaining and the egg still passes the rolling test, you are ready to sand. Again wash the egg carefully to remove all grit.

Sanding

Sanding is essentially a repeat of the grinding process except that you are using finer grits to remove fine scratches left by the grinding. Starting with the 400-grit wet sandpaper belt on the sanding drum, sand until you can only see fine, uniform scratches on the surface, when you examine it with a magnifying glass. Then, after washing the egg to remove any grit, move to the 600-grit sanding belt and sand until the surface of the egg is smooth. Moving directly from 400-grit sanding to polishing sometimes leaves tiny indentations that pick up polishing compound and cannot be polished away.

When the egg's surface is marble-smooth but not glazed, you are ready to polish. But first give the stone an extra hard scrubbing with warm water and detergent. Sometimes ground-off mineral dust fills in small cracks and becomes hidden by the abrasive water mixture on the stone's surface. If your scrubbing uncovers such filled-in cracks, they will need to be sanded out before polishing.

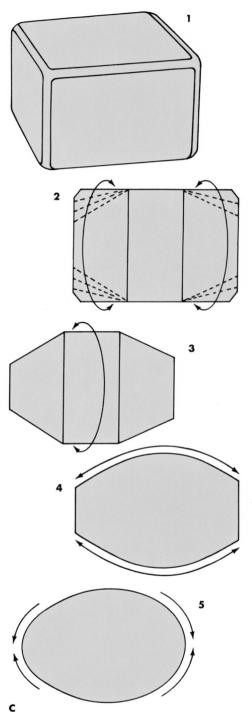

C
Figure C: To grind an egg, follow these steps: (1) bevel sharp edges off the rough block; (2) shape front and rear thirds, and then (3) the middle third of the egg; (4) rock egg back and forth while rotating it to smooth ridges between thirds; (5) round off the ends of the egg.

6: Stages in making a cabochon of Ohio flint include, from the top down: the sawed slab of mineral, mineral sawed as close to oval shape as possible, mineral ground to oval shape, cabochon polished after shaping and sanding.

Polishing

Mix cerium oxide with water in an empty coffee can until you have a cloudy pink to yellow mixture with a watery consistency. Dip the egg in the mix, then let it dry for about 8 seconds. The egg should have a thin coating of polishing powder when it dries. If it takes longer than 8 seconds to dry, the mix is too watery; if it dries in less than 8 seconds, it is too thick. When it is right, start the leather-covered padded polishing wheel and, while it is running, apply the polishing mix lightly with a nylon brush. A new piece of leather will take more mix, a worn piece less. Don't get the leather too wet; a damp surface gives the best polishing action. (Too dry a surface may scratch.)

Polish the egg using the same rotating and rocking motions you used for grinding and sanding. Keep a good pressure on the egg but let up a little if the egg starts to pull. When you begin to feel a tugging action, it means you are starting to get a polish. If this hasn't happened after 15 or 20 minutes, stop, clean the stone and examine it closely again. It may not have been sanded long enough.

The degree of polish will vary with the mineral. Don't expect a mirror-like polish on such soft minerals as dolomite, lazulite, lapis or malachite unless you are prepared to do an unusually careful fine-sanding job. But the harder minerals like agate, jasper, chalcedony and quartz can be made mirror-bright readily. When you are satisfied with the finish, clean the egg thoroughly in warm water and detergent and decide where and how you want to display it.

Jewelry, Lapidary and Metalwork
Gemstone cabochons

Cabochons are traditionally oval-shaped gemstones with flat bottoms and rounded tops. But, as the color photographs below and on page 1041 show, the sizes vary widely and so do the shapes. As long as the top is rounded, the shape may be wide or narrow, shallow or deep, rounded, triangular, or even teardrop or heart-shaped. Although the oval is easiest to shape and polish, the basic techniques for making any of these shapes are the same.

You use the same equipment for making cabochons you used for making gemstone eggs. But in addition you will need: dopsticks (3- to 4-inch lengths of hardwood dowel rod in diameters from ⅛ to ⅝ inch); a stick of dopping wax for holding the stone on the dopstick; an alcohol lamp or dopping stove for melting the wax; a

7: The area selected for the cabochon should enclose an interesting pattern as it does on this dramatically patterned piece of Brazilian agate.

Some colorful cabochons, still dopped (stick-mounted for working on dopsticks) that are being made by the author and his students. Moving clockwise, from the pink rhodochrosite at left, the minerals are: golden tiger's eye; green amazonite; blue and white lapis; amazonite; pale blue chalcedony; and black dolomite with shiny pyrite inclusions.

8: To mark an outline on stone, hold the pencil with tip touching bottom of template opening. Clear spray lacquer protects the marking as you saw, but remove it with alcohol before dopping.

9: Holding the stone flat on the saw table, move it slowly into the blade until a notch is made. Although the blade doesn't have teeth, keep your fingers clear of it to avoid a burn or abrasion.

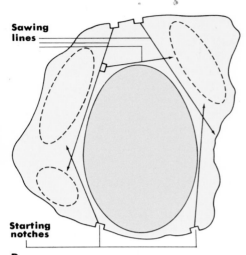

Figure D: Plan as few saw cuts as possible to get close to the cabochon oval. Dotted lines show cabochons you might cut later if you avoid wasting material. Make the starting notch at right angles first, then saw along the straight lines.

flat metal plate about 3 or 4 inches square; a pair of tweezers; and a plastic template with cutout patterns for various sizes and shapes of ovals, circles and other designs.

Photograph 6 opposite shows the sequence of stages in cutting, shaping and polishing a cabochon. Start with a flat slab of mineral, ⅜ inch or less thick, that has an interesting pattern or color. Rock shops sell such slabs or you may saw one out of a large chunk (page 1045). Move the pattern template around on the slab until the oval outline you want frames an interesting pattern (photograph 7). Holding the template in position, turn the slab over to see whether the corresponding area on the other side has about the same pattern. The second side will be the top of your cabochon; you mark the oval on what will be the underside of the cabochon; if there's a choice, mark the better of the two sides. (There are dual templates that slip over the slab and show you the area the oval outline will cover on both sides; check with your rock shop if you want one.) Make sure that there are no bad flaws or cracks within the oval area you have selected. Then mark the oval with an aluminum pencil as in photograph 8.

Draw lines for the saw cuts you will make to get close to the oval outline, but no closer than ⅛ inch (Figure D). Put a 6-inch blade in your diamond saw and enough water in its tank to cover the blade to a depth of ½ inch. Start the saw and place the slab flat on the saw table, with the marked face up. Then don your safety goggles and, with the slab held firmly with both hands, feed the mineral at right angles into the saw blade very slowly to establish the starting notch (photograph 9). If a round edge keeps you from starting along a marked line with the slab at right angles to the blade, notch the edge first at a right angle, then cut through the notch along the marked line, as in Figure D. Feed slowly, at a rate of ¼ inch per minute for hard minerals, ½ inch per minute for softer ones. Don't let the slab twist the blade; trying to make one of these blades saw a curve may ruin the blade.

When you have sawed as close to the oval as possible, remove the larger portions of extraneous material that are still left by nibbling, as in photograph 10. Then scrub the stone with warm water and detergent, and rinse it.

Grinding the Outline

Use the 100-grit silicon carbide grinding wheel to grind down toward the outline of the oval. Wear goggles and an apron, and brace your forearms firmly with your hand resting on the grinder's steady rest if it has one (Figure B, page 1045). Turn on the grinder and then its water supply, adjusted so the wheel throws a fine misty spray. Holding the stone firmly with the fingers of both hands, feed it against the grinding wheel with a sweeping, wiping action that carries the stone across the front face of the wheel (photograph 11). If the stone's edge has a sharp point, work it off by grinding toward it from either side, rather than by putting the point against the wheel. Grind so the edge of the stone remains at right angles to the face of the stone. Keep grinding until the edge of the stone is within 1/16 inch of the oval pencil mark all around. Then, using the 220-grit wheel, grind a tiny 45-degree bevel around the base of the stone, as in Figure E, page 1050. The bevel should touch the edge of—but not remove—the aluminum pencil mark. Its purpose is to keep what will become the sharp lower edge of the cabochon from chipping when mounted.

10: After notching edges on the saw, use nippers or tile pliers to nibble (break) off the small bits of excess material between the notches.

11: To grind down to the cabochon oval, apply the edge of the gemstone to the wheel with a wiping action that keeps the stone moving along the curvature of the oval. Keep the side of the stone at right angles to the wheel.

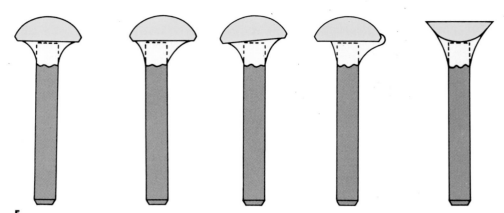

E

Figure E: Left, the dopped (stick-mounted) stone should be at right angles to the dopstick and centered on it, with wax supporting it evenly all around. Note bevel at base of stone. The middle three drawings show poor dopping. Far right, how to dop a cabochon before polishing its bottom.

Dopping the Stone

To shape the top of the cabochon, you will first have to mount it on an appropriately sized dopstick. Ideally, the diameter of the dopstick should not be more than one half the width of the oval. Hold the tip of the dopping wax over the alcohol lamp until the wax becomes shiny and soft enough to pull a blob of it onto the end of the dopstick, as in photograph 12. Roll the soft wax on the flat metal plate to smooth the edges of the blob while keeping most of it on top of the dopstick. Pick up the oval stone near its edge with tweezers. Gently heat the stone and the wax blob on the stick at the same time until the wax will stick to the pencil-marked side of the stone when you press them together, as in photograph 13. Shape the wax to support the stone evenly all around, as in Figure E. Make sure the bottom of the stone is at right angles to the dopstick, and that the penciled oval outline remains visible. The job is easier if you have a dopping stove, photograph 14. If the stone won't stick to the dopstick, coat its bottom with a thin layer of pure shellac before heating.

12: Heat the tip of the dopping wax over an alcohol lamp until it is soft enough for you to pull a blob of wax onto the end of the dopstick.

13: After heating stone and wax on the dopstick until both are pliant, press together until the wax cools slightly. Then shape wax as in Figure E.

14: This dopping wax stove heats both the wax (foreground) and the stones (background) at the same time, making the task of dopping easier.

Shaping the Curved Top

For stones ⅜-inch or more thick, I find it helps to grind the curved top of the cabochon in three successive bevels, Figure F, followed by the final rounding of the top. Two bevels will work for thinner stones. For either thickness make the first bevel around the base of the stone at a 10- to 15-degree angle from the perpendicular. For thicker stones, the second bevel, starting about one third up from the base, should angle more sharply and the third bevel, starting about two-thirds up from the base, should be even more sharply angled than the second. The division into thirds and the angles of each bevel do not have to be precise. But the three bevels leave shallow ridges between bevels you can easily round into a cabochon.

15: To grind bevels on the top of the cabochon, hold dopstick close to wax area and use wiping action to keep stone moving around each bevel.

16: Use the sanding drum, first with 400- and then 600-grit wet sanding belts, to remove pits and scratches left from grinding the cabochon.

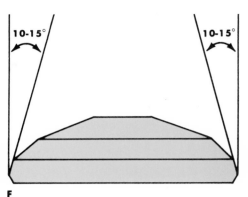

F
Figure F: To shape the top of cabochons ⅜ inch or more thick, make three bevels as shown. For thinner stones, make two bevels. For either, maintain 10- to 15-degree angle of the first or bottom bevel. After beveling, round the top.

If the mineral is soft, you may be able to bevel it on the 220-grit wheel; if hard, use the 100-grit wheel. Hold the dopstick close to the waxed area at the top with both hands, one acting as a prop or fulcrum, the other being used to turn the stone as you grind, photograph 16. Keep the stone moving, using the same wiping action you used in shaping the egg, page 1047, as you work your way around the circumference of each bevel. Then clean the stone and move to the 220-grit grinding wheel (or the 400-grit sanding drum if the stone is a very soft one). Level out the ridges between the bevels and start shaping the final curve of the cabochon, using the same sweeping and turning motions you used for the final shaping of the egg, page 1047. But do not change the 10-to-15 degree bevel angle at the base of the stone. Holding the stone at eye level and looking at it from both sides and both ends, check frequently to make sure the arc that is formed either way is centered.

When you are satisfied with the curvature, clean the cabochon and sand out the pits and scratches on the 400- and 600-grit sanding belts (photograph 16) as you did the egg (page 1048). Polish the stone as you polished the egg, using the cerium oxide/water mix applied to the leather-covered padded polishing wheel (page 1045). After polishing and final cleaning, place the cabochon still on its dopstick in the freezer compartment of your refrigerator for a few hours or overnight. Then to remove it, tap it on the table and the stone will separate cleanly from the wax.

There's no need to polish the flat underside of a cabochon. But if you want to, the stone can be mounted upside down on the dopstick (Figure E, far right) and then sanded or polished.

Cutting Other Shapes

Hearts, crosses, squares, rectangles, triangles, arrows and other shapes can be cut and polished with the same equipment used for cabochons. Mark out and saw the pattern as you did the oval for the cabochon. If the top is to be rounded, grind the curvature with the same wiping and rotating motions used to shape the cabochon top. For the indentation at the top of the heart and the right angles forming a cross, use the edge of the grinding wheel as in Figure G. These corners and crevices are not easy to reach with the drum sander. So try attaching 400- and 600-grit sanding discs to your polishing wheel with peel-off cement, and then use the edge of the wheel discs for sanding. For polishing, the leather replaces the sanding discs.

Mounting a Cabochon

You can buy jewelry findings from craft supply houses in the form of rings, brooches, tie clips, earrings and the like to which cabochons may be glued with epoxy cement. Or the cabochon may be wrapped in a wire cage, as at left in Figure H, and suspended from a pendant chain. (Such a cage can also be formed around tumbled stones.) Still another method is to use a piece of copper or silver as a backing for the stone, cutting out sections that can be folded over the stone to form prongs that hold the stone in place, as at right in Figure H.

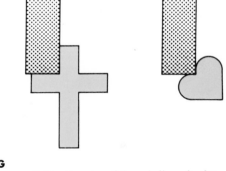

G
Figure G: Use the edge of the grinding wheel to shape such intricate areas as the corners in a cross or the top of a heart.

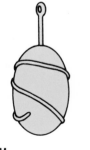

H
Figure H: Two ways to mount a cabochon without gluing: Left, form a cage of 16- or 18-gauge gold or silver wire around the stone, then bring wire up the back of the stone and form a small loop for hanging stone on a pendant; Right, cut an oval of copper or silver larger than the cabochon, then cut small flaps in the metal and fold them up over the stone to hold it in place.

1051

Polished flats, like these of Brazilian agate, can be made into a colorful and musical set of wind chimes, as shown in Figure J, opposite page.

17: Abrasive mix is applied to a rotating lap wheel from a plastic squeeze bottle while hand-held mineral spreads it across the lap.

18: This round rhodochrosite flat could be fitted with a jewelry finding to make a pendant.

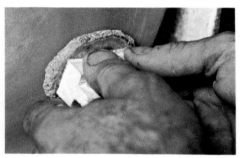

19: To hold a small flat while polishing, attach a wood block handle to it with dopping wax.

Vibrating lap surface

Stones

I

Figure I: With an electric vibrating lap, grit or polishing compound is spread on the lap, the stones are placed on top of the grit, and the vibrations do the work of grinding or polishing.

Jewelry, Lapidary and Metalwork
Gemstone flats

Lapping flats is the unglamorous term for a process that produces some of the most beautiful results found in lapidary work. Essentially it involves grinding and polishing the flat surfaces of slabs or chunks or minerals until the colors and patterns emerge in all their splendor, as in the color photograph above. If a slab is small enough, it can make an attractive pendant. Larger slabs can be inlaid into table tops for a terrazzo effect, made into wind chimes as in Figure J opposite, or, if thin enough and translucent, arranged as dramatic, backlighted displays. The polished chunks can be made into book ends, paper weights or desk set pieces.

You can buy the slabs or chunks from rock shops, or saw your own as was done for the gemstone egg (page 1045). If the slab is no larger, say, than the one in photograph 18, it can be ground, sanded and polished with the same equipment used for making eggs and cabochons (page 1045 and photograph 19). For larger pieces, you need a rotating or vibrating lap (photograph 17 and Figure I). These have a cast iron or steel lap wheel to which silicon carbide abrasives are applied. Holding or resting the mineral against the abrasive-covered, moving wheel grinds it smooth. For polishing, a cloth- or leather-covered wheel replaces the cast iron or steel one, and cerium oxide or some other polishing agent is used.

Some combination lapidary units whose saw blades and grinding wheels rotate horizontally come equipped with lap wheels. Vibrating laps are sold as separate units starting at about $40. If you plan to use a lap wheel, get a pound each of silicon carbide in 100, 220, 400, 600 and 1000 grits. For polishing, get ½ pound of cerium oxide, a tube of peel-off cement (Krylon and On-and-Off are two brands), and one or two Pellon discs the diameter of your lap wheel.

The sequence of grits to use for lapping will be 100-, 220-, 400-, 600- and 1000-grit silicon carbide followed by the cerium oxide polishing agent. All come in powder form to be mixed with water and applied to the lap wheel. I have found it helps to keep each grit mixed in a separate plastic squeeze bottle, as in photograph 17, labeled with the number of the grit. If you can afford it, it also helps to have a separate lap wheel (kept stored in a plastic bag) for each grinding stage, to avoid contaminating fine grits with rougher grits. But lap wheels can be cleaned by rotating them slowly, running hot water and and detergent on them, scrubbing the abrasive off with a brush, then rinsing carefully. Remember also to clean the mineral at each stage and give your hands and fingernails a good scrubbing, too. Nothing is more discouraging than to have one deep scratch from an errant piece of rough grit suddenly appear on the face of a polished specimen.

Mix equal parts of the 100-grit silicon carbide and water and make sure the mixture has a watery rather than a pasty consistency. (If you are using a plastic squeeze bottle, shake the mixture well before applying.) Sprinkle or spread the mixture across the lap wheel and use the slab to work it around onto all areas of the wheel, as in photograph 17. To grind, first hold the flat so that a very slight curve will be formed along one edge; this lets the abrasive get underneath instead of being pushed up over the leading edge of the slab as you move it across the face of the lap wheel. Then hold the flat level and keep a steady but not too heavy pressure on it, moving it back and forth slowly across the face of the lap wheel to keep the wheel from wearing unevenly. If the flat is light and thin, instead of attaching a wood handle to it with dopping wax, try a stone block whose weight will help steady it and apply the right amount of pressure during grinding. Repeat the grinding process with 220, 400, 600 and 1000 silicon carbide grit until all scratches are gone, cleaning carefully between each grinding step. Test the evenness of the work at each stage by cross-hatching the slab's face with an aluminum pencil. All lines should be removed by the next sanding. After the 1000-grit stage, the stone at this stage should have a finely frosted, matte coating spread evenly over the surface, with no change in texture to indicate hollow spots that need more work.

The Final Polish

Cement the Pellon disc to a clean lap wheel with peel-off cement, mix up cerium oxide with water to a thin watery consistency and brush or sprinkle this lightly on the Pellon disc. Use the flat to spread the polish over the entire disc. Polish the flat by holding it firmly against the lap but don't apply so much pressure that the stone heats up rapidly; too much heat may crack the stone or melt the dopping wax holding it to its handle. Clean and check the surface frequently; if part of the stone doesn't seem to be polishing, rotate the stone so the lap feeds into it at a new side. If the stone has been properly sanded, it should begin to show a polish in a few minutes, but a uniform gloss over the entire surface will take quite a bit longer. The actual time varies with the mineral and how well you have sanded it. When you are satisfied with the uniform gloss, give the stone a final cleaning with warm water and detergent. Rinse this off and your flat is ready for display.

Agate Wind Chimes

To make a set of wind chimes, you need four flats of about the same size, and polished on both sides. They should be of a relatively tough material like agate, jasper or chalcedony, and they should be no thicker than ⅛ inch if you want a lively tinkle from them when they strike together. You will also need a jewelry clasp to attach to each flat, epoxy cement to do the attaching, about 8 feet of nylon fishing line, a slice of wood or length of dowel or bamboo about 7½ inches long, and a hook from which to hang the chimes.

Drill four ⅛-inch diameter holes, spaced about 1¼ inches apart, along the center line of the wood or bamboo. Glue a jewelry clasp to the narrowest edge of each polished flat. Cut two 28-inch lengths of nylon line and attach them to the flats as shown by the red lines in Figure J. Cut one 10- and one 13-inch length of line and route through holes in wood and attach as shown by the blue lines in Figure J.

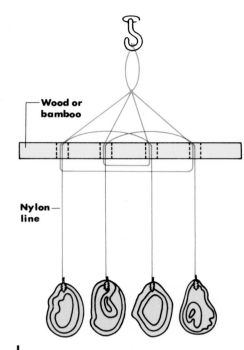

J
Figure J: To make a set of wind chimes from polished flats, route nylon lines through holes in wood as shown, adjusting lengths for balance before knotting. Knot the lines supporting the chimes about two inches above the wood, using their remaining ends to form a loop that goes over the hook above.

Faceted oval cut of smoky quartz and a brilliant cut of zircon. Zircons are frequently heat-treated to transform them into blue stones.

How gems are faceted

If you mount a gemstone on a dopstick and hold it at an angle against a turning lap wheel, a flat face or facet will be cut in the stone. Turn the stick, hold it against the lap again at the same angle, and a second facet is cut. Continue the process and you will have a row of matching facets around the stone, as at right. Raise or lower the angle of the dopstick, repeat the lapping and turning process, and you will have a second row of facets. Remount the stone on the dopstick upside down so that its unfaceted side faces out and you can then facet the bottom or pavilion of the stone as you did the stone's top or crown.

That brief description of faceting makes the process sound much simpler than it really is. Faceting is almost always done on trans-

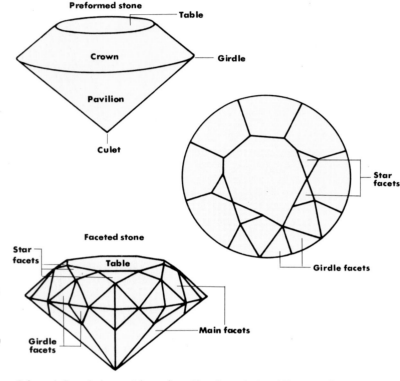

To facet a brilliant cut, the stone is first preformed from the rough mineral. Then a ring of main crown facets is cut around the stone, followed by a ring of star facets, then a ring of girdle facets. The stone is then remounted upside down in the dopping arm (left) and the pavilion facets are cut.

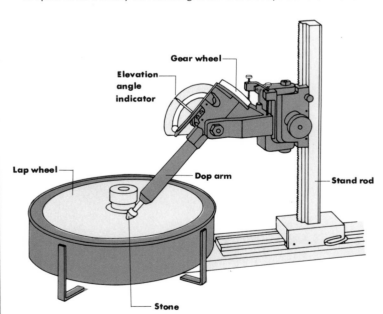

must be preformed (see above), before any facets are cut. The precise angle and location of each facet must be rigidly controlled, using a dop arm attached to a lapping unit, as at left. The drawing of faceted stones above shows a few of the steps involved in cutting the facets on the top or crown of a brilliant cut. The facets on the bottom or pavilion must correspond exactly with matching facets in the top or crown.

Such work is complex but not beyond the reach of the dedicated amateur lapidarist who can afford it. Faceting equipment prices range from around $350 and up, and the precious and semi-precious mineral materials used are usually relatively costly. If you are truly interested in such faceting work, obtain several of the books listed opposite. They do an excellent job of explaining the complexities of basic and advanced faceting techniques.

parent, often costly, stones with such special equipment as is shown above. The faceting must be planned so that no obvious flaws will appear under the flat table of the stone (see right). Also no facet angle should coincide with the natural line of cleavage of the mineral, which will vary with different minerals. Then the stone

LAPIDARY TECHNIQUES

How spheres are made

The technique for making spheres is similar to the technique for making eggs (page 1045). A block of mineral is selected that is roughly square or can be sawed to a square that will enclose a sphere of, say, 1 or 2 inches diameter. The circles or spherical outlines are marked on all sides of the block. Then all corners, edges or projections are sawed or ground off to achieve a roughly ball-like shape. To convert this into a smooth sphere, two heavy-walled cast iron pipe caps whose outside diameter is about ¼ inch smaller than the diameter of the sphere are used. A steel rod welded to the back of one cap permits it to be mounted in a lathe or drill press chuck. The pipe should rotate at speeds no greater than 1750 to 1800 revolutions per minute for spheres up to about 1 inch in diameter, but more slowly, at about 600 rpm, for spheres 3 inches in diameter.

A curved bevel is filed on the inside edges of both pipe caps to help them conform to the shape of the sphere. Rags are stuffed into both pipe caps and a wet mixture of 100 or 220 silicon carbide grit and water in the thin slurry consistency is applied to the ball-like shape to be ground and to the open ends of both pipe caps. Then

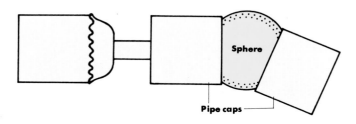

Sphere

Pipe caps

with one cap mounted in the lathe or drill press and the other held by hand, the ball is ground as above, until the rougher contours have been smoothed. More abrasive mix is added to the sphere and the mouths of the pipe caps from time to time. As the surface of the sphere becomes smoother, finer grits are used. If the edge of the pipe caps (which are also being ground by the work) become sharp, they are rounded off with a file so fingers that come in contact with the work will not be cut.

When all scratches and pits have been removed, the pipe caps are cleaned and a section of leather is bound around the mouth of each pipe; the leather should be firmly attached but not be so taut that it won't give somewhat when the sphere is pressed against it. A mixture of water and cerium oxide or some other polishing agent is used on the leather covering the mouths of the pipe sections and the sphere is polished as it was ground. If the sphere is too small to handle easily, it may be mounted on a dopstick and polished on a leather-covered polishing wheel (as was done for the cabochon, page 1051). But more than half of the sphere should be exposed for polishing. After about two-thirds of the sphere area has been polished, the sphere is remounted with the unpolished side out and the polishing job is finished.

Drilling holes in gemstones

Modern epoxy cements have made it easy to mount gemstones without drilling holes in them (see page 1043). But there are applications in advanced lapidary work where holes must be drilled in the stone. For soft stones like marble and malachite, hardened flat steel drills, operated slowly and frequently resharpened, are sometimes used. For harder stones, drills made of thin steel tubing are rotated slowly in a thin slurry of 100-grit silicon carbide, or diamond dust mixed with olive oil, to make the hole. The rate of drilling is quite slow, with the drill being lifted frequently to allow it and the stone to cool, and to let the abrasive enter the hole being drilled. Power for the drilling is supplied by a variety of methods, ranging from bow drills similar to those the ancient Egyptians used, to lathes and special drills whose speed can be controlled for the type of mineral and type of drill being used. The books listed below provide more detailed information on drilling techniques and equipment.

Carving, engraving, sculpturing

These advanced techniques use some of the basic steps previously described—sawing and grinding to the rough shape—but then introduce additional refinements. To control the shape, a template of the design is made, and the work is checked against it frequently. After rough grinding to the general shape, curves, indentations and other intricate portions of the design are worked with small ball-, oval-, wheel-, and cylinder-shaped, diamond-embedded tools. Or mild steel rods (called needle rods) to which various mixtures of abrasives are added are used. Where holes are called for, they are drilled as indicated above. Interiors of bottles or vases are first drilled, then enlarged by inserting ball-shaped grinding tools at various angles through the drilled opening. Sanding is done, sometimes by hand, with silicon carbide abrasive cloths and rubber-bonded abrasive wheels. Polishing is done on leather-, felt-, or muslin-covered polishing wheels using cerium oxide or some other polishing agent.

Books to Look For

Sources of information on characteristics of gemstones and basic and advanced lapidary techniques include:

The Art of the Lapidary by Francis L. Sperisen, The Bruce Publishing Co., Milwaukee, Wisc.

Gem Cutting, A Lapidary's Manual by John Sinkankas, Van Nostrand Reinhold Co., New York, N.Y.

Gem Cutting Is Easy by Martin Walter, Crown Publishers, Inc., New York, N.Y.

Related Projects

For related entries and projects, see "Jewelry" and "Mineralogy."

Anna Grebanier Schäfer was born in Germany, where she taught kindergarten until she began working with leaded glass. She studied with Jean-Jacques Duval in New York and later taught in his studio as his assistant. She has participated in East Coast craft exhibitions and divides her time between teaching at New York City's Craft Students League and creating commissioned leaded glass works.

LEADED GLASS
Luminous Hues

I shall never forget the first time I entered a leaded glass supply store. It was on a sunny day, and as I stepped into the store, I was enveloped in a shimmering kaleidoscope of color. Sunlight pouring through the glass samples arranged along the window sills brought to life the rich purples, greens, yellows, browns, incredible reds and cool blues. Even the clear glass panes seem to pick up a unique appearance from association with the colorful pieces. And, as I watched, passing clouds altered the light, subtly imposing a new atmosphere on the room. But this new atmosphere was—like the first one—joyously vibrant and yet totally peaceful. I spent the next few hours absorbing the quiet excitement of leaded glass.

The magic of leaded glass—to stir the emotions and at the same time convey tranquility—explains its long association with religious architecture, an association that began in the twelfth century. By the year 1200 the mystical religious significance medieval man attached to leaded glass windows had given this art form a prestige few crafts ever attain. The magnificent stained glass windows in European cathedrals built in the Middle Ages still evoke a sense of wonder in those who view them. No matter what the style or subject matter of the design, the intrinsic beauty of the glass endures.

This Tiffany-style lampshade is made of many small pieces of glass and was constructed with the copper-foil method described on page 1062. Anna Grebanier-Schäfer used a special mold when she made this shade; directions for making a simpler shade that requires no mold begin on page 1066.

Leaded glass is the result of a technique whereby pieces of stained glass (glass impregnated with color in the factory during the manufacturing process) or clear glass are held together with lead to form a design. In addition to holding the glass together, lead functions as a part of the overall design; it forms a distinct outline around each glass piece and can add to or detract from the beauty of the finished work, depending upon the skill and talent of the creator.

A leaded-glass candle box dramatizes the beauty of golden candlelight. Pieces of stained glass, clear glass, and stained glass "jewels," held together with copper foil and solder, result in a spectacular means of imparting atmosphere to a room. Additional candle boxes, and directions for making them, are on pages 1064 and 1065.

The lead used for this purpose comes in two forms: as strips called leading, caming, or lead cames, and as solder which must be melted and is used in conjunction with copper foil. The techniques employed in using both forms are explained in the Craftnotes on page 1062 and in the project directions that follow. Until this century, craftsmen relied entirely on lead cames to hold the cut pieces of glass together. This heavy, bulky form of lead limits the design possibilities in that only large pieces of glass can be handled easily.

Around the turn of the century, Louis C. Tiffany began using a new method of holding pieces of glass together. This method enabled him and others to create designs with flowing lines and intricate shapes. It ushered in a new era of glass design, as exemplified by the graceful Art Nouveau style so characteristic of Tiffany's work. (The lampshade pictured on page 1056 is an example of this type of design.) In this method, sometimes called the "Tiffany foil method," the edges of each piece of glass are encased in narrow strips of copper foil and are then bonded together with melted lead solder that adheres to the foil. Because this allows smaller pieces of glass to be joined with greater ease and accuracy, the results are more delicate than those obtainable with the bulkier, less flexible lead cames. This copper-foil method is the most popular method today and in most cases I prefer it because it allows greater design possibilities. I recommend it, especially for beginners, and teach it in all my classes.

Tools and Materials

The list of the tools and materials required for working in leaded glass (photograph 1) seems quite long, but I feel the results can be so beautiful and exciting that acquiring them is worth the expense. Glass, glass cutters, breaking and grozing pliers, soldering gun or iron, copper foil, solder and leading, and pattern scissors are available at stained-glass supply shops. The remaining supplies can be purchased at art supply stores and hardware stores. You probably have some items on hand, such as newspaper, pencil, steel wool, pushpins, nails, sponge, household detergent, and white paper.

Glass: There are two main types of both clear and stained glass. One type is antique glass, so named because it is hand-blown by skilled craftsmen as it was in medieval times. It is full of interesting variations—air bubbles, waves and streaks —and one sheet can vary in color and in thickness. Most antique glass is imported from France, England and Germany; it is the more expensive of the two types of glass, and it is the one I work with most often. Cathedral or commercial glass is machine-made and is available in many colors and degrees of transparency. It is very even in thickness, and comes in many textures. I seldom use it, although it too is beautiful on its own terms. Within these two main types, glass may be further categorized according to other characteristics. *Opalescent* glass is cathedral glass that is almost opaque. It is full of streaks and whorls of colors, which give a sense of movement that doesn't require backlighting to be visible. For this reason, it is often used in lamps and other items that will be viewed frequently in reflected light. *Streakies* are a type of antique glass that contain streaks of delicate colors. Imported from England, they are highly transparent and have imperfections such as swirls, ripples and bumps; many streakies are so beautiful that some craftsmen can scarcely bear to cut them into pieces to use as part of a design. *Hammered glass* is a type of cathedral glass, one side of which has a texture of uniform indentations. You must cut this type of glass with the smooth side facing up. *Jewels or roundels* are small diamond or disk shapes that are often thicker than sheet glass. They may be faceted or impressed with designs on one or both sides, and prices vary according to their size, color and quality. As their name suggests, they resemble precious jewels. See "Where to buy leaded glass supplies," left.

Materials for pattern-making: To make the cartoon—a full-size drawing of the design—you will need white paper, pencil, straight-edge, and perhaps a ruler. For the actual pattern (pieces that are cut out and used as a guide for cutting the glass) use heavy paper such as a manila folder, heavy brown wrapping paper, or 80- or 90-pound kraft paper. Use special pattern scissors (Craftnotes, page 1061) for cutting the pattern pieces. In addition, for transferring the cartoon to the heavy pattern paper, carbon paper and pushpins are needed.

Materials for cutting the glass: Glass cutting is probably the most difficult step in making leaded glass, so have all the following supplies on hand: newspaper, a piece of ½-inch-thick plywood measuring about 2½ by 3½ feet, a table brush for brushing away glass shards, breaking pliers for breaking off pieces of glass that are too small to grasp with the fingers, grozing pliers to straighten uneven cuts, glass cutters (those with carbide cutting wheels last up to five times longer than those with steel wheels; buy the kind with a ball on the handle) and kerosene for lubricating the cutting wheel.

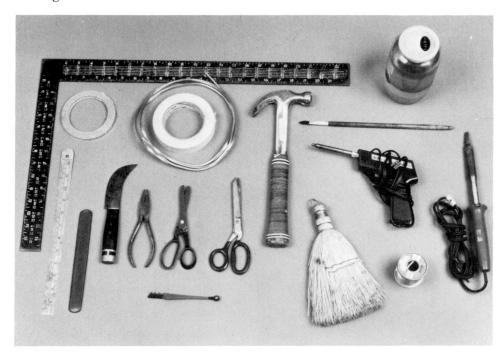

1: Tools and materials required for working with leaded glass are pictured at left. Upper left: metal square. Upper right: liquid flux (oleic acid). Top row, left to right: ¼-inch adhesive-backed copper foil, masking tape and lead came; hammer; brush used for applying flux. Bottom row, left to right: metal ruler; soft wood stick; lead knife; grozing pliers; pattern scissors; regular scissors; glass cutter (below scissors); table brush; soldering gun; soldering iron and solder (below soldering gun). The soldering gun and iron come with a stand; use it when the iron or gun is hot.

Materials for leading and finishing: The copper-foil method of leading requires a roll of ¼-inch-wide adhesive-backed copper foil, 60/40 solid core solder (60 percent tin and 40 percent lead), liquid flux (I use oleic acid) and a brush for applying the flux. Flux is an essential ingredient in the soldering process; it cleans the metal and thus promotes close adhesion between the solder and the metal. Before soldering, always brush flux onto the areas to be soldered. For melting the solder, use a 100-watt soldering gun or iron with a ⅜- or ¼-inch chisel tip; be sure it comes with a stand to rest on between uses. For the lead came technique (the window panel on page 1063 and the lampshade on page 1066 are edged in lead cames) you will need ⅛-inch U-lead (sold in 6-foot lengths) and a lead knife for cutting the lead into strips of the required length. To stretch and straighten the came, a special device is available, but I use two pliers. In addition, strips of 1-by-3-inch wood (the length and the number depend upon the project); hammer and nails are used to hold the pieces of glass in place while the lead is being applied. Use steel wool to rub dirt and finishes off metals so they do not interfere with the soldering process. A damp sponge touched to a hot soldering iron or soldering gun will cool it off if it gets too hot. To clean the finished glass, use a strong solution of liquid detergent. Some people prefer to use whiting (a chalky powder that is applied to the glass with a brush) for cleaning the glass, but I find the detergent works just as well. Clean the finished leaded glass thoroughly; you don't want the beauty of your project marred by a residue of flux, oxides, and other deposits that invariably accumulate. The last step in working with leaded glass is to antique the finished project. Copper sulfate is applied to the lead with a cotton swab to give the lead a muted coppery patina.

Before beginning any of the three projects that follow, I suggest that you practice the techniques described in the Craftnotes on pages 1060 through 1062. You can use ordinary clear window glass for this purpose; it is available at any neighborhood glazier and is much less expensive than stained glass.

CRAFTNOTES: CUTTING

Setting up

One of the most important steps in cutting glass is to set aside a convenient place in your home for this activity. Glass is not as dangerous as many people think it is, but to prevent accidents, try to work in a room with a door that can be shut to keep out children and pets. Set up a sturdy work table that is a comfortable height for you to work at while standing—glass should not be cut from a sitting position. Common sense will forestall many cuts. For example, never run your finger along the edge of a piece of glass to check its smoothness. After cutting glass, brush any resulting fragments off the work table with a brush, not your hands. Handle the glass gently and carefully. Soldering also requires common sense precautions: Don't put a hot soldering iron or gun anywhere but on the stand designed to hold it, and keep it away from paper patterns that could be ignited. Place plywood on top of the work table and cover it with several layers of newspaper—glass cuts much better if it is on a surface that yields a little. To keep the cutting wheel of your glass cutter in good condition, have available a small jar holding a piece of cloth and some kerosene. Dip the cutting wheel into the jar between cuts to lubricate it and keep the wheel running smoothly.

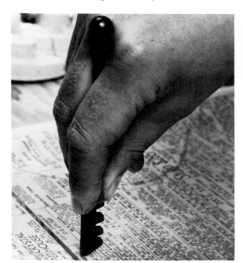

Cutting glass

A glass cutter is the primary tool used in cutting glass. The glass cutter is used to make a controlled scratch, called a score, on the surface of the glass along the breaking line; the glass follows the line as it is snapped apart. As pictured above, hold the glass cutter between your index and middle fingers, with your thumb pressing it from beneath. Hold the cutter in a vertical position, not leaning backwards toward you. Use a relaxed wrist motion; pressure should come from your shoulder, not your wrist. Lean into the cutter with the weight of your body. To begin a score, which can be made freehand or be guided by a straight-edge, hold the glass against the news-paper with one hand to keep it from shifting. Place the cutter in a vertical position on the glass about 1/8 inch from the far edge. Move the cutter toward you, applying firm and consistent pressure. Always run the cutter off the near edge of the glass and onto the newspaper. Then go back to the far edge to the point at which you began the score line, and run the cutter backwards over the far edge. Never stop a score in the middle, and never try to go over the same score twice. After a certain amount of practice, you will be able to recognize the sound of a successful score.

Because scored glass tends to "heal" it-self, it is important that you snap each cut immediately after scoring. To do this, hold the glass by putting a thumb on each side of the scoreline (above). Form a fist with each hand and pull outward and downward, applying even pressure until the piece snaps apart.

Sometimes the glass cannot be broken by hand, no matter how much pressure you apply. In this case, the score must be deepened by tapping. Tapping is done with the ball end of the glass cutter. Keeping the scored side up, hold the glass in one hand, supporting it on both sides of the score (above). Balance the cutter in the other hand, guiding the ball to make taps along the scoreline from underneath. Don't tap with much force—the idea is to "run" or fracture the initial score, not break it completely. When you have tapped the entire length of the score, the glass can usually be broken by hand.

Cutting glass forms new edges, and these new edges will be filled with tiny, razor-sharp slivers. Remove these slivers by scraping one glass edge against another (above).

THE GLASS

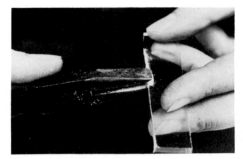

Should there be unwanted bumps, or if the break didn't follow the scoreline exactly, use the grozing pliers to improve the edge. Holding the glass in one hand and the pliers in the other, carefully grip the edge of the glass between the jaws of the pliers (above). Grind the glass little by little, taking small bites until the edge is shaped to your requirements.

Using and making a pattern
Next, practice cutting pieces of glass using a pattern as a guide. Cut a practice pattern (a simple rectangle is a good shape) out of heavy paper. Place the pattern on top of the glass and score the glass in the same way you scored it without a pattern. Begin all scores at the far edge of the glass and keep the wheel of the cutter moving along the pattern edge (above). When you reach the end of the pattern, don't stop—continue the score, running the cutter off the edge of the glass nearest you. Break the score immediately. Then cut along each side of the pattern, running the cutter off the edges each time and snapping apart each score immediately after it is made. This may seem wasteful, but you will soon learn to economize by placing each pattern piece so it allows no more than ½-inch of waste at the edge of a piece of glass. (If you try to place the pattern closer to the edge than this, it will be difficult, if not impossible, for you to grip and break off the piece narrower than ½-inch, even with breaking pliers.)

Once you feel comfortable about handling glass and have become adept at cutting with a practice pattern, you are ready to start your first project, using a real pattern and stained glass. First, you need a full-size working design, called a cartoon. You might want to begin with the panel shown on page 1063. You may, of course, prefer to use your own design. If you do, remember that designing for leaded glass is a disciplined art, and there are certain decorative and structural principles governing what you can and cannot do. Use simple, geometric shapes. The books listed on page 1065 include other patterns for novices and some rules to follow when creating your own designs. When you have drawn a full-size cartoon, you may color it with pastels or watercolor paints to approximate the color of the glass from which the pieces will be cut. Then number each area on the cartoon.

Now you are ready to make the pattern. Place heavy paper on the plywood board, and put a sheet of carbon paper, face down, over it. Place the cartoon, face up, on top of the carbon paper and fasten all three layers at each corner with a pushpin or thumbtack. Trace over the lines and the numbers of the pattern, thus transferring them to the heavy paper (above). Each pattern piece will be cut out later, so the numbers will tell you where each piece belongs in the design and you will avoid ending with a jigsaw puzzle. Before removing the papers from the board, take out two pins and make sure all lines and numbers have been transferred to the bottom sheet of paper. If everything is visible, unpin the top layers, remove the carbon and heavy paper, and tape the original cartoon to the board to serve as an assembly guide.

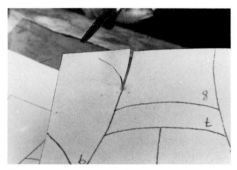

The next step is to cut the pattern into pieces. First cut along the outside line with regular scissors. But for the inside cuts, between the pattern pieces, use the special pattern scissors. It is designed to remove a sliver of paper between the pieces (above), which allows the space between the cut pieces of glass that will be filled with copper foil and solder. Cut on top of the lines, using short strokes with the very back of the blades. Remove and discard the sliver of paper after every few strokes; it will clog the blades if you let it grow too long.

When all the pattern pieces have been cut, put each one in place on the cartoon to see that all pieces match. Now cut a piece of glass to match each of the pattern pieces. Start with the simplest shape. Usually one side of the glass will be easier to score than the other, so make a tiny test score in the corner of the glass to determine which is the better side. If you have purchased a whole or half-sheet of glass, or if you happen to get an unusually large scrap, cut a strip from it first and then cut the desired shape from the strip. As you tap and break, let the larger area of the glass rest on your work table if it is too heavy to hold in one hand. After you cut a piece of glass from a pattern, number it with a grease pencil or write the number on a piece of tape attached to the glass. Place the cut glass and the used pattern aside so you won't cut the same piece twice. When you have cut out all the pieces, compare them to the proper pattern pieces. If you have cut a piece of glass a bit too large, grind the edge down to the proper size with the grozing pliers. Clean your work area with a brush, and you are ready to foil and solder the pieces together.

CRAFTNOTES: FOILING AND SOLDERING

Foiling

Start with a roll of ¼-inch pre-cut adhesive-backed copper foil. Later you may want to experiment with 6-inch-wide foil from which narrow strips can be cut with scissors or a razor blade. The latter is the traditional foil used by craftsmen; it is less convenient but more economical and versatile.

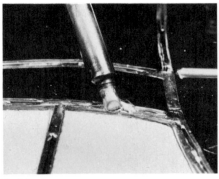

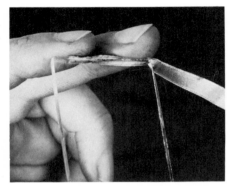

Begin by pulling off the paper that protects the adhesive backing of the foil. Press the sticky side of the foil onto the edge of a piece of glass, centering it there (above). Wrap the foil around the glass in one continuous strip; overlap the ends by ¼ to ½ inch. Press the foil down on both sides of the glass with your fingers, then smooth the foil with a piece of soft wood or the handle of a toothbrush.

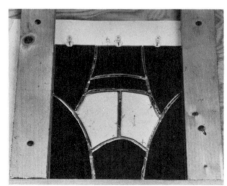

When all the pieces have been foiled, place them on top of the taped-down cartoon. Nail 1-by-3-inch lengths of wood around three of the sides. Secure the fourth side with pushpins (above).

Soldering

The next step is to prepare the soldering gun or iron by heating it and tinning the tip. Brush the tip with flux and touch the solder to it, running a bit of the melted solder over the surface of the tip. If the solder does not adhere, let the iron cool a bit and try again. When the iron is ready, use solder to tack the pieces of glass to each other along their edges. To do this, apply flux sparingly with your brush on all foil sides. Hold the soldering gun or iron in one hand, and a spool of solder wire in the other. Place the end of the solder on the foil and hold the heated tip of the gun or iron next to it. The solder will melt and flow onto the foil, forming a bead (above), which holds the pieces in place.

When all the pieces have been tacked together, complete the soldering process. Apply more flux to the foil and melt more solder with the heated tip of the gun or iron, running it over all the foil lines except those around the outside edge, next to the wood frame.

Should there be any gaps between pieces of glass, fill them with pieces of foil which have been folded in half with the adhesive sides together. As you solder, occasionally wipe the tip of the gun

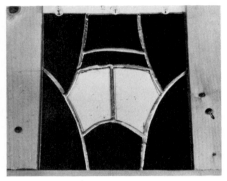

or iron with a damp sponge. This cools the tip and cleans off excess flux and solder. Avoid using too much solder—it is easier to add more than to remove it. Occasionally the melted solder will run through to the other side. If this happens your iron is too hot. Let it cool a bit. If you find the solder is not adhering to the foil, use a bit of steel wool to clean off any dirt, grease or oxides that might be clinging to the copper. A finished line of solder should be quite smooth and almost half-round (above).

When you have finished one side, let the solder cool for about five minutes; then wipe off excess flux with a paper towel. Remove the pushpins, slide the leaded glass out and turn it over. Solder the other side as you did the first, but omit the tacking since the pieces are already secured. Let the second side cool. Finish the project following the individual project directions.

Lead came

Two of the projects in this entry, the window panel on page 1063 and the lampshade on page 1066, are edged in strips of U-shaped lead came. Caming is extremely soft, and easily becomes bumpy and twisted from handling. To straighten it out, you need two pliers and one friend. Each person holds one end of the lead with the pliers. Pull the lead, stretching it so it straightens. To prepare it for fitting on the glass edge, lay the strip of stretched lead on a table and pry open the channel by running the end of a toothbrush handle along its length.

Note: If, for any reason, you know your work on a leaded glass project will be interrupted for a week or longer, be sure to wipe off excess flux. If you allow a coating of flux to remain on the lead for a long time, it will oxidize and cause the lead to discolor.

Glass and Plastics
Window panel

$ ☒ ⚐ 🔥

A simple window panel is a good first project for anyone interested in learning to work with leaded glass. Enlarge the pattern in Figure A to obtain the 6-by-7¾-inch design shown in the photograph at right; for a slightly smaller design (5½ by 7 inches) enlarge one of the patterns given for the planter or candle box in Figure D, page 1065. Tools and materials needed are shown and described on pages 1058 and 1059; three wood slats are used, each about 8 inches long.

Follow the steps in the Craftnotes to cut the glass, foil the edges and solder the pieces together (pages 1060 to 1062). When both sides have been soldered, remove all but one long wood slat, and clean your work area. The panel will be finished with ⅛-inch U-shaped lead came, designed to be used as an edging. Straighten the caming as described in the Craftnote on page 1062. To edge the first side, cut a strip of lead measuring ½ inch longer than the side. Use a special lead knife or a utility knife with a replaceable blade. Lay the lead on the table, place the blade on top and gently slice through the soft lead with a side-to-side rocking motion. Slide the glass into the lead (photograph 2) and flatten the lead with a stick of soft wood. Apply flux where the lead came meets a soldered line (the arrow in photograph 2 indicates this point on the first side). Apply a bit of solder at this junction, which forms one of the strongest points in the structure. Lead came is pure lead (unlike the solder, which is 60 percent tin and 40 percent lead) so it burns easily; solder carefully and cool the iron tip frequently with a damp sponge. When the lead has been attached to both sides of the panel with solder, trim off the excess lead at each end with the knife. Encase the edges of the remaining three sides in strips of lead came the same way, opening the ends of the lead to accommodate the thickness of the previous lead so corners are overlapped. Remember to press the lead down before soldering at the junctions. Then trim off excess lead, apply flux and solder the lead together at each corner.

Anna Grebanier-Schäfer designed this 6-by-7¾-inch leaded-glass window panel. Its small size and simple design make it a beginner's delight. The individual glass pieces are held together with copper foil and solder; the finished piece is edged with U-shaped strips of lead called cames.

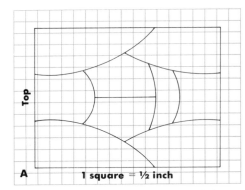

Figure A: Enlarge this pattern for the window panel on paper that has been ruled in ½-inch squares. Copy the design, one square at a time, transferring the lines from the small grid above onto the larger grid.

Top

A   1 square = ½ inch

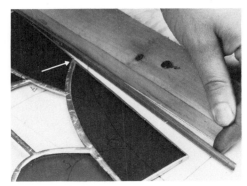

2: Lay the U-channel lead on its side against a wooden slat; then slide the glass into the U. Push hard to make sure the edge of the glass is against the base of the U. Press the edge of the lead down with a stick of soft wood.

Finishing
If you wish to hang the panel in a window, solder two hooks to the came, one at each corner. Cut two paper clips with wire cutters, or hold them with pliers and bend off the parts to be discarded to form two elongated U's. Rub the hooks with steel wool to remove any coating. Apply flux to each hook and the top corners of the panel, and solder the hooks to the lead. Clean both sides of the panel thoroughly with a strong solution of detergent. This removes the flux and other residues that may have accumulated. But do not let hot water run on the panel for very long—it might dissolve the adhesive under the foil. Dry the panel completely and antique the lead with a copper sulfate solution, applied with a brush or cotton swab. Clean the glass once more with a gentle touch—the copper sulfate affects only the surface of the lead.

Suspend the panel in a window with lengths of nylon thread or thin chain.

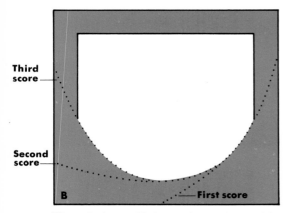

Figure B: An outside (convex) curve is one of the more difficult glass cuts and requires several steps if you are just beginning to work with glass. Make a series of short tangential scores and cuts as indicated by the dotted lines rather than one long, continuous curved score. Such an approach will give you a somewhat ragged edge, but it can be evened out with the grozing pliers.

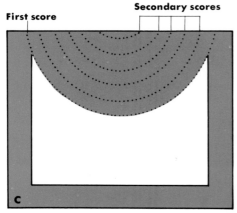

Figure C: An inside (concave) curve is another difficult glass cut, for novices and experienced craftsmen alike. First make one continuous score along the curved pattern edge. Remove the pattern and immediately tap below the score with the ball end of the glass cutter; begin at the center of the curve, and tap gently in either direction. Then make a series of secondary scores within the hollow of the first one. Tap these secondary scores, and with breaking pliers grasp the glass near the smallest curve and break it out. Break the remaining curves, one at a time, exercising more and more caution as you approach the first score. Finally break the first score, smoothing the curve with the grozing pliers if necessary.

Glass and Plastics
Candle box or planter

The candle boxes and planters pictured below are all constructed the same way. The only difference is in the choice of glass—a planter requires clear glass for the top pieces to let unfiltered light reach the plants. Tools and materials needed are shown and described on pages 1058 and 1059; three wooden slats are used, each about 8 inches long. No lead came is used in this project.

Follow the directions for cutting glass, foiling and soldering given in the Craftnotes on pages 1060 to 1062. For each box, make four panels, following one of the patterns in Figure D opposite. Note that in some of the boxes and planters I used a "jewel" or roundel rather than a piece of glass cut from a pattern. You could substitute flat pieces of stained glass cut in the shape shown in the pattern, but I recommend that you use jewels or roundels if they are available. They add texture and dimension that is exciting—especially in a candle holder, where refracted candlelight gives a spectacular effect as shown in the color photograph, page 1057.

If you choose to work with the planter design containing inside and outside curves, follow Figures B and C to make these cuts. Cut the pieces containing an outside curve before attempting the inside curve, as the former is the less difficult of the two. For each piece, place the pattern on top of the glass and make the curved cut first. Then complete cutting the glass by making the straight cuts.

Once the four individual panels have been foiled and soldered, they are ready to be soldered together into a box. My students always wonder how this can be accomplished, since I have only two hands and it seems at least six are needed. Here are a few tricks that make the process easier. Heat your soldering gun or iron and cut a string of solder into several ½-inch pieces; let the pieces cool. Clean the work surface and remove all but one wooden slat. Place one panel face down on the plywood, with

Four identical glass panels plus a bottom piece are soldered together to form each open candle box measuring 5½ by 5½ by 7 inches high. The candle box at top left is also shown in the photograph on page 1057; note how a change in the location affects the quality of the refracted light.

A beautiful way to display plants is to place them in leaded-glass planters. By cutting the upper pieces from clear glass, you let the plant in the container get the light it needs to thrive. A layer of pebbles, broken pottery, or gravel in the bottom will help you avoid overwatering.

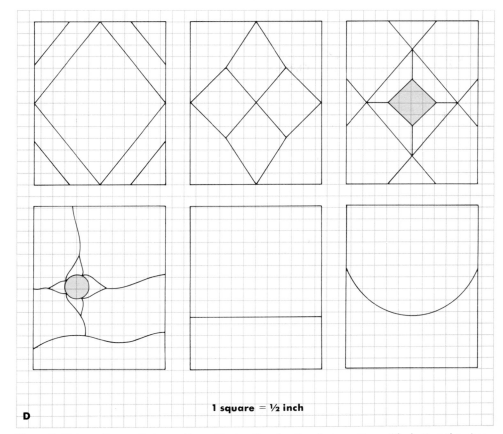

Additional references
The following books are recommended for advanced leaded glass techniques and for additional design ideas:

How to Work in Stained Glass
Anita and Seymour Isenberg
Chilton Book Company
Radnor, Pennsylvania 19089.

Working With Stained Glass
Jean-Jacques Duval
Thomas Y. Crowell Co.
666 Fifth Avenue
New York, N.Y. 10019

1 square = ½ inch

D

Figure D: Enlarge the candle box patterns (the top three) or the planter patterns (the bottom three) on paper on which you have drawn a grid with squares measuring ½ inch. Transfer any design one square at a time, copying the lines from the small grid onto the larger grid. Shaded areas indicate pattern pieces which may be cut from glass or for which textured glass "jewels" or roundels may be substituted. The last planter pattern has both an outside curve and an inside curve. Follow directions with Figures B and C when you make these cuts.

the edge of one side against the wooden slat. Secure it with a few pushpins on the other side. Hold the second panel against the wooden slat at a right angle to the first panel. Apply flux to both panels where soldered foil lines meet. (This is the strongest point.) Take a pre-cut piece of solder and put it at the fluxed juncture. With the heated soldering tip, melt the solder and thus join the two panels (photograph 3). Repeat these steps with the two remaining panels. Then put the two pairs of joined panels together in the same way, forming a box open at both ends. Finish soldering the joints of this box, covering all the foil lines with a smooth flow of solder. Next, place the box on a piece of pattern paper and trace around the inside bottom edges with a pencil; this will be the pattern for the bottom piece. Cut out the pattern, then foil the glass and tin the foil by melting a thin coating of solder over it. Tin the bottom edges of the box, and place the bottom inside it. Solder the bottom to the box on the inside; invert the box and solder the bottom to it on the outside.

Clean the inner and outer surfaces of the planter or candle box with a strong solution of detergent, but don't expose the glass to hot water for a long period of time or the adhesive on the foil might dissolve. Dry the box. To "antique" or dull the solder, apply a copper sulfate solution with a brush or cotton swab. Clean the glass once more, but not so thoroughly that the antiquing is removed.

For a planter, line the bottom with a piece of plastic wrap to prevent possible water leakage. Make sure the plastic extends partially up the sides, just up to the clear glass. Then place small pebbles, gravel, or broken pottery in the bottom before filling it half-way with soil. This provides drainage, and helps you avoid overwatering. To keep the candle box clean and free from wax build-up, set a small ashtray or candle-holder in the bottom to catch wax drippings.

3: With two panels to be joined held at right angles to each other, hold the heated soldering gun or iron in the other hand and melt a pre-cut length of solder at the point where the soldered foil lines meet.

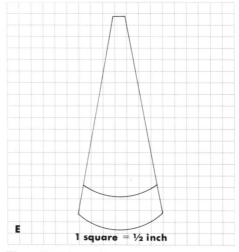

Figure E: Enlarge this pattern for the lampshade panel on paper that has been ruled in ½-inch squares. Copy the design, one square at a time, transferring the lines to the large grid.

1 square = ½ inch

E

4: From this inside view of the taped lampshade panels, you can see the first set of masking-tape strips (applied while the panels were laid out flat) and the second set of strips (applied after the first and last panels were brought together in a cone shape so their edges met).

5: Adjacent lampshade panels at the top of this photograph have been tacked together with lumps of solder and the lumps of one joint are being smoothed down with the soldering tip. The lower panels are only partially tacked. The shade is held so the joint being soldered is horizontal.

This simple leaded-glass lampshade can be made without using an expensive lamp mold for support. To achieve the flower shape, eleven petal-like opalescent glass panels were temporarily joined on the inside with masking tape. Solder was then used to join them permanently; a continuous strip of U-shaped lead came edges the scalloped bottom.

Glass and Plastics

Flower-petal lampshade   💲 🕐 🧍 ⚗️

The rather simple shapes of the glass pieces used in this lampshade make it seem deceptively easy to make. However, all of the pieces must fit together precisely and so they need to be cut very accurately. Even those who have a healthy amount of glass-cutting experience will find this project a challenge.

The tools and materials required are shown and described on pages 1058 and 1059. Two 10-inch-long wood slats are needed. I used two shades of opalescent glass in this project. To wire and assemble the lamp, once the shade is finished, you need: one 2-inch-diameter vase cap (stainless steel or stainless steel with a brass finish); stainless-steel flux; ⅜-inch threaded tube about 1½ inches long; light bulb socket without a switch; decorative loop; two decorative hooks; two toggle bolts (for hollow plaster ceilings) or two-ended screws (for beamed ceilings) that fit into the decorative hooks; wire cutter; wire stripper; screwdriver; line switch; lamp cord long enough to extend from the socket to the ceiling, across the ceiling to the wall, and down the wall to an electrical outlet; swag chain long enough to extend from the loop at the top of the lamp to the ceiling and across the ceiling to the wall; a globe bulb.

Making the Panels

The lampshade consists of eleven identical panels; each panel is made of two flat pieces of glass. Following the directions in the Craftnotes, pages 1060 and 1061, make a cartoon by enlarging the pattern for the panel (Figure E) on plain paper. Then cut a pattern for each of the two panel pieces from heavy paper. Cut eleven upper pieces from the same color of glass; refer to Figure B on page 1064 for advice on cutting the outside curve of these pieces, making the curved cut first and then the straight cuts. Then cut eleven lower pieces from the other color of glass; refer to Figure B on page 1064 for cutting the outside curves and Figure C for the inside curves. When all of the pieces have been cut, foil them as directed in the Craftnote on page 1062. When foiling the large upper pieces, overlap the foil on the outside curve; on the small bottom pieces, overlap on the inside curve. Following the soldering directions in the Craftnote on page 1062, make eleven panels by soldering the two panel pieces together where their curved edges fit together. To keep the two pieces from shifting while you solder, nail two wooden slats to the board at an angle matching the long edges of the larger piece. Slide two glass pieces into the open triangle formed by the slats as far as they will go, and anchor the bottom glass piece with one or two pushpins. Apply solder to one side, let cool; turn the panel over and solder the other side.

Assembling the Lampshade

When you have finished eleven panels, wipe the flux off thoroughly. Put the eleven panels side by side and face down on the plywood board, arranging them in a fan shape with the side edges butting. Secure the panels in this position by hammering nails into the plywood all around and close to the edges of the fan shape. Then place strips of masking tape across the panels. Overlap the strips about ¼ inch, making parallel rows until nearly the entire surface is covered with tape. If the tape does not stick well, clean the glass more thoroughly—some of the flux has not been removed. Next lift the taped panels off the board. Bring the first and last panel together, forming a cone. Place several more strips of masking tape across the first and last panel, overlapping the first set of strips (photograph 4).

Set the lamp on its scalloped, bottom edge. Use solder to tack adjacent panels together at the point where the soldered foil lines meet (where two panel pieces have been joined). Then tack the panels together along the length of all the adjacent edges, placing lumps of solder close together (photograph 5). After the tacking is completed, run the heated soldering tip along the tacked lines, melting the lumps so they flow and flatten into smooth lines. After the adjacent outside edges have all been soldered (do not apply solder to the scalloped edge at the bottom), remove the tape. Finish the inside of the lamp by applying solder along the length of the panel edges. If you find it difficult to reach into the top part of the lampshade, use the heated soldering tip to cut a length of solder into ½-inch pieces. Place these pre-cut pieces of solder on the hard-to-reach joints, and melt them onto the foil.

When both inside and outside panel edges have been soldered, edge the scalloped bottom edge with ⅛-inch U-shaped lead came. Stretch and straighten the lead as directed in the Craftnote on page 1062. Placing the beginning end of the lead in a valley between the scallops, press the lead firmly onto the glass. The lead is quite soft and may be curved and pushed into the valleys with a finger or with a toothbrush handle. Use tape to secure the lead to the glass as your work progresses around the edge. When the bottom of the lamp is completely edged in lead, cut off any excess at the end. To do this, mark the cutting point on the lead by nicking it with a lead knife; place the lead on the table and with a side-to-side rocking motion, gently slice through the lead with the knife. Then replace the end of the lead on the lamp edge. With solder, tack the lead came to the soldered foil lines where they meet in the valleys. Then flood the came with solder covering it completely and smoothing down the previously tacked points. Fit the vase cap over the opening in the top of the lamp and tape it in place. Then apply solder wherever the vase cap touches the soldered lines of the lamp. To do this, rub the vase cap at these points with steel wool to remove the finish. Brush stainless steel flux on the metal to be soldered, and solder the vase cap to the lamp. Clean the inside and the outside of the lamp and the soldering tip with liquid detergent immediately (stainless steel flux is very strong). But do not allow hot water to run on the glass for long—the adhesive on the foil might dissolve. Dry the lamp thoroughly and apply copper sulfate solution to the solder with a brush or a cotton swab. Clean the lamp again, but do not apply much pressure or the antiquing might come off.

Wiring the Lamp

To assemble and wire the finished lamp, follow the directions in Figure F for screwing the threaded tube into the vase cap, screwing the loop and socket onto the tube, attaching the swag chain to the loop, and connecting the lamp cord to the socket core. Tighten the terminal screws and reassemble the socket. Next, attach a decorative hook to the ceiling directly above where the lamp is to hang; use a toggle bolt or two-ended screw. Attach the chain to this hook so the lamp hangs at the right height. Attach another hook to the ceiling near where it meets the wall above an outlet. Drape the chain across the ceiling and attach it to this second hook. Attach the line switch to the cord at a convenient height. Screw a globe bulb into the socket, and plug the cord into the outlet.

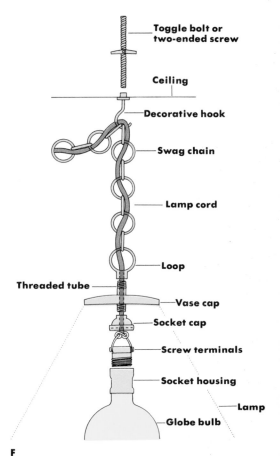

F
Figure F: This exploded-view diagram shows how the parts used to wire the lamp are assembled. Screw the threaded tube halfway into the vase cap. Screw the loop onto the top end of the tube, and the socket cap onto the end inside the lamp (the socket disassembles). Split the end of the lamp cord with a knife, and with wire strippers remove ½ inch of plastic coating from the ends. Open a link in one end of the swag chain with pliers and close it over the loop. Weave the lamp cord through the chain and pass the stripped ends through the tube and out of the socket cap. Make an Underwriter's knot with the split ends of the cord by passing each end of the wire through a loop in the other end, as shown. Slip the socket core out of its metal housing; connect an exposed wire to each terminal screw in the direction in which the screw turns, and reassemble.

Labels in Figure F: Toggle bolt or two-ended screw · Ceiling · Decorative hook · Swag chain · Lamp cord · Loop · Threaded tube · Vase cap · Socket cap · Screw terminals · Socket housing · Lamp · Globe bulb

LEATHER WORKING
Luxurious Durability

Leather, made from animal hides (called skins, if the animals are small ones) is one of man's favorite craft materials. Its timeless appeal lies in its luxurious texture, warm color, clean natural aroma, and exceptional durability. Leather-like synthetic materials abound, but few approach leather's natural beauty, which actually tends to improve with age.

The crafting of leather began early in man's history. Egyptian carvings dating from 3000 B.C. show leather being processed, and some of the leather shoes and sandals made by these early Egyptians are on display at the British Museum. Around 3000 B.C., the Sumerians were using leather tires for their chariots; the Roman legions in Caesar's time sailed the seas on ships with leather sails. Australian aborigines and primitive tribes of Africa and South America have used leather for shields, armor and shelter.

Primitive peoples transformed animal hides into leather following the same steps we use today. The hides are cleaned and the hair of the animal removed. The skin is then tanned. Tanning involves impregnating the skins with a special tanning solution which preserves them and keeps them supple and pliable. The Romans tanned hides with a solution made from barks, berries and roots, and the word tan is derived from the Latin word "tanare" meaning oak bark. Another tanning process, described in Homer's Iliad, involves softening the skin with oil beaten and rubbed into it. A mechanized version of this procedure is used today to produce chamois and latigo. The two most widely-used methods of tanning today are vegetable tanning and chrome tanning. As in Roman times, vegetable tanning still involves the use of oak bark extracts. Chrome-tanned leather has been processed in a chemical solution of chrome salts; it is rapidly replacing vegetable-tanned leather since it is a faster and less expensive process. For a description of vegetable- and chrome-tanned leather, refer to the Craftnotes on page 1076.

Although leather objects made by ancient peoples were primarily functional, man soon learned the decorative potential of leather; today objects made from leather combine function with beauty. Indeed, they are sometimes purely decorative, like the sculptured leather man, opposite, and the painted bracelet, right. In most cases, however, the leathercrafter seeks to create a useful as well as a decorative object, the appliqued pillow (page 1071), like the braided belt (page 1072), and the briefcase (page 1077). All these projects use relatively heavy leather sewn by hand; on pages 1074 and 1075, you will find a Craftnote on how to sew thinner leather, used mostly for garments, with a machine.

Hope Stevens is a graduate of Syracuse University, where she studied advertising and design. While taking her master's degree in art education at New York University, a course in leather working sparked her enduring interest in that medium. She provides boutiques and individual customers with a steady supply of personally designed, handcrafted leather goods.

Leathercrafts
Painted bracelet ¢ ▢ 🧍 ♨

Painting on leather is one of my favorite ways of decorating this material. I use acrylic paints for everything—belts, bags, pillows, and as shown here, bracelets. Acrylic paint can be applied full strength, straight from the jar or tube, or it can be thinned with water to achieve the effect of watercolor.

To make the painted bracelet you need the following equipment (available in art supply stores): paper for the pattern; carbon paper; replaceable-blade knife; fine-pointed (No. 1 or 2) watercolor brush; and a can of clear acrylic spray. From a leathercraft supply shop, you need: one piece of undyed 2-ounce vegetable-tanned leather measuring at least 8-by-3-inches; sharp leather (or fabric) shears; a circular punch; waxed nylon or linen thread; a harness needle; and a ¾-inch buckle. See Craftnotes, page 1076, for a description of the equipment.

This painted bracelet is in the form of a mini-belt for your wrist. Use the flower design shown here or substitute one of your own. Directions for making the bracelet are on the following page.

Leather becomes remarkably pliable when soaked in water, and can be curved and molded into sculptural forms. Jim Murnak designed and cut a simple 26-inch-high human figure from leather and poured sand into the sewn leather form. Directions for the sculpture are on page 1079.

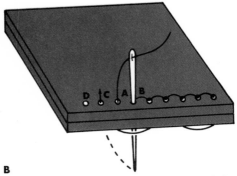

B

Figure B: Backstitch: Working from right to left, bring the needle up at A, insert at B, up at C. Complete the next stitch by inserting the needle down at A, and then up at D. Begin and end each thread length by going over the first and last stitch a few times.

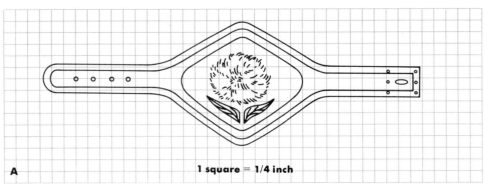

A　　　　　　　1 square = 1/4 inch

Figure A: To enlarge the pattern for the bracelet, use a ruler and pencil to draw a grid whose squares measure ¼-inch. Draw the pattern on the grid one square at a time, following the lines on the ⅛-inch grid shown here. The bracelet fits wrists measuring from 5½ to 6½ inches; for larger or smaller wrists, add or subtract the additional or lesser amount at the buckle end (at the right).

Make a paper pattern for the bracelet by enlarging Figure A. Tape the pattern to the smooth (grain) side of the leather with carbon paper between. Transfer the outline of the bracelet, the holes and the slit, and the outlines of the painted design to the leather. With shears, cut out the bracelet shape. Prepare the bracelet for the buckle by making the holes and the slit (see pattern); use the No. 0 tube of the circular punch to make the holes and the replaceable-blade knife to make the slit.

Paint the bracelet, using your own colors or those shown in the photograph on page 1069. For the large border areas and the leaves, use broad strokes so the paint flows on smoothly; when painting the flower, use short, feathery strokes for the petals. Let the paint dry and set for two or three hours. Then coat the bracelet with the acrylic spray to protect the paint. When the spray coating is dry, pass the buckle end of the bracelet through the buckle, inserting the buckle tongue in the slit. Fold the end over so the six holes match and form a row of three holes. Using a 6-inch length of doubled thread, sew the buckle to the bracelet. Use a backstitch (Figure B) when sewing the three holes.

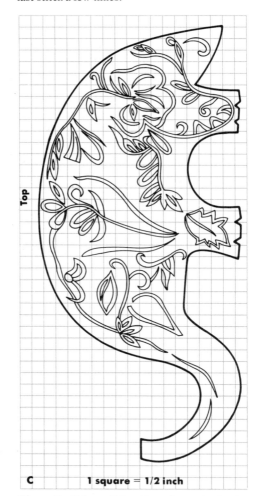

C　　　　1 square = 1/2 inch

Figure C: Enlarge this pattern for an elephant applique by copying it on paper ruled in ½-inch squares. Draw the pattern on the ½-inch squares, one square at a time, following the lines on the smaller grid shown above.

Leathercrafts
Animal applique pillow　　　$ ▯ ☥ ♨

Suede pillows of any size and shape can be made by hand and embellished with simple animal shapes. For example, a sprightly imaginary elephant decorates the 22-by-22-inch square suede pillow shown opposite. Using children's books, posters and greeting cards as sources for design ideas, you could enjoy a whole menagerie parading across your bed, floor or sofa.

Each pillow requires the following equipment, available from leathercraft supply shops: two pieces of 3-ounce suede cut the same size and shape for the pillow front and back; and a piece of 4-ounce top-grain (smooth-surfaced) cowhide in a contrasting color for the animal applique. The contrasting leather should be vegetable-tanned because this type of leather retains impressed designs; you'll need a piece measuring 9-by-19 inches. You will also need a swivel knife and a deerfoot—two tooling instruments—and a sponge for dampening the leather. Sharp leather or fabric shears are used to cut the leather. A hole spacer (5 spaces per inch), tapestry awl, block of soft wood, a wooden, leather or synthetic mallet, waxed linen or nylon thread, and a harness or No. 18 tapestry needle are needed to sew the leather. See Craftnotes on page 1076 for a description of the equipment. The remaining materials may be purchased at dime stores and include: paper for the pattern; pencil; ruler; masking tape; rubber cement; and polyester stuffing.

Enlarge the elephant in Figure C, including the tooling design. Place the piece of contrasting leather on a flat surface with the smooth side up. Dampen the leather with a wet sponge and tape the pattern to it. With a pencil, go over all the lines on the pattern, impressing them in the leather. Remove the pattern and cut out the

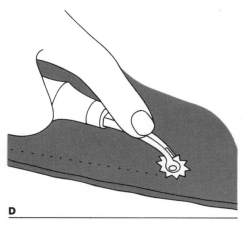

Figure D: Run the wheel of the hole spacer all around the edge of the leather, leaving impressions ¼-inch in from the edge.

Hope Stevens enlivened a plain suede pillow by sewing on a whimsical elephant applique cut from leather that she tooled herself.

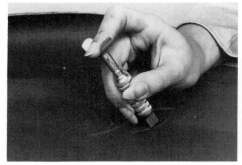

1: The swivel knife is used to cut lines into the leather. Apply pressure with the forefinger, which rests on top as shown. The blade is turned between the thumb and the remaining fingers.

2: Hold the deerfoot as you would a pencil. The scribe (pointed end) of the deerfoot is used to deepen the uncut lines of the design; it is also used to open and spread the cut lines.

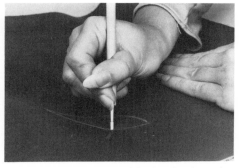

3: The spoon-shaped end of the deerfoot is used to create designs in relief by depressing the leather surrounding the areas you wish to appear raised.

elephant shape. To tool the impressed design, use the swivel knife as shown in photograph 1 to cut deep lines in the leather wherever a dark line is desired. (Be careful not to cut through the leather completely; practice tooling on a scrap piece of leather to familiarize yourself with the instrument.) Deepen the remaining uncut lines, using the scribe, or pointed end, of the deerfoot (photograph 2). If you would like to raise certain areas, this may be done by depressing the surrounding area with the flat or foot end of the deerfoot (photograph 3). If you wish, dye or wax the applique following the Craftnote on page 1076.

Rubber-cement the applique in the desired position to the right side of the pillow's front section. Place the pillow front on a flat hard surface, and, with the hole spacer, mark holes ¼-inch in from the edge all around the applique (Figure D). Place the pillow front on the block of wood and with the awl and mallet, pierce holes where marked by the spacer through both thicknesses of leather. Using 24-inch lengths of doubled thread, sew the applique to the pillow front with a backstitch (Figure B, page 1070).

Wrong sides facing, place the pillow front and back together with all edges even. Pierce holes ¼-inch apart all around the perimeter of the pillow, ¼-inch in from the edges; use only the awl and mallet—a hole spacer will not mark suede successfully. Sew up three sides of the pillow using a whip stitch (Figure E) and doubled thread. Begin and end each length of thread by going over the first and last stitch twice. Stuff the pillow with polyester stuffing, and whipstitch the fourth side closed.

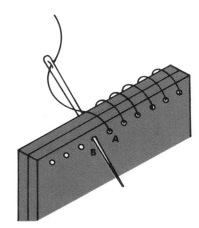

Figure E: Whipstitch: Bring the needle out to the front at A, then bring the needle around to the back and insert it through B. Continue from hole to hole, whipping the thread around the edges.

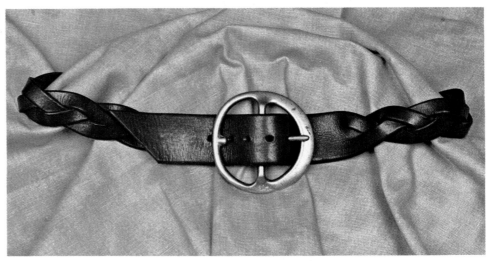

A mystery or magic braid belt is easy to make. Hope Stevens utilized the technique to make the handsome belt you see here; it could be adapted for use in watchbands, bracelets and necklaces.

Weaving, Braiding, Knotting
Magic braid belt

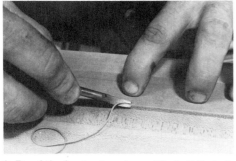

4: Bevel the front outer edges of the belt (including the ends), and the four strip edges using the No. 2 edger. This removes a sliver of leather, as shown, leaving a smooth beveled edge.

This trick or magic braid belt looks difficult, but it really is quite easy once you know the secret. The magic lies in the fact that only the center portion of the belt is slit and braided, with the ends left intact. Try it on a scrap piece of fabric or leather; you will be surprised how easily the strips fall into place.

From a leathercraft supply shop, you will need a belt buckle measuring 3 to 3½ inches wide; a strip of leather cut from 6- to 7-ounce vegetable-tanned leather (the length is determined as described below, the width is determined by the width of the buckle); a No. 2 edger to round the leather edges; leather, wooden or synthetic mallet; circular punch; dark-brown liquid dye; leather wax or oil; medium-size rivets and a rivet setter. (See Craftnotes, page 1076, for descriptions of tools.) In addition, you will need these dime store items: pencil; clean soft cloth; masking tape; and rubber gloves. Also needed are a steel mending plate (used as an anvil); a metal-edged ruler; and a replaceable-blade knife—all found in hardware stores.

Preparing the Belt
The best way to determine the proper waist size is to measure an old belt the wearer uses with comfort. Lay the old belt out flat and measure it from the end of the buckle tongue to the hole that is most used. This is the waist size.

Cut the strip of leather the desired width and 10 inches longer than the waist size (this allows for the shrinkage which results from the braiding process). Place the leather, smooth side up, on a flat surface with cardboard underneath to protect the surface when cutting the leather. With pencil and metal-edged ruler, mark two parallel lines as far apart as the desired width of the belt. Using the metal edge as a guide, cut along the two lines with the replaceable-blade knife. Cut the ends of the belt in the same manner, making the buckle end square, and the other end diagonal (refer to the photograph above).

The next step is to slit the belt into three lengthwise strips. With the ruler, divide and mark the belt into thirds. Beginning approximately 7 inches from the tip of either end, slit the belt along the marked lines using the replaceable-blade knife. To keep the leather from splitting further (the leather is subjected to considerable strain during the braiding process), punch a No. 1-size hole at each end of each slit with the circular punch. Bevel the front outer lengthwise edges of the belt with the edger (photograph 4), the front outer edges at the two ends, and the four strip edges. Prepare the belt for the buckle as shown in Figure F. Then dye both sides of the belt following the Craftnotes on page 1076.

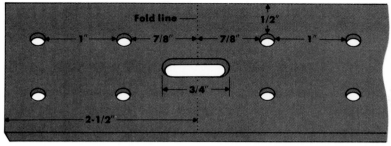

F

Figure F: Mark a fold line 2½ inches from the square end of the belt. Across the center of this fold line, make a slit for the buckle tongue: use the circular punch to punch a hole at each end of the slit, then make cuts with the replaceable-blade knife, joining the holes. Punch the eight holes for the rivets as indicated.

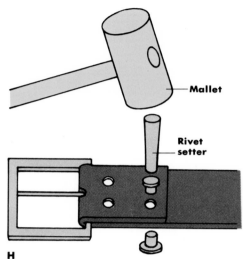

H

Figure H: Place one half of the rivet on the steel plate under the belt. Press the holes in the belt down over the half rivet. Press the second half of the rivet down onto the first half; then, pound the rivet setter with a mallet as shown, forcing the two halves of the rivet together.

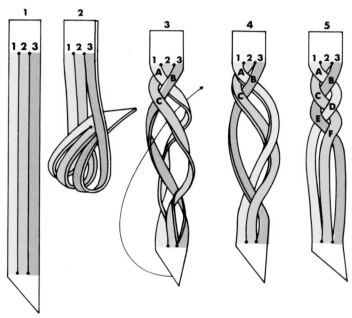

G

Figure G: Follow these steps to complete one entire cycle when working the magic braid. *Step 1:* The belt leather has been slit into three equal strips. Label the strips 1, 2, and 3 with pieces of masking tape. *Step 2:* Pass the lower end of the belt through the slit that separates 2 and 3, as shown. *Step 3:* Carry strip 1 over 2, forming a bend or curve (bight A). Carry strip 3 over 1, forming bight B. Carry strip 2 over 3, forming bight C. You will notice that undesirable twists have formed at the bottom. To remove these twists, follow the arrow, passing the lower end of the belt through the slit between 2 and 3, below bight C. *Step 4:* The twists have been removed by step 3. *Step 5:* Continue braiding, passing strip 1 over 2, (bight D), 3 over 1 (bight E), and 2 over 3 (bight F). One braiding cycle is now complete.

Braiding

To begin braiding, dampen the belt slightly to make it more pliable. Follow steps 1 to 5 in Figure G. Continue braiding, repeating steps 2, 3, 4 and 5 until the strands are not long enough to complete another braiding cycle. Make sure to braid as tightly as possible, so that when you reach the end you have enough leeway to smooth the braid and equalize the braid pattern.

Finishing

Rub leather oil or wax into the leather to protect it. The first step in attaching the belt buckle is to fold the buckle end along the fold line, smooth side out. Then place the fold on the metal plate and pound it flat with the mallet, making sure the eight holes line up. Unfold the end and pass it through the belt buckle, fitting the buckle tongue through the slit; then refold the end around the bar of the buckle, again lining up the holes. Set rivets into each of the pairs of holes as shown in Figure H. After the buckle has been attached, punch belt holes in the opposite end, referring to the old belt for spacing.

Sewing garment leather by machine is no more difficult than sewing fabric by machine—in some ways it is even easier. For example, leather edges won't ravel, so there is less finishing and seams can be narrower. The close texture of leather makes marking—usually a tedious step—a breeze. Put away your iron—there's no need to press leather. One manufacturer has developed a garment suede that can be machine washed and dried. Chamois skins (used for polishing cars and available at hardware stores) make butter-soft garments, and are also washable.

To machine-sew leather, you will need the usual sewing supplies (available at sewing shops and sewing departments of department stores): a modern sewing machine, capable of sewing heavy fabrics; sewing machine needles (a regular needle for the trial garment, and a wedge-shaped leather needle); dressmaker's carbon paper and pattern wheel; dressmaker's pattern; fabric for a trial garment (see pattern for yardage); straight pins; silk, heavy-duty mercerized, or cotton-wrapped polyester thread. For cutting garment leather, use sharp fabric or leather shears; for pounding seams flat, use a mallet with a synthetic, wood, or leather head. The following equipment is also needed: pencil; waterproof felt-tipped pen; tracing paper; ruler; transparent or masking tape; and rubber cement.

Choosing a pattern

Most dressmaker patterns designed for fabrics are easily adaptable to garment leather and garment suede. Avoid patterns calling for stretchable knit fabrics, as these patterns are designed for fabrics with more stretch than leather will provide. Unless you intend to use a leather that is very lightweight, soft and supple (such as "sheer suede" or chamois), choose patterns specifically designed for heavier fabrics, and in which the pattern pieces are small (see drawing, right). If they are available, it's a good idea to use patterns designed for real leather and suede, vinyl or imitation leather fabrics. These have convenient construction details built right in and were designed with the very special properties of leather in mind. All other patterns will need to be altered by you in a time-consuming procedure, but one that can be well worth it if you like the pattern. Using the directions that follow, you can make a luxurious, economical, well-fitted leather or suede garment that will afford you years of wear and enjoyment.

Making a trial garment

It is best to make alterations on a trial garment made from an inexpensive fabric. Every pin mark and stitch will leave a hole in the leather, so there can be no ripping out of mistakes or adjustment of improperly fitting pieces. Most often a heavy, firm, canvas-weight cotton fabric is used, but felt is a highly recommended alternative because it resembles leather in weight and texture; like leather, its cut edges don't fray. Cut the pattern pieces from the fabric. With dressmaker's carbon paper and a pattern wheel, transfer all the pattern markings—darts, buttonholes, notches, pockets, center front and back—to the wrong side of the fabric pieces. Machine-baste the parts together. Make any standard fitting adjustments you would make if sewing the garment from fabric. Then make the following additional alterations, marking the adjustments right on the trial garment with a ball-point pen.

Leather garments, especially pants, look best if they are fitted closely to the body. Remember, too, that leather tends to stretch and sleeves and pant legs will shorten up to one full inch because of the bending action of the knee and elbow, so these pattern pieces will need to be altered accordingly. Since the cut edges of leather and suede don't fray or unravel, you may choose to dispense with hems entirely. But you might prefer the look of a finished hem; in this case, allow 1 to 2 inches (directions for making a hem follow).

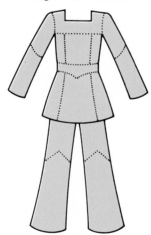

Since leather is a natural, not manufactured material, it comes in irregularly shaped pieces and limited sizes. It has at least a few flaws, holes, or scars which were incurred during the animal's lifetime. Leather is expensive; garments made from

many small pieces are more economically constructed because the pieces are easier to lay out on the usable portions of the skin. Therefore, if the pattern you have chosen has large pieces, divide them into small sections (as shown at left). For instance, add a yoke, a center seam, a waistline or a waistband; split a leg or a sleeve above or below (not at) the knee or elbow. Experiment first by tracing the fashion sketch on the pattern envelope; draw your additional seamlines on this tracing. Try for an attractive, balanced effect. Remember that the garment has a back view; don't neglect it. When your sketch is ready, mark the seamlines you have added on the trial garment, indicating that a ⅜-inch seam allowance must be added when cutting the parts from leather.

Finally, turn the trial garment inside out and trim seam allowances to ⅜-inch. The normal ⅝-inch allowed for fabric seams is unnecessary, bulky, and uneconomical when sewing leather, unless you use a very lightweight leather. Mark the inside of each piece; then take the garment apart. The disassembled trial garment pieces, with all adjustments indicated, will be used as a pattern to cut out the leather.

Preparing leather pieces

Lay the leather on a large flat surface, wrong side up. Each pattern piece is cut out individually from a single thickness of leather; unlike fabric, leather is never folded double when cutting out pieces. With a felt-tipped pen, mark the faults in the leather on the wrong side of the skin. Lay all the major pattern pieces on the lengthwise grain of the skin, (the grain that runs parallel to the animal's backbone, page 1077). Small pieces, such as cuffs, pockets, and collars can be placed in any direction. If working with suede, lay out the pieces as for a napped fabric.

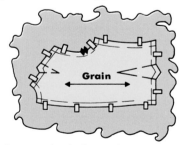

The best method of securing pattern pieces to leather is with tape; place pieces of masking or transparent tape about every 6 inches (as shown above). With very sharp fabric shears, leather shears, a

SEWING GARMENTS BY MACHINE

single-edged razor blade, or a mat knife, cut around the pattern pieces, cutting right through the tape as you go. (Where you have added a seam, mark the additional seam allowance on the leather and cut along marked line rather than the pattern edge.) Next, transfer the markings to the leather with a felt-tipped pen. To do this, insert a pin through the pattern and scratch the wrong side of the leather to mark the symbols. Connect the scratch marks with a ruler (for straight lines); draw curves free-hand.

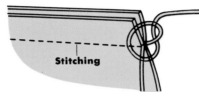

Sewing

Fundamental sewing techniques are employed, along with a few special methods and shortcuts; in general, follow the step-by-step instructions that come with all patterns. Before sewing the garment pieces together, practice the techniques on scrap leather using the same thread, needle and thicknesses of leather as you would in the final garment. Insert the wedge-pointed leather needle in the machine, set the stitch length at 7 to 10 stitches per inch, adjust the pressure regulator and upper and lower thread tensions as you would when sewing heavy fabrics (see the directions in the machine's instruction manual). Make sure the machine is clean and free of oil or lint. When sewing, keep the machine going at a slow even speed. Tie off all thread ends (above); do not backstitch, as this weakens leather seams.

Seams

Pieces may be sewn together with two basic types of seams: plain seams and lapped seams. **Plain seams** should be used when you want the seam to be strong yet inconspicuous (such as when setting in sleeves or sewing the crotch seam of pants) or when the leather is lightweight and needs the extra support that plain seams give. Plain seams are sewn with right sides together, edges even. The pieces to be seamed are held together temporarily with tape. When stitching is finished, the seam allowance is opened, rubber-cemented and pounded flat with a mallet. **Lapped seams** are more decorative than plain seams, and also more practical in that they are less bulky; they are therefore ideal for heavyweight leathers. Use

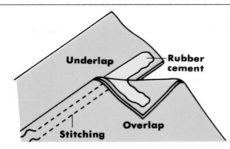

lapped seams also wherever you wish to enhance the garment's pieced look, and especially for the seams you added to the trial garment (yokes, center seams, waistbands, split pant legs and split sleeves).

To make a lapped seam (shown above), first trim off the seam allowance of one of the sections to be joined. Place the trimmed section (overlap), with the overlap's trimmed edge along the underlap's seam line. Baste in place by applying rubber cement to the underside of the overlap and the top of the underlap. Rubber cement discolors leather surfaces, so make sure it stays within the overlapped areas. Let dry; press both pieces together. Make two rows of stitching about ⅛ inch and ¼ inch from the cut edge of the overlap.

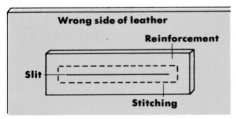

Buttonholes: These can simply be a slit in the leather. If the buttonhole will be subject to a lot of wear, rubber-cement a small rectangle of leather underneath the opening, as above. Cut a slit through both, and stitch around the area to secure the reinforcement.

Zippers: Fold back the seam allowances for the zipper opening, apply rubber cement to the underside and just beneath. When dry, press the surfaces together and pound them flat with a mallet. Tape the zipper, face down, over the seam and sew in place. Remove tape.

Interfacing: Leathers rarely need extra stiffness; but they may stretch. Stabilize areas vulnerable to stress and wear such as necks, cuffs, and armholes with an interfacing of fabric. Instead of basting the interfacing to the garment, trim off the seam allowances and apply rubber cement near the seam edges.

Facings: Save leather by using fabric or grosgrain ribbon for facing armholes, necklines, waistbands.

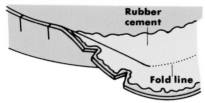

Hems: Mark the foldline of the hem on the wrong side of the leather, and apply rubber cement to the inside surfaces of the hem. Let dry and fold up the hem, pressing it with your fingers (pound it with a mallet if the leather is heavy). On curved hems, remove small triangular pieces at the cut edge so the hem lies flat (as above).

Linings: Most leather garments should be lined to eliminate clinging, stretching and crocking (tiny fibers that rub loose from leather), and for a finished appearance. Choose a fabric that is dry-cleanable (or machine washable, if your garment is made from the machine-washable suede). Cut out the lining using the same pattern pieces you used for the leather, minus the details such as pockets. Sew the lining pieces together to form a basic shell in the same shape as the leather garment. Attach skirt or pants linings before applying waistband or facing. Sew jacket linings to facings after the jacket is complete.

How much leather?

Leather comes in irregularly-shaped pieces and is sold by the square foot; fabric comes in standard widths and is sold by the yard. In order to determine how much leather is required to make up a dressmaker's pattern (which is designed for fabric), a formula is used to convert the fabric yardage specified on the pattern envelope to the required leather footage. Most woven fabrics are 44-to-45 inches wide (pattern designs specifically for stretchable knit fabrics are unsuitable for leather). To convert 44- to 45-inch-wide fabric, simply multiply the specified fabric yardage by eleven, and then add twenty percent (for loss in cutting). Thus, if the pattern calls for 3 yards of fabric:

```
        3 yards
      ×11
       33
   ×    .20   loss allowance
      6.60
       33    add to 33
      39.60  or 40 square feet
```

CRAFTNOTES: TYPES OF LEATHER, TOOLS, AND SUPPLIERS

The skins of many animals can be made into leather, but those that are commercially raised for meat are most common, since their hides are available in large quantities. Thus, cowhide, sheepskin, and calfskin are the most readily available. But you might like to try working with lambskin, deerskin, goatskin, snakeskin, pigskin or horsehide—when you can get them.

Cowhide, the most popular leather, is available in many types and thicknesses. **Latigo** is cowhide tanned in animal oils, and is a strong, flexible leather that can be used for belts, purses, sandals and other items. **Vegetable-tanned cowhide** is a dry, stiff leather and is the best type to use for tooling and stamping. It is used for belts, watchbands, cases, shoe soles and luggage. **Chrome-tanned leather** has been tanned with chrome salts, which renders leather tough, firm, and water-resistant (not waterproof). Chrome-tanned leather is used for shoe uppers, gloves, and garments, and is usually dyed at the tannery; the salts leave the edges of the leather with a bluish-green tinge.

Suede is a type of leather whose surface has been buffed or sanded to produce a velvet-like texture.

Garment cowhide is thinner and more supple than that used for bags, belts, and shoes. Most garment leather is dyed and sueded when you purchase it. The thinness of the leather is obtained by slicing a thick hide into layers. "Splits" are layers that have been taken from the flesh side of the hide, and are usually sueded on both sides. "Top grain" leather, which is the topmost layer, has only the flesh side sueded, with the grain side left smooth on top. **Sheer suede** is lightweight, soft and so supple that it handles almost like fabric. For techniques that will help you in sewing garments from leather, see the Craftnotes on pages 1074 and 1075.

Dyeing and finishing

Chrome-tanned and sueded leather are usually dyed at the tannery. Therefore, if you like the natural color of undyed leather, or if you require a color that isn't readily available, choose vegetable-tanned or oil-tanned (latigo) cowhide; both are sold undyed in natural tan and light yellow. The materials required for dyeing leather are: leather dye, natural or antique finish; shearling (this is a wool pad specially made for applying dyes, oils, and waxes to leather because it absorbs more liquid than plain cloth; you can make a substitute by placing a sponge inside a cloth); newspaper; and rubber gloves to protect your hands.

Spread sheets of newspaper over your work surface to protect it from the dye. Dip the shearling or cloth-covered sponge into the dye. Apply the dye to the leather, making increasingly larger circular swirling motions. When the entire surface and the cut edges of the leather have been covered with dye, allow to dry. The color of the dye will lighten as it dries, so apply a second coat of dye if the color isn't as deep as you would like it to be. Allow to dry completely. The next step is to finish the leather by applying a leather wax or oil to lubricate, soften and protect it. Apply either one with a shearling and rub in well.

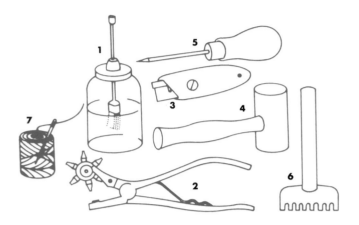

Tools

The basic leathercrafting tools needed to complete the projects in this entry are pictured above or in the project directions.

Rubber cement (1, above): A refillable glass jar with a brush embedded in the lid is the most economical form to buy.

Rotary punch (2, above): This plier-like tool is equipped with a rotary head that has tubes in graduated sizes. To use a rotary punch, insert the leather between the jaws and squeeze the handles together.

Replaceable-blade craft knife (3, above): Use this knife for cutting heavy leather. Leather or fabric shears may be used on lightweight leather.

Leather, synthetic, or wooden mallet (4, above): Because of their softer heads, use one of these mallets to flatten rubber-cemented leather seams, and to pound a thonging chisel or awl through leather to form slits or holes for sewing.

Awl (5, above) and **thonging chisel** (6): To prepare the leather for sewing, pierce single holes with the awl or multiple slits with the thonging chisel by pounding the tool into the leather with a mallet (4, above). Work on a block of cork or soft wood to avoid wearing down the tool. Thonging chisels have 1 to 10 prongs spaced 1/8- or 3/32-inch apart.

Thread (7, above): Linen or nylon thread is used for sewing leather. It is available pre-waxed (coating the thread with beeswax lubricates it and makes sewing easier), and in black, brown, and white. Nylon or linen thread is sold in two weights: heavy and fine. Harness needles are elongated needles with blunt points; many leathercrafters use a tapestry needle as a substitute.

Tooling instruments: The two tooling instruments called for in this entry—the deerfoot and the swivel knife—are shown in use in photographs 1, 2 and 3 on page 1071. Pressing the points of these instruments into dampened leather results in lasting impressions or cuts in the surface of the leather.

Hole spacer (Figure D, page 1071): Also known as a stitching wheel, this tool leaves evenly-spaced impressions in the leather to guide you when piercing holes with an awl or rotary punch.

Edger (photograph 5, page 1072): An edger or edge beveler cuts off a thin sliver of leather along edges, leaving them smooth and rounded. Edgers come in sizes from 1 to 5—the higher the number, the larger the cut; use high-numbered ones for heavy leather and low-numbered edgers for thinner leather.

For leather sources, see the page opposite.

Leathercrafts
Envelope briefcase $ ☒ ⚐ ⚗

Jim Murnak was born and educated in Pittsburgh, Pennsylvania. He worked as an art director for advertising agencies until 1971, when he decided to devote all his time to working in leather—which had been a hobby for some time. He later opened his own shop in New York City's Greenwich Village. Jim is a self-taught leathercrafter, specializing in custommade camera holsters, bags, attache cases and briefcases.

Jim Murnak built the wooden frame for this custom-made attache case, upon which he then constructed the outer leather shell using his advanced techniques and skills.

Most of my briefcases are custom-designed and constructed on a wooden frame. The case shown at top right is one example. For the Family Creative Workshop, I designed a simpler version (below), made of vegetable-tanned cowhide. The leather was dyed and sewn by hand into an envelope shape; if you prefer, the leather can remain its natural undyed color. Chrome-tanned leather may also be used.

Before beginning to make the briefcase, assemble all the materials and tools you will need: six or seven square feet of 5- to 6-ounce undyed cowhide; a sharp wooden stick, such as an orange stick; leather dye; shearling (a sponge inside a cloth may also be used); a thonging chisel; a rubber, leather, wooden or synthetic mallet; linen thread; harness needle (or blunt-pointed No. 18 tapestry needle); 3-inch brass dog leash clasp and dee-ring (sold at leathercraft supply stores). You will also need: cardboard or posterboard; pencil; metal-edged ruler; a replaceable-blade knife, and rubber cement. All may be purchased at artists' supplies stores. The project also requires a sponge, a block of soft wood, rubber gloves, and newspaper.

The distinguished envelope briefcase shown in the photograph below is a simpler version of Jim Murnak's custom-designed attache case shown top right.

Leather suppliers
Leather is sold by the square foot in the form of a whole hide, half hide (called a side), back, and belly (see below). Sometimes scraps, which are useful if you only wish to make small items, are packaged in a bag and sold by the pound.

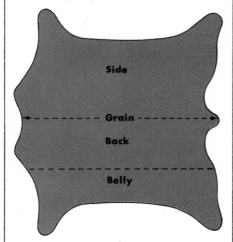

Side

Grain

Back

Belly

The thickness or weight of leather is indicated in ounces; 1-ounce leather measures 1/64-inch thick, 2-ounce leather measures 1/32-inch thick, 4-ounce measures 1/16-inch thick, and so on. Leather may be purchased directly from tanneries, leathercraft supply shops, and general craft supply stores and hobby shops. Consult the classified telephone directory of the largest town or city nearest you, under the listing "Leather." You may order leather tools and supplies through either of these leathercraft mail order houses: Berman Leather Company, 147 South Street, Boston, Mass. 02111. Tandy Leather, 508 6th Avenue, New York, N.Y. 10011.

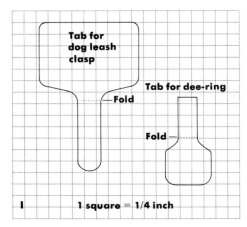

Figure I: Enlarge the tab patterns for the envelope briefcase by copying them on paper ruled in ¼-inch squares. Draw the pattern on the larger grid, one square at a time, following the lines on the smaller grid shown above.

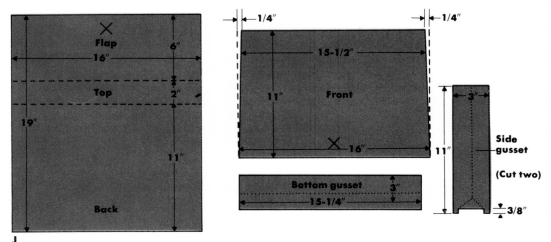

Figure J: Follow these measurements when cutting out the patterns for the pieces of the envelope briefcase shown on page 1077. The X's indicate tab positions; dotted lines indicate folds.

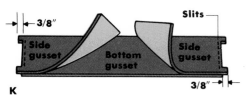

Figure K: Wrong sides facing, rubber-cement the side and bottom gusset pieces together as shown. With a thonging chisel and a mallet, cut slits along the seams to be sewn.

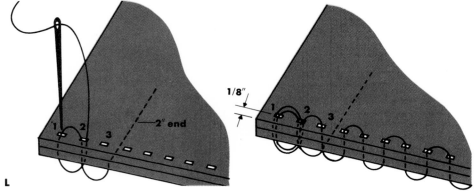

Figure L: *Step 1:* To start sewing a seam, leave about a 2-inch end at the inside, between the two pieces to be sewn. From between the layers of leather, push the needle through the bottom piece of leather at hole 3. Then pull the needle up through 2, bringing the thread to the top. Insert the needle down through 1, up through 2, then down in 1 again. *Step 2:* To continue stitching, reinsert the needle in 2, then down through 1, then up through 2 again. This forms two stitches at the beginning of the seam, and secures the thread. Continue stitching as shown, passing the thread through each hole once, until the seam is completely sewn. End the thread in the same way it was started, making two stitches at the end of the seam and bringing the end to the inside, between the two pieces of leather. Trim ends close to the seam.

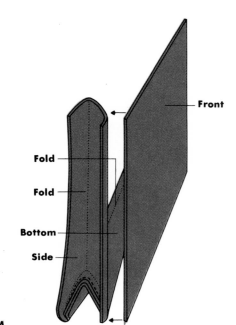

Figure M: Fold the side and bottom gusset pieces as indicated by the dotted lines on the pattern (Figure J). Apply rubber cement to the wrong side of the side and bottom gusset pieces, and to the front piece, close to the edges that will be sewn. Press the front and gusset pieces together, along the rubber-cemented edges.

Make patterns from cardboard or posterboard following Figures I and J. Place the leather on a flat surface, grain (smooth) side up. Dampen the leather slightly with a wet sponge. Lay the pattern pieces out on the leather; tape them in place, if you wish. Then trace the pattern outlines onto the leather using the sharp wooden stick. With the replaceable-blade knife, cut out the leather pieces, using the metal-edged ruler as a guide for the straight lines.

After the leather pieces have been cut out, dye them the desired color, then wax or oil the leather to protect it (see Craftnotes, page 1076). If you prefer the color of natural leather, omit the dye, and simply wax or oil the leather.

Next, the leather pieces are sewn together. With the wrong sides facing, rubber-cement the side gusset pieces to the bottom gusset piece along the edges to be sewn; refer to Figure K for position. Place the rubber-cemented pieces on a block of soft wood and use the thonging chisel and the mallet to cut slits in the leather along the seam ⅛-inch in from the recessed edges. Thread the needle with doubled thread that is 1½ times the length of the seam to be sewn, and use a running stitch (Figure L) to sew the bottom gusset to the side gussets. Before stitching the front piece to the side and bottom gusset pieces, the dee-ring must be attached. Slip the dee-ring on the tab extension and fold the extension under.

Apply rubber cement to the wrong side of the tab so it remains in a folded position. Sew the tab to the front of the briefcase at the point marked by the X on the pattern

(Figure J). Use a running stitch (Figure L) as before, and make sure to catch the folded extension in the stitching. Wrong sides facing, rubber-cement the front to the side and bottom gusset pieces (Figure M). Using a running stitch sew the pieces together along the side and bottom edges, ⅛-inch in from the edges.

Sew the back piece to the side and bottom gusset pieces as you did for the front. Sew a decorative running stitch around the flap, ⅛-inch in from the edge.

Slip the dog leash clasp on the tab extension; fold the extension under and secure with rubber cement as for the dee-ring. Using a running stitch, sew the tab to the front at the point marked by the X on the pattern (make sure to catch the folded extension in the stitching).

Leathercrafts
Sculptured leather man $ �X 👥 ⚱

Leather molding—an interesting technique that is used most often in forming leather for sandals, shoes, hats, and handbags—was used to form the sculpture pictured on page 1068. Elasticity is a natural property of leather; immersed in water, it becomes quite stretchable and is easily shaped.

The equipment required to make the sculpture includes: two 12-by-28-inch pieces of 5- to 6-ounce vegetable-tanned leather (undyed); a sharp wooden stick, such as an orange stick (the eye end of a large needle may also be used); leather dye in dark brown, or another color of your choice; leather wax or oil; shearling for applying dye (a sponge placed inside a cloth makes a good substitute); thonging chisel; rubber, leather, wooden or synthetic mallet; pre-waxed linen thread; and a harness needle (or a No. 18 tapestry needle). You will also need: rubber gloves; sand, fine gravel, or cat litter (for stuffing); sponge; paper; pencil; ruler; cardboard or posterboard (or a cut up cardboard box); a replaceable-blade knife; rubber cement; newspaper; and a broom.

To begin, enlarge the pattern (Figure N); or use your own design. Cut the enlarged pattern out of the cardboard or posterboard. Place the two pieces of leather together, flesh sides facing. Rubber-cement the pieces together in a few places to keep them from shifting as you trace around the pattern. Now dampen the top piece of leather slightly with plain water. Place the pattern on top of the dampened leather, taping it in place, and trace around the pattern edges with the wooden stick or needle eye. Cut out the two pieces simultaneously, using the replaceable-blade knife. Dye the leather, and then apply wax or oil, following the directions in the Craftnote on page 1076. With the two pieces placed together, cut slits through both layers of leather using the thonging chisel and the mallet. Working all around the edges of the figure, place the line of slits ⅛ inch in from the leather's edge. The leather is sewn with lengths of doubled thread measuring about 24 inches long. Using a running stitch (Figure L) sew the leather together, beginning at one X on the pattern (Figure N), working all around the bottom of the figure to the other X. Leave the top of the head (above the X marks) open for inserting the broomstick and stuffing.

Stuffing the Figure
Dip the figure in water and insert the end of a broomstick in the limbs to open the passages and prepare them for stuffing. Remove the broomstick and pour the stuffing into the figure through the opening in the head. Agitate the figure to work the stuffing into the passages and make sure they are all solidly filled. Sew up the opening in the head with a running stitch. Dampen the leather figure with a sponge (don't dip it in water again—the stuffing would absorb moisture and not dry for years). Shape the figure as desired, referring to the photograph on page 1068 as a guide when bending the knees, elbows and neck into position. Allow to dry thoroughly (you can use a hair dryer to speed up the process). Then prop up the completed figure against a wall, or purchase a doll stand (available at display supply houses or large toy shops) for displaying it.

For related projects, see the entries "American Indian Crafts," "Belts and Buckles," "Carryalls," "Fur Recycling," "Jewelry," and "Mittens and Mukluks."

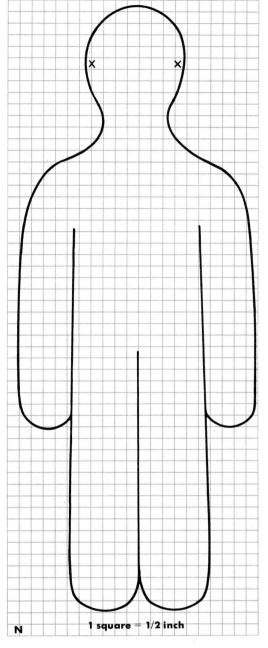

N 1 square = 1/2 inch

Figure N: To enlarge the pattern for the leather sculpture, draw a grid whose squares measure ½ inch. Copy the pattern shown onto the large grid, transferring the lines one square at a time. The X's indicate where stitching begins and ends.

LIGHTED INDOOR GARDENS
Flowers and Foliage the Year Round

Charles M. Evans, a horticulturist who is as conversant with wattage ratings as with plant characteristics, is a partner in Pot and Plant *in New York, where he acts as lighting consultant and interior landscape designer as well as chief horticulturist. He has written articles and books on house plant care and has lectured at the Brooklyn Botanical Gardens in New York.*

Not so long ago, indoor plants depending largely on artificial light were exotic—and somewhat unnatural—phenomena. Even in the lush conservatories of the Victorians, plants thrived or failed depending on how much natural sunlight could be provided.

But times and technology have changed. In the 1920s, during a massive research undertaking at Beltsville, Maryland, plant scientists began to unravel the mysteries of light in terms of plant needs. Research moved from the realms of the theoretical to the practical after World War II, with the development of lights especially designed for use by indoor gardeners. With the advent of dependable man-made sunlight, it became possible to garden successfully indoors the year round, in rooms receiving no natural light at all. Even bankers and hotel keepers began throwing out their dusty artificial foliage, replacing it with living plants.

In homes, artificial light can be used to extend the growing season of plants that normally become dormant as sunlight levels drop in the fall. It can supplement daylight, making it possible to grow foliage plants where no plant would normally thrive and flowering plants where only foliage plants would otherwise grow. It makes winter indoor gardening possible even in a north-facing room at a time of the year when the rays of the midday sun are low and feeble. It can even be the sole light source, bringing the joy of houseplants to city apartment dwellers cut off from direct sunlight. Indeed, some artificial-light gardeners have amazed flower show judges by exhibiting plants that seemingly could not have been grown exclusively under artificial light—but were.

As gardening lights have become more widely available, indoor gardens, plain and fancy, have become increasingly popular. Gardening lights have made it possible for many city people largely cut off from outdoor living greenery to create a mini-environment indoors where nature dominates. Gardens may be as simple as a nursery (page 1085) where plants are started and light-hungry houseplants are given an occasional booster of artificial light; or as complex as the wall garden opposite, where an entire room has been transformed with a lavish collection of plants. In between are gardens that can decorate a bookshelf, a corner—and even one that can be placed oasis-like in the middle of a room (page 1090). Gardens of all these types are included in the projects that begin on page 1085; the Craftnotes on page 1093 will tell you how to help it flourish, once your garden is a reality.

A Handful of Sun

Artificial light was first used by indoor gardeners to supplement natural light when seedlings were being started in early spring, usually with some temporary and makeshift arrangement. Today, in a permanent installation, it can be decorative as well as a beneficial source of light for plants. I know one woman who used gardening lights to brighten two dark rooms as well as to rescue her failing plants. The lights, installed at the windows, gave the illusion of sunlight streaming into the rooms—and her plants flourished, too. Another homeowner used indoor gardening lights to avoid removing a tree outdoors. The tree, an old and graceful specimen that had shaded the home for many generations, became so large it darkened the adjacent rooms. Removing the tree or pruning it were possible solutions; simulating indoor daylight was another—and it solved the problem.

Perhaps the most startling example of the potential of growing plants entirely with artificial light was displayed in a garden grown by scientists in the 1960s. It was located 800 yards from the South Pole—and under 20 feet of polar ice.

The question of the possible ill effects that artificial light might have on plants has been examined and reexamined by plant scientists. Some of the results are inconclusive, but the evidence available now indicates that far from being harmful to plants, artificial light is extremely beneficial. The consensus is that as long as the necessary light waves are present in the right proportions, the *source* of the light is immaterial to the plant.

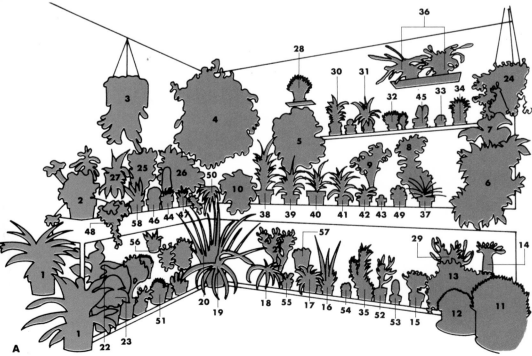

Housebound plants can be as lush as outdoor types with artificial light. Mercury vapor flood-lights supplement light for the window-level plants; beneath the shelves, succulents and cacti, lighted solely by fluorescent lights, are displayed.

A: Plants of the indoor garden pictured above and keyed at left include aglaonema frasierii (1), begonia (2), burro's tail sedum (3), kangaroo ivy (4), Ming aralia (5), Texas Star begonia (6), dumb cane dieffenbachia (7), gold-dust dracaena (8), jade plant (9), beefsteak begonia (10), Queen Victoria century plant (11), golden barrel cactus (12), Norwood fern (13), euphorbia (14), variegated jade plant (15), snake-plant sansevieria (16), earth-star cryptanthus (17), tillandsia (18), agave (19), sansevieria cylinderica (20), jade plant (21), dumb cane dieffenbachia (22), rex begonia (23), sedum (24), aralia (25), aglaonema (26), tiger aloe (27), zebra haworthia (28), aloe plicatilis (29), tiger aloe (30), aloe jacunda (31), stapelia (32), bishop's cap (33), aloe (34), aloe ciliaris (35), gasteria caespitosa (36), agave stricta (37), tiger aloe (38), agave (39 and 40), spider plant (41), sansevieria (42), bishop's cap (43), old-man cactus (44), rainbow cactus (45), star cactus (46), ariocarpus cactus (47), sedum (48), mammillaria cactus (49), spider plant (50), fish-hook cactus (51), opuntia cactus (52), notocactus (53), astrophytum (54), jade plant (55), aloe (56), parlor ivy (57), and aloe (58).

Light and water needs: flowering plants

Plant	Light level	Watering information
African Violet	M	S
Allamanda	B	S
Amaryllis	B	S
Azalea	B	F
Bougainvillea	B	S
Camellia	B	F
Chrysanthemum	M-B	S
Columnea	M	S
Crocus	M	F
Flowering maple	B	F
Fuchsia	B	F
Gardenia jasminoides	B	F
Geranium	B	I
Hibiscus	B	S
Hyacinth	M	F
Hydrangea	M	F
Lilian	M	F
Narcissus	M	F
Poinsettia	M	F
Wax Begonia	M	S
Waxplant	B	S

B: Bright
M: Medium
L: Low
F: Frequent; soil should stay wet
S: Sparingly; soil should be kept barely moist
I: Infrequent; soil should be allowed to dry
  between waterings.

Rays	Spectrum	Primary function	Primary source
Ultraviolet	Invisible	Generally harmful to plants	Sun lamps
Blue-violet	Visible	Plant growth; photosynthesis	All fluorescent lights; mercury vapor lights
Green	Visible	No known function	
Yellow	Visible	No known function	
Orange	Visible	No known function	
Red	Visible	Flowering	Full-spectrum fluorescent and incandescent lights.
Infrared	Near-visible	Flowering	Full-spectrum fluorescent and incandescent lights.

The color bands represent the different light waves that make up the visible portion of the light spectrum. The gray areas on either end show the near-visible (infrared) wavelength and the invisible (ultraviolet) wavelength. Essential for plant life are the blue, red and infrared rays.

Light Colors

Many of the facts needed for successful light-gardening were discovered in the Beltsville research program. The most important finding had to do with plant responses to light waves of varying lengths, which led to the establishment of principles of balanced lighting.

White light, or daylight, as prism-gazers know, is a blend of all the rainbow colors of the visible light range—violet, blue, green, yellow, orange and red (see table above). It was discovered at Beltsville that of these waves, the plant is physiologically indifferent to green, yellow and orange, but needs light waves primarily in the blue-violet range for growth and photosynthesis and in the red range for flowering. The third essential wavelength, infrared light, is part of the near-visible spectrum; it is tied into the blooming cycle in a way science does not yet fully comprehend. Experiments are continuing to determine just what the infrared function is, and what effects, if any, other colors may have on plant growth.

In practical terms for indoor gardening, the light needs of plants mean that

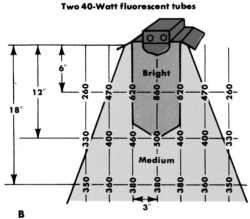

B

Figure B: The light provided by a fluorescent tube decreases at the ends of the tube as well as with increasing distance from it. Plants requiring bright light should be nearest the tube and placed under its middle portion. The colored areas indicate where plants needing bright and medium light can be grown. The source shown is a reflector fixture holding two 40-watt tubes.

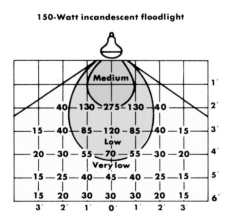

C

Figure C: Incandescent floodlights are often used to supplement other light. They are not adequate as the sole light source for most plants. The colored areas indicate where plants needing medium and low light may be grown under a 150-watt incandescent floodlight.

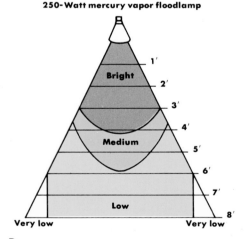

D

Figure D: There are no standardized foot-candle charts for the light intensity provided by mercury vapor floodlights, but the colored areas indicate approximately the areas in which plants needing bright, moderate and low light may be grown. The light source used for this chart is a 250-watt mercury vapor floodlight.

non-flowering foliage plants can be grown under standard fluorescent lights alone; both warm-white and cool-white fluorescents provide a great deal of light in the blue range. Flowering plants, however, need an additional light source in the red range—sunlight, an incandescent source, or a full-spectrum fluorescent—if they are to blossom freely.

Light Strength

Just as plants vary in the color of light they need, they differ in terms of the strength of light required for good growth and in how long they should be exposed to it. Light strength is designated in foot-candles—a measurement indicating how many standard candles, situated one foot away from a surface, would be needed to throw a given amount of light on that surface (Figures B, C, and D). Some plants require relatively little light, since their natural habitat is in the shade of taller plants, as on a forest or jungle floor. Others require a medium amount of light, while still others—primarily the meadow or desert plants—require a high level of light. In planning an indoor garden, providing the right light for the plants selected is essential. Low-light plants, such as those of the philodendron family, can be grown with as little as 50 foot-candles of light, although, like most low-light plants, they are healthier with about 200 foot-candles. For any of the plants needing medium light, such as coleus and various ferns, plan to provide from 250 to 500 foot-candles of light. True light-lovers, including a great many of the flowering plants, won't be happy with anything less than 500 foot-candles of light, and they do even better with more light—up to thousands of foot-candles..

Day Length

With a round-the-clock sun at your disposal, you must be careful not to abuse it. All plants need the rest that darkness brings, and alternating darkness and light is critical in getting a flowering plant to blossom. At one time it was thought that plants would not flower unless they were exposed to about 16 hours of light each day. But for some plants, the critical flowering factor is the dark that follows the light. Chrysanthemums and poinsettias, for example, are not likely to bloom if they are exposed to more than 12 hours of light per day, and do better with only eight hours of exposure. Most flowering plants are day-neutral, and will bloom in either long (16-hour) or short (8-hour) days, or anything in-between. Generally, foliage plants thrive best with a 12-to-16 hour day. The day-neutrals can be placed with short-day flowering plants, with long-day foliage plants, or by themselves in a middle range.

The Right Mix

To raise plants under artificial light, then, you need to achieve the right mix of light colors, provided at a compatible intensity for the proper amount of time. This means being familiar with the light sources themselves, as well as with what your plants need. If no daylight is available, light color requirements are traditionally met by combining warm-white or cool-white fluorescents, for blue light, with standard incandescents, which provide a small but adequate amount of red light. These can be teamed in a one-to-three ratio (one watt of incandescent light for every three watts of fluorescent light). In recent years, lights made specifically for indoor gardening have become popular; some provide all of the essential light colors with one unit. Among these are the full-spectrum fluorescent lights that simulate sunlight to a remarkable degree, providing all of the wavelengths present in daylight—and providing them in the right proportions. Since these units cost about the same as standard fluorescent lights, I recommend them. They can be used for foliage and flowering plants alike.

An alternative that some people are trying is the mercury vapor lamp with a built-in ballast, designed especially for indoor gardening. This emits a great deal of blue light but little red light, so it is best used with foliage plants. The advantage of the mercury vapor lamp is that it produces such a strong beam of light that it permits growing plants 7 or 8 feet from the light source. This has opened new possibilities in indoor gardening, such as the floor garden shown on page 1087. (If you try such a mercury vapor light, pay close attention to any hazard warnings given by the manufacturer.)

Light and water needs: foliage plants

Plant	Light level	Watering information
Aralia	M	S
Asparagus Fern	B	S
Burro's Tail	B	S
Caladium	M	F
Chinese Evergreen (all varieties)	L	S
Coleus	M-B	S
Copperleaf	B	S
Dracaena (all varieties)	M-L	I
English Ivy	M	S
Ficus (all varieties)	M-B	S
Grape Ivy	M	S
Moonstones	B	I
Old Man Cactus	B	I
Peperomia (all varieties)	M	S
Philodendron (all varieties)	M-L	S
Prayer Plant	M	S
Purple Passion	M	S
Silver Pothos	L	S
Snake Plant	L	S
Spider Plant	M	S
Wandering Jew (all varieties)	M	S

B: Bright
M: Medium
L: Low
F: Frequent; soil should stay wet
S: Sparingly; soil should be kept barely moist
I: Infrequent; soil should be allowed to dry between waterings.

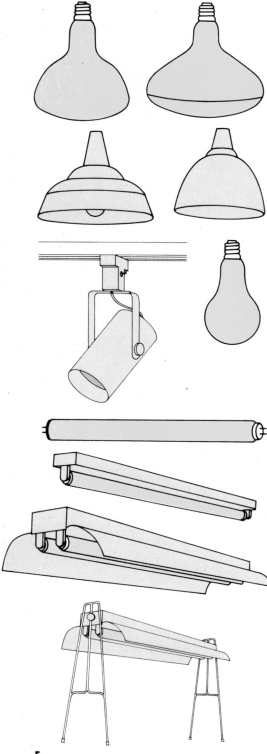

E

Figure E: Gardening lights and fixtures include (top row) self-ballasted mercury vapor floodlight; reflectorized incandescent floodlight; (second row) deep-dome reflectors; (third row) track-light fixture; incandescent bulb; (fourth row) fluorescent tube; (fifth row) channel fixture; (sixth row) reflector fixture; (bottom) reflector fixture with side supports that can be set on a table or shelf.

Light Forms

Lights that can be used for indoor gardening come in a great array of shapes, sizes and strengths, ranging from an 18-watt midget to giant bulbs producing thousands of watts of light. Ordinary incandescent bulbs, often used as a supplemental source of red light for flowering plants, produce enough heat to harm plants. When they are used they need to be shielded from the plants with a glass or plastic barrier. A better choice is the reflectorized floodlight type of incandescent bulb, silvered on the bottom so heat is reflected upward and away from the plants.

Fluorescent tubes, often used as a source of blue light, need to be properly ballasted—the ballast converts house current to a voltage the tube can handle. That means they can be used only in a compatible fixture. But given such a fixture, full-spectrum fluorescents can eliminate the need for any incandescent source.

Only the self-ballasted type of mercury vapor light bulbs should be used for indoor gardening—other types can be hazardous. And even the self-ballasted type should be used only in a floodlight-type fixture that has the socket shielded with a porcelain collar; a paper collar might catch fire. Let it be noted, too, that a mercury vapor bulb is quite expensive.

If a high-wattage bulb of either the mercury vapor type or the incandescent floodlight type is used, make sure the fixture is rated to carry that wattage without being damaged.

Typical lights and fixtures are shown in Figure E. A fixture designed for an incandescent floodlight of high wattage can also house a mercury vapor floodlight. Fluorescent tubes and fixtures are sold in standard lengths (18-inch, 2-foot, 3-foot, 4-foot and 8-foot) with the wattage increasing by 10 watts per foot. (A 2-foot tube is a 20-watt tube; a 4-foot tube is a 40-watt tube.) Fluorescent fixtures are available in a channel form or reflector form; the latter directs the light downward and is painted white to increase light efficiency. I generally prefer the two- or four-tube channel fixtures; they are most adaptable and less obtrusive. I paint the wall or ceiling in back of the fixtures with flat white paint to compensate for the loss in lighting efficiency.

Juggling the Factors

How much light you need to supply will depend on what plants you grow. Any of the light sources recommended can be used in multiple units to supply the required intensity, so how you choose to supply the light will depend largely on the decorative appearance you want to achieve. For a shelf arrangement, or in any location where the light source must be close to the top of the plants, use fluorescent lights, as they are the coolest of the light sources and will not harm plants even as close as 1 inch. The floodlight type of bulbs—mercury vapor or incandescent—are not practical for close-up gardening mainly because they produce too much heat. They are a very good choice, however, for lighting plants from a distance, as near a low-light window or in a floor garden.

If you notice that a plant is not getting enough light (the telltale sign is a tall, spindly growth, rather than a lush, full-bodied look), or that it is getting too much heat (the plant will wilt and its leaves will curl), one of these techniques will maximize light and minimize heat:

If you are working with floodlights of any type and your plants begin drying out, replace a high-wattage bulb with weaker bulbs that add up to the same total wattage as the original. Light intensity will remain the same, but the heat will decrease since it is being dispersed over a greater area.

If you are working with foliage or day-neutral plants and they need more light, try leaving the lights on for a longer period of time. This will have the same effect on the plants as increasing the light intensity would, without raising the heat level.

Generally you arrive at the right heat-light ratio by experimenting, but you can use the following rule of thumb as a starter: If your hand, held at leaf-top level under the light source, feels warm, the garden is too close to the light. Move your hand down until it feels cool; that is as close as plant leaf-tops should be to the light source. In most cases, plants should be placed no closer than 18 inches to a floodlight; no farther than 18 inches from a fluorescent light. There are variations in this, however, as shown in the skylight garden on page 1090.

Lamp Placement and Maintenance

To be most effective, light must be directed. Floodlights should be placed so the light comes at the plants from an angle, shining on the maximum amount of foliage. Floodlights placed directly overhead shine only on the topmost leaves, causing lower leaves to die from lack of light. In the case of fluorescent lights, however, the light source is large enough so the light can be directed straight down.

Remember to replace fluorescent tubes at the end of their warranty period, after which they may burn at only 20 percent efficiency. Floodlights, however, produce maximum light until the day they burn out, and most have a guaranteed life-span. Dust, along with time, is an enemy—it weakens light intensity, so bulbs and tubes should be dusted frequently and washed occasionally.

Accessories

Timers, used to turn lights on and off automatically, are a particularly convenient accessory. They are available in hardware stores. Any type of 24-hour timer may be used, as long as it is rated to handle the total number of watts used in the garden. To use a timer to operate more than one light fixture, plug a four-way socket into the timer, and plug the light cords into the socket.

Another accessory—and a vital one—is the tray that holds the potted plants and gravel. This must be leakproof and rustproof and may be made either of galvanized tin or plastic, depending on your needs. Plastic is inexpensive and readily available—trays are sold in all hardware stores. Galvanized tin trays, made to order by a tinsmith, can be shaped and sized to fit a special design. For some gardens (pages 1087 and 1090), you can make a tray of two-by-fours and heavy polyethylene plastic.

If you want to measure light intensity exactly, you can do so with a foot-candle meter; they are available at nurseries and plant-lighting supply stores.

Greenery and Growing Things

The nursery $ ⊠ ☻ ⚗

I start cuttings and seedlings in an indoor plant nursery, and also use it to revive full-grown plants that are ailing. Because the size of the plants under the light fixture may vary by several feet from time to time, I wanted an easily adjustable light source, and hooked the fixture to two strong chains anchored to a ceiling beam. To change the height of the fixture, I simply hook it into different links of the chains. (A similar, though less flexible, fixture is shown at the bottom of Figure E. This type fixture can be set over plants on shelves or tables and requires no construction as it comes complete with side supports.)

To make the nursery, you will need two lengths of chain (long enough so the fixture is 12 inches above the top of the potting tray at its lowest level), two screw eyes to attach the chain to the ceiling; four S-hooks for attaching the chain to the screw eyes and to the fixture; a sturdy table; plastic or galvanized tin trays to hold the plants; gravel; a drill and bit; a pre-wired light fixture and tubes. What size fixture you need will depend on your growing area. Fluorescent lights are used, and with one 40-watt tube, 18 inches above leaf-top, you can grow a row of plants the length of the tube and for 4 inches on either side of the tube. In the arrangement shown (Figure F), I used a reflector fixture to accommodate two 4-foot tubes, giving me a growing area 4 feet long and 1 foot wide.

To hang the fixture, measure the distance between the attachment points provided on it, and mark the ceiling to indicate these points. Drill pilot holes to start the screws into a ceiling beam or rafter. Turn one screw-eye into each hole. Use S-hooks to attach the chain to the screw-eyes and to the fixture (Figure G). Center the table under the fixture, fill trays with gravel, and put potted plants or cuttings on the gravel.

If you plan to keep the nursery lighted a specific length of time each day, you may want to add a timer. Then you can simply plug the lights into the timer, the timer into a wall outlet, set the timer and walk away. Your plants will get the light they need without your having to remember to turn the lights on or off.

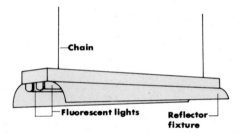

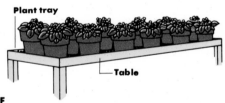

F

Figure F: This type of gardening arrangement, more functional than decorative, is ideal as a nursery or plant hospital area, since the fixture can be raised a notch at a time to accommodate growing seedlings—or a tall but light-starved plant.

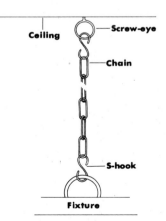

G

Figure G: S-hooks join the fixture-supporting chain to ceiling-mounted screw eyes, and are also used to attach the chain to the fixture.

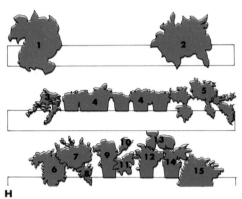

The greening of this bookcase can be credited to the use of full-spectrum fluorescent lights, mounted on the underside of each shelf and hidden with valances. Plants are identified in the diagram below.

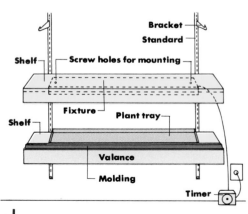

H

Figure H: Garden plants above include: philodendron (1 and 2); lipstick plant (3, 5, 6 and 15); African violets (4); ornamental pepper plant (7); wandering Jew (8); Cleopatra begonia (9); coleus (10); wax plant (11); wax begonia (12); Iron Cross begonia (13); pothos (14).

Figure I: To make the bookcase garden, anchor standards to the wall and fit knife brackets in the slots to hold the shelves. These shelves, with fixtures attached, are simply set on the brackets. Trays, molding and a timer complete the garden.

I

Labels in Figure I: Bracket; Standard; Screw holes for mounting; Shelf; Fixture; Plant tray; Shelf; Valance; Molding; Timer

Greenery and Growing Things
The bookcase shelf garden

The easy-to-do light-gardening arrangement shown at left is attractive and functional. The materials required will vary according to your particular set-up, but the basic components are: standards and knife brackets, ¾-inch plywood shelving; one 2-tube channel fixture per shelf (Figure I), wired with an 8-foot cord and plug; full-spectrum fluorescent tubes; ¼-by-6-inch plywood to make valances the length of the shelves; an equal amount of decorative molding; finishing nails; screws; leakproof and rustproof trays; gravel; a level and a timer.

The unit shown was designed to accommodate one two-tube, 4-foot channel fixture per shelf, providing a growing area of 4 feet by 8 inches. The shelves are 60 inches long to allow overlap on the brackets and space for books or decorative accessories. Shelf dimensions can be changed to fit your own design, but be sure to use the right size fixtures with them. For an 8-foot shelf, put two 4-foot fixtures end to end. For a narrow shelf, up to 8 inches wide, use one two-tube fixture; for a wider shelf, bank fixtures side by side (four tubes will light a shelf 12 to 14 inches wide). If you are working with a shelf longer than 4 feet, put up extra standards, spacing them to provide adequate support.

Decide how many shelves you want, how wide they should be, and how long. This will tell you what length standards you need (allow 20 inches between shelves) and how many you need. Use one standard every 49 inches (Figure I). Use standards and brackets made of steel as the aluminum type may not hold the heavy plant trays, and use heavy-duty standards and brackets for any shelf over 60 inches.

Putting Up the Shelves
Before anchoring the standards to the wall, pencil guidelines for drilling the pilot holes. The standards can be used as patterns for this, and, simultaneously, be aligned, a necessity if the shelves are to be level. Hold each standard to the wall, positioning it exactly where it is to be mounted, and mark the pilot hole positions through the pre-drilled holes in the standards. When the pilot hole locations have been indicated, draw vertical lines where the standards will rest and horizontal lines connecting the pilot holes to indicate how the shelves will lie. Check for level with the vertical and horizontal gauges of your level. Drill the pilot holes and anchor the standards. Saw the hooks off the brackets with hacksaw.

If possible, the standards should be anchored directly to wall studs. These are normally 16 inches apart. Begin by anchoring one standard to a stud. Next, allowing the least possible distance between brackets that will accommodate the light fixture, anchor the second standard a scant 49 inches from the first. If the bracket spacing is tight, the second standard should also fall on a stud. If not, secure it with butterfly-type toggle bolts that will open behind the wall to support the weight. Once the standards are in place, insert the knife brackets (Figure I).

Before attaching the fixtures to the shelves, paint one side of each shelf (to be the underside) with flat white paint. This provides a reflective surface and maximizes light efficiency. If possible, also paint the wall backing the unit.

Attach the fixtures to the undersides of the shelves, first drilling pilot holes in the wood through the pre-drilled holes in the fixtures. Fasten the fixtures to the shelves, but don't insert the tubes at this point.

Cut the wood for the valances that will hide the fixtures in pieces long enough to run the length of the shelves, then nail them in place with finishing nails. To finish the shelves, you may want to add cove molding and paint or stain it to match the shelves and valances. If so, choose plant trays somewhat narrower than the shelves to allow space for the molding.

Insert the fluorescent tubes in the fixtures, put the trays on the shelves, fill the trays with gravel and potted plants, and the unit is complete. The shelf garden, provided with strong, color-balanced light, can be filled with both foliage and flowering plants—even those with a high light requirement, as long as the plants are close enough to the light source (see foot-candle charts and plant light-requirement tables, pages 1082 and 1083).

Greenery and Growing Things
The corner garden

The corner garden, easily made, can be very dramatic. Since plants can be grown 7 or 8 feet from the light source, the plants selected can even include small trees.

To make the corner garden you will need two 250-watt self-ballasted mercury vapor bulbs (be sure to get the self-ballasted type, since an unballasted mercury vapor bulb can cause fires or line damage). In addition, you will need track-type light fixtures (specify that you want them with a weighted base); common nails in various lengths; gravel; a timer; the plants and a galvanized tin tray. Should you have difficulty getting such a tray, you can make your own with the following materials: three two-by-fours (the length of these pieces will vary according to the size of the garden you want); three one-by-twos and three lengths of strip molding, all cut to the same length as the two-by-fours; 10-mil polyethylene; finishing nails.

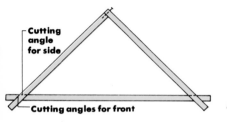

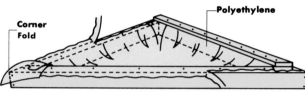

J

Figure J: To make a triangular tray frame, miter three two-by-fours at the angles shown above and fasten them together with finishing nails. Tack polyethylene lining to the top of the frame, tucking and cutting away excess material at the corners. Overlay the plastic with one-by-twos and add strip molding to cover the seam where the framing pieces meet.

Begin with the tray. If you have it made by a tinsmith, get galvanized tin so that the tray will not rust. Have it made 3 to 4 feet long on the wall sides of the garden, depending on how large a growing area you want. The tray should have a curved front and a 2- to 3-inch lip all around to prevent leakage. If you decide to make your own plant tray, it can be triangular, a shape easier to build than one with a curved front edge.

To make the tray, determine the dimensions of each piece by deciding how far you want it to project into the room. Mark each wall, and measure the distance between these two points to determine the length of the front edge of the tray. Have the two-by-fours, one-by-twos and strip molding cut to these dimensions, allowing 6 to 12 inches extra on all pieces for mitering (Figure J).

Start the frame by nailing the side pieces together at one end to form a 90-degree angle, overlapping the two pieces and nailing them on their 4-inch faces. Put the joined sides in the corner they will occupy and mark the ends. Then move them out from the walls and set them on any convenient 4-inch props. Put the front piece in place (Figure J), sliding it under the side pieces and, with pencil and straight-edge, draw the lines where the pieces overlap and should be cut. In doing this, draw the miter lines so that the front of the tray, rather than the ends of the side pieces, is visible when the tray is in position. Following the lines carefully, cut the two-by-fours, then miter the one-by-twos to match the angles. Now align the mitered two-by-fours and nail them together.

Line the tray with 10-mil polyethylene, available in hardware and dime stores, cutting it to a triangle at least 10 inches larger all around than the two-by-four frame. This will allow it to be pulled up along the 4-inch sides of the tray, and over the top edge, in one watertight piece, necessary because the tray will be filled with water to supply humidity for the plants (see Craftnotes, page 1093).

Lay the polyethylene over the frame and press it down to the floor in the center of the frame. Smooth it out towards the sides of the frame, then bring it up along the inside 4-inch walls and up onto the top edge, tucking it at the corners (Figure J). Don't worry if the lining is less than beautiful. The one-by-twos laid over it will hide any folds. Tack the polyethylene to the top edge of the frame, using small brads or a

K

Figure K: The corner garden is suited to the display of tall, dramatic plants, such as the sentry palm shown (1). Also included in this garden are dracaena (2), croton (3), English ivy (4) and philodendron (5).

L

Figure L: The basic elements of the corner garden at the top are a pie-shaped galvanized tin tray and two wall-mounted mercury vapor lamps. A homemade plant tray is shown in Figure J.

staple gun. Trimming the plastic so it does not stick out beyond the frame, overlay it with the one-by-twos, cut to align with the two-by-four frame. Secure the one-by-twos to the two-by-fours with finishing nails. If desired, use molding to hide the seam where the one-by-twos and two-by-fours meet. Paint or stain the tray to match the room.

Position the light fixtures on the wall so the light strikes the plants at an angle, lighting as much foliage area as possible (Figure K). One floodlight will suffice if you are using plants with low light requirements, but two are better. Mounting the lights 3 feet out from the front of the garden will provide maximum exposure. Since the fixtures have weighted bases, they can be hooked on a screw or toggle bolt in the wall. The lights can be turned on and off with a timer. If you decide not to use a timer, have line switches mounted on the light cords, since the switches on the fixtures would be hard to reach.

Place the tray in the corner spot selected for it, fill it with gravel and set potted plants on the gravel. Because the mercury vapor lamps provide light that is strong in the blue range, only foliage plants should be used in this garden.

Greenery and Growing Things
The window garden

An indoor garden placed below and in front of a window is ideal for dramatizing a wall and masking a lackluster view at the same time. And it takes advantage of whatever daylight there is. The heart of the arrangement is the soffit, the box-like structure at the top that spans the garden space, enclosing and concealing fluorescent gardening lights mounted on the ceiling (Figures M and N).

The soffit is attached to the ceiling and side walls that frame the garden. The length is, of course, determined by the length of the wall the garden is on; the depth (measuring from the garden wall to the front of the soffit) is determined by the fixtures used. To garden at this distance, unless only low-light plants are grown, at least four 48-inch full-spectrum fluorescent lights are necessary in addition to daylight. These should be mounted in two two-tube, 4-foot channel fixtures. To accommodate those used in the arrangement pictured here, a soffit 12 inches deep is adequate (Figure M).

The following materials list is based on a soffit 12 inches deep and 10 inches wide (measuring from the ceiling to the bottom edge of the soffit). To calculate the missing dimensions—those that would vary from room to room—refer to Figures M and N, and measure the appropriate areas in the room you will be using. If the fixtures you plan to use are wider than 10 or 11 inches when held side by side, adjust dimensions accordingly. All parts of the soffit must butt each other, so it is essential that measurements not be scant.

For the soffit frame (Figure M), you will need one one-by-two the length of the wall and two one-by-twos, each 7 inches long, for the ends. For the panel rim you will need four one-by-ones, two 12 inches long and two the length of the wall. For the front and bottom panels of the soffit (Figure N) you will need one piece of ½-inch plywood, 10 inches wide and the length of the wall; eggcrate louvers, 12 inches by 48 inches, and one piece of ½-inch plywood, 12 inches by the length of the wall minus 4 feet. Two two-tube channel fixtures, each 4 feet long, and four 48-inch full-spectrum fluorescent tubes light the garden. You will also need a timer to turn lights on and off or line switches on the light cords.

Measure your window wall and light fixtures to get exact material dimensions and have the lumber cut to size at a lumber yard. The eggcrate louvers may have to be ordered. They should total the length of the lights and be wide enough to rest on the rim at the bottom of the soffit (Figure N)—4 feet by 12 inches in the plan given here. Such louvers are available at plastic and lighting supply houses.

To make the soffit, begin with the one-by-two frame that supports the panelled sections. Measure out 1 foot from the window wall at several points and draw a line across the ceiling at this distance from the wall. Check to see that the line is equidistant from the window wall at all points, then nail the long one-by-two to the ceiling so the front 1-inch edge is aligned with the pencilled guideline and a 2-inch

Plants grouped in front of a window bring a sense of openness and light even to a shaded window without a good view. Full-spectrum fluorescent lights, hidden by the decorative soffit, provide sufficient intensity for moderate and low-light plants. (Plants included in this garden are identified in Figure O, opposite.)

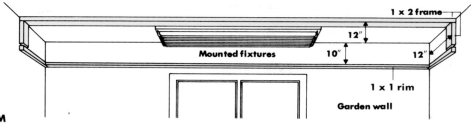

Figure M: The framework for the soffit is made of two sections, the one-by-twos to which the front panel is attached, and the one-by-one rim to hold the panels that close in the bottom. A fourth one-by-one, at the front edge of the soffit, is attached to the front panel before it is mounted.

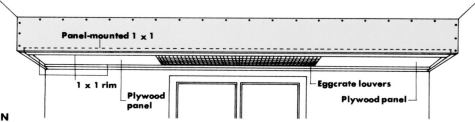

N

Figure N: The front panel is nailed to the one-by-twos. Eggcrate louvered panels, framed by the plywood panels, rest on the one-by-one rim. The louvers are positioned directly under the light fixtures.

surface is against the ceiling. On each side wall, nail one of the 7-inch one-by-twos, placing it under the ceiling-mounted one-by-two, and checking to be sure it is plumb, using the vertical gauge of your level. You will now have a three-sided frame 12 inches out from the window wall. Measure down 10 inches from the ceiling, and paint the ceiling and walls that will be inside the soffit with white paint to increase light efficiency. Also paint each of the plywood panels on one side, henceforth the side that faces into the soffit.

Mount the fixtures on the ceiling, centering them over what will be the garden area. Use fasteners appropriate for your type of ceiling, and be sure that they go into a structural framing member as the fixtures are fairly heavy. Do not insert the tubes into the fixtures at this point.

Attach one long one-by-one to one edge of the plywood that will front the soffit, first trimming off two inches to allow it to butt the one-by-ones that will be added to the side walls. Center the one-by-one on the front panel, leaving an inch free at each end, and nail it to the side painted white, aligning its bottom surface with the edge of the plywood. Fasten the plywood to the three one-by-twos at the front of the frame (Figure N), keeping the one-by-one on the bottom inside edge. This forms the front rim on which the bottom panels will rest; and at this point the rest of the one-by-one rim can be nailed in place. Run a 12-inch length from the front panel one-by-one back to the rear wall. Nail it in place temporarily and check for level before securing it to the wall. Add the rear and remaining side-wall one-by-ones in the same way. Insert the lights into the fixtures and slip the louvered panels into place directly under the lights, resting them on the rim. Measure the distances between the end of each louvered panel and the side wall adjacent to it, then cut the 12-inch-wide plywood into pieces long enough to close in the soffit on either side of the louvered panel. Slip the plywood into place on the soffit rim.

The components for the gardening shelf will vary according to whether or not your window is over a ready-made prop, such as a radiator, shelf or window seat. If there is such a prop, the shelf that holds the garden trays can simply be set in place on top of the prop; otherwise, two large steel L-brackets, mounted on the wall under the window, will hold the plant tray at windowsill height. Have the shelf, made of ¾-inch plywood, cut to size at a lumberyard. For the lighting installation shown here, it should be 12 inches wide and 4 feet long. Put the plant trays on the shelf. If you have a very wide windowsill, the trays can rest directly on it. If a radiator is beneath the tray, an asbestos lining should be used between it and the tray to prevent heat from harming the plants.

O

Figure O: Plants pictured in the window garden opposite include green spider plant (1), Swedish ivy (2), grape ivy (3), Norwood fern (4), maranta (5), schefflera (6), piggyback (7), grape ivy (8), and dracaena warneckii (9).

The skylight garden is made of two units, a light fixture, suspended from the ceiling to simulate a skylight, and a watertight gardening box. The light intensity is strong enough for most light-loving plants; if not, they can be moved closer to the light source with blocks of varying heights. Tall plants and trees may need to be pruned to allow smaller plants to get a share of light.

Greenery and Growing Things
The skylight floor garden $ ● ♦ ⚗

A floor garden illuminated with a simulated skylight is not difficult to assemble, but the materials and fixtures are not inexpensive. To make each skylight fixture (the garden pictured at left incorporates two), you will need: two two-by-fours, 49 inches long; two boards ½-by-8-by-50 inches; two boards ½-by-8-by-49 inches; two one-by-twos 45½ inches long; two one-by-twos 49 inches long; two plastic eggcrate louvered panels, each 2-by-4 feet; four channel type four-light fluorescent fixtures, each 48 inches long and wired with a cord long enough to plug into timers near a wall outlet; 16 full-spectrum fluorescent tubes, each 48 inches long; eight screw eyes; eight S-hooks; finishing nails; wood screws; electrical fixture chain.

Begin construction by attaching all fixtures (minus the tubes) to the 4-inch side of the two-by-fours (Figure P). Attach the fixtures so each bridges both two-by-fours, and so all are spaced equally along the length of the two-by-fours. Align the two-by-fours precisely before attaching fixtures. The two-by-fours will form the top of the skylight. To make the sides, attach two 49-inch boards to the two-by-fours (Figure P), nailing them to the ends of the two-by-fours with finishing nails. To these pieces, nail the two 50-inch sides, using finishing nails and driving the nails into the edges of the 49-inch sides. You will have a frame 8 inches high, 49 inches square on the inside and 50 inches square on the outside. Turn the frame over and nail two 49-inch one-by-two strips to opposite sides of the interior perimeter of the frame, using finishing nails. Put the two 45½-inch one-by-two strips on the other two sides, forming a ridge where the eggcrate louvers will rest (Figure Q and photograph 1).

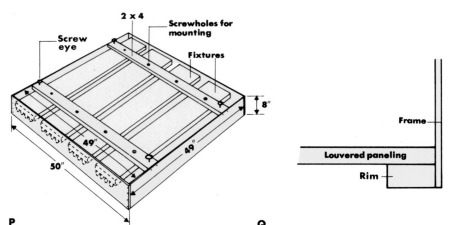

P
Figure P: To make the skylight fixture, nail or screw light fixtures to two two-by-fours, then frame them with boards 8 inches wide and ½ inch thick. Put screw eyes in the two-by-fours.

Q
Figure Q: Nail one-by-twos to the inside bottom perimeter of the frame, forming a rim to hold the louvered panels. Position the one-by-twos so the narrow dimension faces the ½-inch frame.

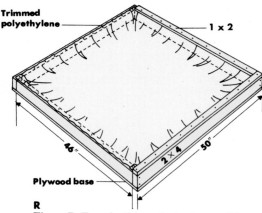

R
Figure R: To make the gardening box, nail four two-by-fours together, overlapping them as shown, attach the base, then line the box with 10-mil polyethylene, using a single sheet so the box will be watertight.

To hang the fixture, attach four heavy-duty screw eyes to the ceiling, making sure these go into a ceiling rafter because the fixture is heavy. Then screw the remaining four screw eyes into the top of the two-by-fours (Figure P). Use chain to hang the fixture, attaching it to the screw eyes in the ceiling and top of the skylight fixture. Adjust the height; the combined wattage strength of these lights permits gardening up to a distance of eight feet.

Put the lights into the fixtures and insert the eggcrate louvers so they rest on the rim of the frame. Plug the fixtures into a timer (or timers, if necessary) and plug the timer into a wall outlet.

A galvanized tin pan, 4 feet square, with 3-inch-high sides, positioned on the floor directly underneath the skylight, can be used for the garden bed. You may prefer to make a lined wooden flower box (Figure R). For this you will need four two-by-fours, two 50 inches long and two 46 inches long, four one-by-twos, two 50

1: When viewed from beneath, the skylight fixture looks like this. The eggcrate louvers hide the light fixtures and tubes. The frame can be stained or painted to match the room.

2: Corner molding, a single piece of wood shaped into a right angle, can be used to cover rough edges where the one-by-twos overlap the two-by-fours and polyethylene of the gardening box.

inches long and two 46 inches long, a 50-inch-square piece of ¾-inch plywood; 10-mil polyethylene, at least 5 feet square and four pieces of corner molding or strip molding to give the box a finished look. Nail the two-by-fours together to form a box, using finishing nails, with the longer pieces overlapping the short pieces. Nail the plywood base to this, turn the box over and position it under the skylight. Center the plastic lining over the box frame so that it forms a solid sheathing over the box floor and sides. The box must be watertight. Following the instructions for the corner garden frame (page 1087), secure and trim the polyethylene, then finish the frame with strip or corner molding (photograph 2). Fill the box with gravel, placing potted plants on top of this. To supply adequate humidity for the plants, keep the gravel moist at all times.

S

Figure S: Plants in the floor garden pictured opposite include aglaonema (1), sentry palm (2), corn palm (3), false aralia (4), corn palm (5), weeping fig (6), Swedish ivy (7), Kangaroo ivy (8), Whittman fern (9) and asparagus fern (10).

Greenery and Growing Things
The wall garden

$ ● 🚶 🔬

Having an indoor light garden like the one pictured on page 1081 is second only to having a plant-filled patio or terrace. It permits the gardener to incorporate small trees, foliage plants, flowering plants, succulents, cacti and almost every other type of plant imaginable. The flexibility of the unit is due to the use of two lighting systems—mercury-vapor track lights supplementing natural light for the window-high plants, full-spectrum fluorescent lights for the floor garden.

Since you may wish to make only one of the garden components, the instructions and materials list for each section are given separately. Exact amounts and dimensions of the materials will vary according to the size of your garden wall, but the components can remain the same.

For supplementing natural light for the hanging plants and windowsill-level garden, you will need track-mounted floodlight fixtures with porcelain collars, the track for mounting the fixtures and several 250-watt mercury vapor floodlights, the exact number depending on how large a garden area you have. For a 9-foot main garden wall (pages 1081 and 1092), four lamps are necessary. For a smaller garden, three would suffice.

The track is sold in 4- and 8-foot sections with predrilled holes for easy ceiling mounting. Secure it to the ceiling, approximately four feet out from the window wall, then clip the fixtures into the track and attach one or more timers, depending on the combined total wattage of the bulbs. Angle the fixtures so the light falls on the maximum amount of foliage possible.

The dimensions of the materials needed for the shelf units will vary according to the size of your room. All dimensions given here are for shelving 18 inches wide on the main garden wall and 14 inches wide on the side garden wall. If these widths are compatible with the size garden you plan, buy the materials listed, computing the missing dimension (the lengths of the shelves and support pieces) by measuring your own walls. When figuring footages, refer to Figures T and U, page 1092.

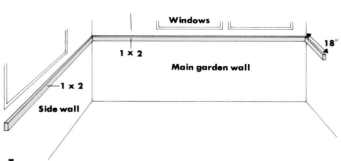

T

Figure T: The wall garden pictured on page 1081 begins with a simple one-by-two frame, mounted on the main and side garden walls. These support the plant-holding shelves; braces are added later for additional support.

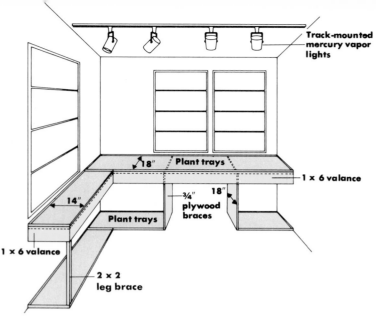

U

Figure U: Plywood shelves, supported by wall cleats, plywood braces and a leg brace hold the plant trays. Track-mounted ceiling lights will supplement daylight coming in the windows; plants beneath the shelves will be lighted with concealed fluorescent fixtures.

For the shelf supports (Figure T) you will need four one-by-twos, one 18 inches long, one 12 inches long, the third long enough to run the entire length of the main garden wall, and the fourth cut to run the length of the portion of the side wall to be shelved. For shelving material ¾-inch plywood is used. For the long shelf, have the plywood cut 18 inches wide, and long enough to span the entire main garden wall; the shorter shelf, also of ¾-inch plywood, should be 14 inches wide and 18 inches shorter than the one-by-two used for the side garden wall, as this area will be taken up by the width of the long shelf (Figure U).

For the shelf braces, use two pieces of ¾-inch plywood, both 18 inches wide and long enough to run from the floor to the underside of the shelf (Figure U). To brace the outer corner of the short shelf, you will need a two-by-two leg the same length as the other braces.

One-by-six valances are used to hide the fluorescents. In figuring out the footages here, have one valance cut long enough to span the main garden wall, one cut long enough to span the short shelf edge (this piece should equal the length of the short shelf plus ¾ inch, not the length of the one-by-two on the side garden wall); and the third, used to enclose the end of the short shelf, cut 14 inches long.

You will also need either galvanized tin or plastic trays to fit the shelves; they should have a 1- to 1½-inch rim.

To make the shelf units, nail the three longest one-by-twos to the three walls (Figure T) just under the windowsill. Check with a level to make sure they do not slope. Paint the undersides of the shelves with flat white paint and let dry; then rest the long shelf on the three one-by-two supports and nail it in place with finishing nails. Wedge the two ¾-inch plywood braces into place beneath the shelf and secure them by driving finishing nails through the shelf and into the edges of the braces. Attach the light fixtures to the underside of the shelf. To do this, hold each fixture in place and mark the wood through the screw holes to indicate where the pilot holes will be needed. Drill the holes and fasten the fixtures to the shelf. Do not insert the light tubes at this time.

Nail the longest one-by-six valance to the edge of the shelf, using finishing nails — and a gentle touch, to avoid damaging the fixtures.

The short shelf, already painted, can be attached now. To do this, first nail the remaining (12-inch) one-by-two to the long shelf valance to provide a support for the short shelf. Position the one-by-two so its top edge is ¾ inch below the top of the shelf, so both shelves will be flush on their top surfaces. Set the short shelf on the two supports thus provided, nail it in place and attach the light fixtures to the underside of the shelf. Put in the two-by-two leg brace, driving a nail through the shelf and into the leg. Attach the two remaining valances along the exposed edges of the short shelf, nailing them in place. To secure the leg, drive nails through the valance into the two outside faces of the leg.

Set the plant trays in place, both on the floor under the shelves and on top of the shelves. Fill with gravel and potted plants.

If you have difficulty obtaining any of the lights used for the projects in this entry, either of the following electrical lighting suppliers will fill mail orders: Duro-lite Lamps, Inc., International Division, 17-10 Willow St., Fairlawn, New Jersey, U.S.A. 07410
Veri-Lux TruBloom, Dept. B, 35 Mason St., Greenwich, Connecticut, U.S.A. 06830.
For related entries, see: "Bottle Gardens," "Greenhouse Construction," "Herbs," "Sprouting," "Terrariums."

CRAFTNOTES: LIGHT GARDENING ENVIRONMENTS

The indoor gardener uses artificial lights to simulate the light his plants would get in their natural environment. But he can supply light at its optimum, not subject to nature's vagaries: its storms, its freezes, its overcast days. Yet, with the best light in the world, plants cannot survive unless the other critical environmental factors—temperature, humidity, water, soil, fertilizer, and a suitable container—are provided.

Temperature levels, critical to plant health, vary over the day; the right daytime temperature is too high at night. Most foliage plants do well at a daytime temperature of 72 to 80 degrees Fahrenheit. At night, it should drop by 10 degrees. For flowering plants, the usual range is 60 to 70 degrees Fahrenheit for daytime, with a 5-degree drop at night. When checking to see that the temperature in the garden area is within these ranges, do not go by the overall room temperature (this may be different than that in the growing area, due to the effects of lights, drafts, air conditioners or radiators). Place a thermometer in the garden or growing area itself. If the temperature is too high, adjusting the heat by providing ventilation will help. Raising the light source, away from the plants, is another solution. If the temperature is too low, but the rest of the room is comfortable, a draft may be the culprit; try weather-stripping the windows.

Humidity is another vital factor—and one that is often wildly misestimated. My clients often are astonished when I tell them that the average home has a lower relative humidity than does the average desert. This fact accounts for one reason indoor gardeners so often forget to provide the proper humidity for their plants. I always recommend a relative humidity of about 40 percent, an attainable level adequate for both garden and gardener. This can be measured with a hygrometer, an inexpensive instrument available at hardware stores. If the humidity is too low—as it almost surely will be—putting plants on damp gravel and misting leaves with water will help. Better still, use a humidifier to increase the room humidity. If placed in the same room with the garden and the doors to the room are kept closed, a humidifier can be very effective.

In order to provide humidity, all of the garden systems described here employ a plant tray filled with gravel. The gravel should be kept damp, with the water level stopping just short of the bottom of the pots that rest on the gravel (water should not touch the pot).

Soil is a vitally important variable; and even though packaged potting mediums are available, it is a good idea to learn to mix your own. The overall goal is a soil mix that is chemically similar to the natural soil environment of the plant, has enough nutrients to feed it adequately, and one that will hold water without packing. For most plants a mixture of ⅓ packaged potting soil, ⅓ peat (which will hold water, releasing it slowly) and ⅓ perlite (which provides good aeration and drainage) is a good potting medium.

The frequency of feeding should not exceed that recommended on the fertilizer package. There are many good fertilizers available, but I prefer alternating them, rather than relying on one alone. I alternate an inorganic, commercial fertilizer at three-quarters strength with an organic fertilizer such as fish emulsion. Fertilize plants only when the soil is moist to avoid root burn. If the plant has gotten dry between waterings, water it a day before you add the water-fertilizer solution.

Watering is a surprisingly difficult art to master. People usually err on the side of too much rather than too little; but either can be fatal since any plant that is kept wet or dry for too long suffers root damage and cannot absorb water or nutrients.

Watering is not a question of how much, but of how often. Plants needing wet soil should be watered frequently; those needing moist soil are watered more moderately, while plants that thrive in dry soil need infrequent waterings. In a perfectly controlled environment this would translate into a timetable of days between waterings. No environment is this controlled, however, and the variations in heat, humidity and light levels and in soil and container types drastically affect watering frequency. The best way to determine when watering is necessary is to put your finger an inch or two down into the soil and feel for moisture. Unless otherwise indicated in the chart, plants need moist but not wet soil and should not be watered until the soil at this level is almost dry. When it is time to water, however, water quite liberally. (See plant requirement charts on pages 1082 and 1083.)

The flowerpot should have a hole at its base, and the plants should be watered until excess water runs out of the hole and onto the gravel.

The element that holds it all together—the pot—is important, too; and what type you use will influence watering to some extent. Always use a pot big enough to hold the roots comfortably; it is easy to knock the soil ball out of the pot to see if the roots are encircling it. If they are, repot in the next larger size pot. To provide for adequate drainage, the pot should have a drainage hole and it should have a layer of gravel or shards—pieces of a broken pot—underneath the soil. Most pots are made of either clay or plastic, and either type is fine. Clay pots, being porous, will not hold water as long as plastic so plan to check for dryness more frequently than if you use plastic pots. But if you use plastic pots, be more careful not to overwater—it is easy to drown a potted plant. Never plant in a metal container unless it has been painted or treated to prevent rust, and never plant directly in copper or brass containers—these metals are toxic to plants.

LINOLEUM AND WOODCUTS
Incisive Design

An adjunct professor at Kean College in Union, New Jersey, Sarah Patricia Duffy was born in Newburn, North Carolina. She received a Bachelor of Fine Arts degree from Howard University, Washington, D.C. and a Master of Fine Arts degree from Pratt Institute, Brooklyn, New York. Ms. Duffy, who likes to be called Pat, also teaches printmaking to children and young adults through community programs. In addition to her teaching activities, Pat creates her own works at The Printmaking Workshop in New York. Her work has been exhibited at the Pratt Manhattan Center, the Westchester Arts Festival, and the Warwick Gallery in London, England.

Linoleum blocks and woodcuts are used for relief printing. Each block has areas that have been cut away called "deeps," and design areas that are left standing called "reliefs." Ink is applied only to the relief areas, and paper is pressed against the block to print the relief design on the paper. In this way an artist or craftsman can reproduce many copies of the designs he has cut in the block.

Relief printing was developed by the ancient Chinese, Assyrians and Egyptians who used both wood and stone blocks. The art then spread to Japan where wood was used exclusively as the medium. Block prints that date back to the eighth and ninth centuries have been found in China and Japan. By the fifteenth century, woodcuts were being produced in Europe. The earliest printed books were called block books because the illustrations and the text on each page were carved from a single block of wood. After the invention of movable type, woodcuts were used only for the illustrations. Albrecht Dürer, a German artist of the medieval period, used this medium. But the custom in his day was for the artist only to draw on the block; then a block cutter, who was not an artist but a member of the carpenter's guild, would cut the block. Today, artists and craftsmen design and cut their own blocks. Eventually, woodcuts for book illustrations were replaced by wood engravings. (A woodcut is gouged from the flat side of the board, along the long grain. A wood engraving, on the other hand, is engraved from the end-grain using engraving tools similar to those used to engrave metal.) Artists still make woodcuts today, but linoleum is becoming a popular craft medium.

Linoleum has long been used as a floor covering because of its flexibility and durability; it is also waterproof, has a fine texture, and is slightly elastic—all of which make it wear well when used as a printing block. The word linoleum comes from two Latin words: *linum* which means flax, and *oleum* which means oil. Linen fibers and seeds from the flax plant are processed into linseed oil which, when oxidized, is mixed with ground cork and spread on burlap to form linoleum.

The projects that follow will show you how to print the whimsical design shown opposite on a scarf with a linoleum block, and how to use woodcuts to imprint greeting cards and a two-color wall hanging.

What You Need

Before you start to assemble the necessary equipment, make sure that you have a suitable work area. You will need a flat table or work bench, fairly smooth and free of bumps, on which you will do both the cutting and the printing. The surface should be large enough so that the plate glass and the paper on which you are printing will fit comfortably at the same time.

Linoleum

For the best results in block printing, use battleship linoleum, a heavy floor covering that comes in ⅛-inch and ¼-inch thicknesses. Its solid color, usually tan or white, makes it easier to see the drawing, and it is backed with heavy burlap. If you plan to make several block prints, linoleum can be purchased at a linoleum store. Small blocks of linoleum ranging in size from 2-by-3-inches to 12-by-12-inches, and glued to ¾-inch plywood, can be purchased at an art supply store.

Wood

Wood that has knots or whose grain is splintered or raised should be used only if you want such marks and raised graining on the final print. To avoid such problems, use a smooth-surfaced board whose grain is not too prominent. Fruitwoods such as apple, cherry, and pear are good because they are smooth, have only a faint grain pattern, and are durable. White pine is a good choice because it cuts easily without splintering. Plywood surfaced with birch or maple cuts nicely, but avoid the wildly grained plywoods like fir. All plywood used should be ¾-inch thick.

An inked linoleum block makes a print of the areas that are left at the original surface level, and,
therefore, pick up the ink. The gouged-out areas or "deeps" are white on the print.

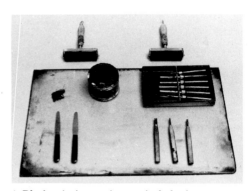

1: Block printing equipment includes brayers (top), ink (in the can), cutting tools (a set of tools is in the box; individual ones are below the box), spatulas (left), and a sheet of plate glass (under the tools).

Tools and Equipment

To cut either wood or linoleum blocks, there are tools—knives, gouges, V-cutters —that can be purchased in a set or singly (photograph 1). Printer's ink is available in a variety of colors and can be purchased in small quantities in tubes from art supply stores. It is the best all-around ink for block printing because it can be used on both paper and cloth. If you are working with children or simply want an easier clean-up, there are several water-soluble block printing inks available. However, oil-soluble printer's ink comes in a greater range of colors and is used for finer work. Since it is oil-soluble, you will need spirits of turpentine, the highly-refined type available in small quantities at art supply stores, as a solvent. Kerosene is an inexpensive and safe cleaning agent for the equipment, the blocks and the hands. Have plenty of clean rags on hand. (Use rags free of buttons, snaps and hooks that might damage the surface of the linoleum.)

If you are printing on paper, use a fairly heavy, dull-finish paper such as rag paper because it absorbs ink readily and gives a more even result. If you want to print on cloth, use a firmly woven cotton, such as muslin, or linen.

For the printing process itself, you will need a piece of plate glass, at least 12 inches square, for spreading the ink (photograph 1). Glass is most practical because it does not absorb the ink and it can be cleaned easily. A brayer, or ink roller, is a solid rubber or rubber-covered wooden roller with a handle. It is used to spread the ink into a thin layer and to apply the ink to the block. A spatula, or ink knife, has a thin flexible blade that is used to measure out and mix the ink. A wooden or rawhide mallet can be used to make an impression on the paper; however, a large serving spoon works just as well.

Graphic Arts
A block-printed scarf ¢ ▨ 👫 🦞

The whimsical scarf on page 1098 is made by block printing the stylized frogs on a 20-by-21-inch piece of muslin. The curved lines and intricate details of the frog are more suited to linoleum because it is softer and easier to cut than wood. To cut linoleum to the 4-by-6-inch size, use a steel ruler or T-square as guide and a mat knife to score the surface. With the linoleum over the edge of a table or work bench, press down evenly on both sides of the scored line; the linoleum will crack down to the burlap. Fold the linoleum on the crack and cut the burlap backing. The linoleum can be used this way, but if you find it difficult to handle, mount the linoleum on a

Figure A: At right is a full-size frog pattern to trace for the linoleum block used to print the scarf shown in color on page 1098.

A

piece of plywood of the same size using white household glue. To prepare the linoleum block for cutting, remove the protective wax covering that is usually found on the surface by wiping it with a rag soaked in kerosene and rinsing it. The linoleum block is now ready for drawing. The muslin for the scarf should be washed before it is printed to remove the sizing. (After it is printed, the scarf can be washed in cold water, or dry-cleaned.)

Two of the frogs will fit on a 4-by-6-inch piece of linoleum. Each time the block is printed, two frogs will appear. This will save time when you make the border on the scarf. If you do not want to cut out two frogs, center one frog on the linoleum block. This will give you more space between frogs on the border if you want it, or allow you to place the frogs in different positions.

Trace the frog (Figure A) onto tracing paper, then put carbon paper on top of the linoleum block, place the drawing on top of the carbon paper, and trace the frog pattern using a sharp pencil to outline the design lightly. (Do not bear down hard enough to leave an impression on the linoleum.) If you want to change the design in any way, sketch the design you want on paper first; then transfer it to the linoleum block using carbon paper. Or, if you feel adventurous, you can draw your design directly on the linoleum block with a pencil. To change the drawing, pencil lines can be erased with a soft eraser.

With the drawing on the linoleum block, place the block on a firm flat surface and hold it gently but firmly with your free hand and begin cutting (photograph 2). Caution: Always keep your free hand behind the blade and cut away from you. Use broad U-shaped gouges to cut out large areas such as the background, and pointed V-shaped cutters to make lines such as the texture of the frog's skin. When cutting around the edge of the design, do not make cuts perpendicular to the linoleum's surface; slope them gradually away from the outline of the design. This gives added strength to the parts of the design that remain higher.

Remember that the areas such as the background that are cut out will appear white on the print although they are darker on the linoleum block. To make the grass-like effect on the background, gouge out the linoleum in long, vertical strips (photograph 2). Although none of the background is left at the original level, the ridges between the strips are higher than the remaining background so they receive some ink and make an impression when printing. The areas immediately surrounding the frog, its eyes, and the edges of its backbone are gouged out deep enough so that no ink is received; they will be completely white on the print.

When the cut linoleum block is ready to be printed, the ink must be put on the block in a thin even film. To do this, spread some ink on the sheet of glass with a spatula so that it measures the width of the brayer and roll the brayer into the ink until its roller is evenly covered with a thin layer of ink (photograph 3). Roll the brayer across the linoleum block in one direction from one end to the other several times until the raised design areas are covered with ink (photograph 4). (Rolling

Sharpening the Tools

A dull tool is hazardous because it may slip and cut your free hand (especially if you are not careful to keep your free hand behind the blade). Not only are sharp tools safer, but they produce a more cleanly cut block.

To sharpen dull blades, you will need an India stone, an Arkansas stone, and a honing slip; all are available at art supply stores. Start with the India stone for general sharpening. Using oil (any household oil will do) to reduce friction, rub the beveled side of the blade against the stone. If both sides of the blade are beveled, rub both sides against the stone. Be careful to maintain the angle of the bevel while sharpening. When you have achieved a sharp edge, use the Arkansas stone and oil to polish it smooth.

To sharpen V-cutters and rounded gouges, use a honing slip that is specially designed to sharpen the inside of these tools. The slip is a stone with one V-shaped side and one rounded side. The grooves in V-cutters and rounded gouges fit over these sides so the entire cutting edge can be sharpened at once.

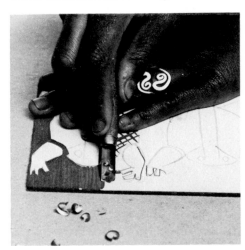

2: With the free hand behind the cutting tool, cut out the linoleum following the drawing lines.

3: To get an even layer of ink on the brayer, roll the ink out on the plate glass.

4: To ink, hold the block lightly with the tips of your fingers and roll the brayer across it.

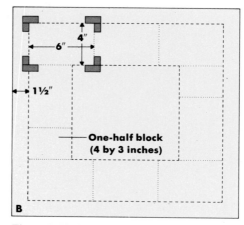

Figure B: Mark the placement of the linoleum block on the fabric with masking tape before you begin to print. To print the half-blocks (single frog) on each side of the border, cover one of the carved frogs with a piece of paper.

the brayer back and forth will lift up the ink rather than deposit it.) Do not put too much ink on the block; the excess ink will drip into the cut areas and may spoil the clear outline of the design when it is printed.

To print the design, place the paper or cloth on top of the inked linoleum block in a location where you want the design to appear (Figure B). Put a piece of scrap paper over the paper or cloth on which you are printing and rub the surface with a large spoon (photograph 5). The block should be rubbed from one end to the other with the same amount of pressure until the entire block has been rubbed; do not skip around. When the block is partially rubbed, carefully lift one corner to check to see if the ink is coming through onto the paper or cloth. As long as a large part of the print remains firmly stuck to the block, this lifting can be done without smearing the print. Keep checking the print as you rub. When you are satisfied with the print, carefully peel off the paper or cloth (photograph 6) and lay it aside to dry. When it is completely dry, repeat the printing procedure for the next print. Make sure the print is thoroughly dry before printing the next block or the previous one will smear. Continue around until the border is complete.

5: Holding the paper or cloth in place, rub the print evenly from top to bottom with a spoon.

6: When the rubbing is finished and you are satisfied with the print, peel off the paper or cloth.

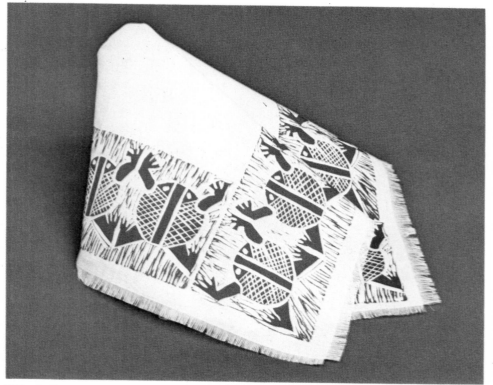

Whimsical frogs peering out from the long swamp grass dance hand-in-hand (or foot-in-foot) around the border of the muslin scarf.

Graphic Arts
Greeting cards

¢ ◻ 🚶 🖌️

Making a woodcut for block printing follows much the same procedure as making a linoleum block. The main difference is that cutting wood requires more effort than cutting linoleum. The grain of wood gives a woodcut print a subtle texture that linoleum block prints do not have. If you do not want this texture to show, you can sand the wood block with fine sandpaper and give it a coat of shellac.

The greeting cards shown on page 1100 were printed from a 4-by-8-inch block of ¾-inch plywood that was cut out following the pattern in Figure C (page 1101). Use heavy-weight watercolor paper at least 8 inches square for the print. The print will take up half the paper; the other half will be folded over to form the card. To trace the pattern in Figure C, use the carbon paper method described on page 1097. If you want to try out your own design, remember that the areas cut out will be white on the print, and the areas left uncut will pick up the ink and print. To see how your finished design will appear on the print, coat the wood block with opaque black india ink with a small brush and let dry. Then use crayons, pastels or any drawing substance that will not depress the wood's surface to draw the design on the wood block (photograph 7).

7: With a crayon or pastel, make the drawing directly on the india ink-covered wood block.

8: With your free hand behind the cutting tool, cut out the solid areas with large, firm cuts.

9: To create texture, gouge out part of the wood leaving part of it at the original level.

Cutting the Block

Before starting to cut the wood block, make sure all the cutting tools are sharp (see page 1097). Always cut with the grain of the wood and away from you. First outline large areas with long continuous cuts. Use a knife, holding it firmly and applying pressure along the length of the cutting line. This continuous cut will act as a stopping line when cutting out the solid areas. Do not cut perpendicularly to the surface, but cut at a 45-degree angle away from the relief areas. This adds support to them while printing. The next step is to cut out the solid areas that are to be removed. (These areas will appear white on the print.) Hold the cutting tool more loosely to gouge out small, shallow sections of wood so that none of the wood remains at the original level (photograph 8). When the solid relief areas that will print and the deeps or cut-out areas that will not print are established, areas of texture can be added. Texture can be created by cutting or scoring relief areas, as in photograph 9. Keep in mind that woodcuts lend themselves to bold images, ones that have strong, jagged lines, irregular edges and a lot of light and dark contrast.

Printing the Block

Before you begin to print, brush the wood block thoroughly to remove all wood chips and splinters. Put a small amount of ink on the glass slab, and roll the ink over an area as wide as the roller until the ink is smoothed out to a thin film on both the glass and the roller (photograph 3, page 1097). The ink should be tacky but not

When they are block-printed with your own design, greeting cards become an especially personal way to communicate with friends.

lumpy. Use the brayer to roll the ink onto the wood block (photograph 10), as you did when inking the linoleum block; the ink should cover the block in a thin layer. If the ink is too thick, it may drip into the deeps and smear the lines of the design.

The block is now ready to be printed. Although the watercolor paper will be folded later to form a greeting card, it is best to work with the flat piece of paper so the ink will not penetrate both layers of paper. Place the paper on the wood block so that the print will be on one-half of the paper. (If your paper is larger than 8 inches square, place the paper so there will be a border on all sides of the print.) Put a piece of scrap paper on top of the printing paper for protection and using a serving spoon or tablespoon, rub the paper-covered block from top to bottom across the full width of the block (photograph 5, page 1098). Check to see that the ink is printing by carefully lifting up one corner of the paper. When you have rubbed the entire block and are satisfied with the print, carefully peel off the paper (photograph 11) and lay it aside to dry. When the print is completely dry, fold the paper in half and write your message on the inside.

10: To cover the wood block with a thin layer of ink, roll the inked brayer across it.

11: When the rubbing is complete and you are satisfied with it, carefully peel off the paper.

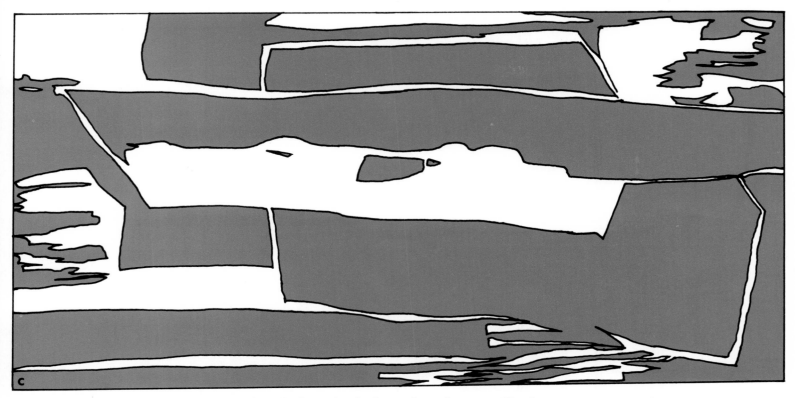

Figure C: This full-size pattern can be used to make the woodcut for the greeting cards on page 1100 and is one of the two blocks used to make the wall hanging on page 1102.

Figure D: This full-size pattern was used to make the woodcut that was printed in yellow on the wall hanging on page 1102. (A woodcut from the pattern in Figure C was used to print the green ink.)

Graphic Arts
A two-color wall hanging   ¢ ◨ ᛘ 🐦

The wall hanging at left is a 19-by-27-inch piece of muslin that has been block printed with two woodcuts in two colors. It is hung from an 18-inch dowel. The green design is printed with the same wood block that was used for the greeting cards (Figure C, page 1101); the yellow design is printed with a wood block cut from the pattern in Figure D, page 1101. The inked woodcuts, ready to be printed, are shown in photograph 12.

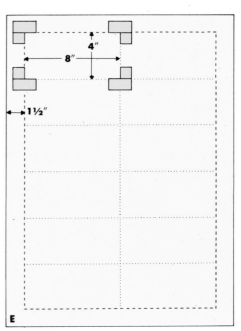

Figure E: To register a woodcut—assuring that the woodcut is printed in the right place each time—lay the wood block on the paper or cloth, and mark the block's corners with masking tape.

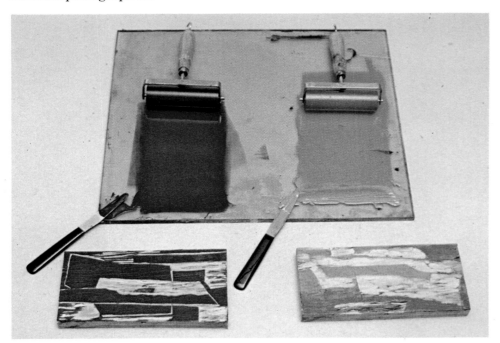

12: To make the wall hanging (opposite), you will need the two woodcuts and two colors of ink.

Since each color is applied with a separate block, the blocks must be placed in a fixed location to make sure the design colors register, or fit together as intended. To accomplish this, place one block, before it is inked, on the spot where it is to be printed. Then with pieces of masking tape, mark the outline of the block as shown in Figure E. (When making a design with more than one block, the over-all size of the blocks should be the same. In this design, both blocks are 4-by-8-inches.) After both blocks have been cut, one wood block is inked, the fabric is placed on the block so that it fits into the taped area, and the print is rubbed with a spoon. When the first print is thoroughly dry, the second print can be made. Allow at least 20 minutes (and up to one hour) for the print to dry. The drying time will depend on the thickness of the ink and the amount of humidity in the air. Test to see if the ink is dry by touching the corner of the print. Dry ink will be duller in color than wet ink. Print all the green blocks from top to bottom first. The solid area at their tops and bottoms will help to guide you when placing the next print. When the green prints are dry, the series of yellow blocks can be printed. Use the same masking-tape method to register the yellow print; apply masking tape lightly so it doesn't take paint off when it is removed. When both colors are dry, trim the fabric close to the edges of the printed area (or hem the edges under if desired). Then staple the top to a dowel or make a top hem for the dowel to fit through.
For related crafts and projects, see "Block Printing," "Greeting Cards," "Mono-printing," and "Woodcarving."

Two woodcuts printed in two colors combine to make a bold wall hanging. The colors are printed separately but registered so they fit together.

Seamstresses as Artists

Lanny Lasky, an artist who specializes in sculpture and collages made from found objects, has exhibited her work in museums and galleries in New York and at Expo '74 in Spokane, Washington. She first developed her free-embroidery technique to decorate her children's clothing, and this is one of the crafts she teaches to teen-agers at the Riverdale Neighborhood House in New York, where she is art director.

The discovery of this Aztec calendar stone revealed secrets of Aztec language and culture to archeologists. It is now in the Museo Nacional in Mexico City.

If you own a sewing machine but have hesitated to use it for decorative stitching, the projects given here may pleasantly surprise you. Machine embroidery looks more complicated than it really is. The necessary techniques can be mastered in a few hours, even if your machine sewing thus far has been limited to simple seams. And elaborate, hand-embroidered effects can be achieved on a machine in a fraction of the time required for handwork.

Machine embroidery received real impetus with the development, after World War II, of sewing machines for home use designed to produce a wide variety of stitches. Although many types and makes of machines are available today, they fall into these categories: straight-stitch machines that sew backward and forward in a straight line with the needle moving up and down only; and standard and automatic zigzag machines that sew backward and forward *and* from side to side in a zigzag pattern. By adjusting the width of the zigzag and the length or closeness of the stitches, you can produce a wide variety of decorative stitches. Automatic zigzag models can be made to repeat the same stitch pattern over and over simply by setting a dial or inserting a disc (also called a cam).

Two popular forms of machine embroidery are included here. The free embroidery designs by Lanny Lasky (pages 1105 and 1107) can be done on a straight-stitch machine. For this technique, the sewer draws a design on fabric and then stitches over the lines by guiding the fabric under the needle.

The second approach, more like hand embroidery, calls for decorating fabric with a wide variety of stitch designs. A standard or automatic zigzag machine is needed to provide the different stitches. The projects by Nancy Weber (pages 1109 and 1111) and Johanna Bafaro (pages 1113 through 1115) incorporate the basic zigzag stitch as well as some repetitive stitch patterns. If your machine cannot duplicate the exact stitches used for the projects described, substitute any similar stitch it can do. Or use a satin stitch (see Craftnotes, page 1109), which is basically a series of very closely spaced zigzag stitches. The skill is in the stitchery—producing a smooth, uniform series of stitches—rather than in the stitch itself.

Sewing Guidelines

Whatever machine you own and whichever projects you make, the following guidelines basic to machine embroidery will help you achieve good workmanship. First learn to adjust your machine to sew decorative stitches by following the directions given in your instruction manual. If your machine is not in good working order, have it repaired before stitching on anything but practice fabric.

For free embroidery the sewing machine must be adapted to let the fabric move freely under the needle. A darning foot (see photograph, page 1106) is substituted for the presser foot that normally exerts pressure on the fabric as it feeds through the machine. The toothed gears, called the feed dogs, that normally advance the fabric are lowered or covered with a metal plate. Then you can move the fabric in any direction.

The most temperamental adjustment is that of thread tension—the tightness or looseness of the thread as it is fed through the machine and into the fabric. Make tension adjustments carefully (see diagrams, page 1108), then take a few stitches on a practice swatch to make sure the adjustment is what you want. Experimenting on a practice swatch is the best way to learn a new stitch. Use the same thread and fabric you will use for the final project.

Finally, wherever possible, do the embroidery before you assemble the article. Decorations can be applied to a finished garment, of course, but it is easier to work on flat, unassembled pieces.

This design, inspired by the Aztec calendar stone at left, was simplified for application on a cotton workshirt. You can trace this actual-size design and transfer it to a shirt or jacket. Instructions for making the project begin on page 1106.

Placed high in the center of the back of a shirt, the Aztec-inspired design is in a good position for effective display.

A darning foot is used for free embroidery because it puts no pressure on the fabric and you can guide it in any direction. A plate covers the teeth that would otherwise move the fabric forward.

For practice, sew your name first in script (top), then outline and fill in block letters (bottom).

Needlecrafts
Free embroidery work shirt

The Aztec calendar stone design turns an ordinary work shirt like the one at left into a prized possession. The design, first worked out on paper, is traced onto the shirt and then all the outlined areas are filled in with the appropriate color of thread. During sewing, the fabric moves freely under the needle. In my first version of this design, reds and pinks along the outer edges contrasted poorly with the blue shirt. So, for my second version, I added the yellow border and the lighter blues, as shown on page 1105. The idea is to begin with a plan but if, as you sew, you see that some colors do not show up or combine well, or if parts of the design are too large or too small, make whatever changes seem right.

Tools and Materials

The workshirt (and the hanging on page 1107) were done on a straight-stitch machine fitted with a darning attachment. For the work shirt you need: a sheet of tracing paper; sheet of dressmaker's carbon paper (or ordinary carbon paper); pencil; scissors; mercerized cotton thread in assorted colors; white thread for the bobbin; and a sharp-pointed sewing machine needle.

Some Practice Runs

A good way to get the feel of the free embroidery work you will do for the Aztec design is to write your name with thread on a swatch of practice fabric. Thread the machine with colored thread and work on a closely woven fabric—a flimsy fabric may pull and pucker from the constant puncturing of the needle. Set the length of the stitch at 0. Since the machine does not advance the fabric, how long or short the stitches are will depend on how fast you guide the fabric. If you move it quickly, the stitches will be long or more widely spaced; if the fabric is moved slowly, shorter, tighter stitches will result.

Reduce the tension to allow the top and bobbin threads to feed easily, without pulling. Here, you will have to experiment as tension adjustments vary from machine to machine; they will also be affected by the weight of the fabric you are using. Work on the right side of the fabric and start stitching slowly. To stitch a script name, as at left, you may find it easier to write the name in pencil first, then stitch over the penciled outline. After finishing the name, go over the letters again, to make them more prominent.

For more practice, outline your name in block letters, as at left below, then fill in the letter outlines with the same color thread as neatly as you can. You may need to go back and forth over each letter several times to set it off vividly from the background. Make the stitches in the direction that looks best to you.

Decorating the Workshirt

The Aztec calendar design for the work shirt is shown actual size in the photograph on page 1105 and can be traced directly on a sheet of tracing paper. To find the center of the shirt, pin the shoulders together, toward the back, and place a pin at the crease in the middle of the shirt. Then, unpin the shoulders, spread out the shirt and place the design where you think it will look best when worn. (Remember that the shirt may be worn tucked in, as in the photograph above.)

To transfer the design (photograph 1), place the carbon paper face down on the shirt and put the design tracing on top of the carbon. Retrace the design with a hard pencil, pressing firmly to make sure it will transfer to the shirt.

To Sew

Set the stitch length at 0. Using a scrap of fabric similar to the work shirt, sew a few stitches, then check to see that the tension is adjusted properly (see diagrams, page 1108). Always begin at the center of a design and work out from it. (This helps to avoid puckering and lets you smooth out any wrinkles and small puckers that may occur.) You may find it advantageous to use an embroidery hoop to hold the fabric taut. Iron the shirt back occasionally as you work.

Start with orange thread and sew the eyes in the center of the design by moving the fabric around in a circle. Change to light blue for the areas under the orange eyes. Then stitch the nose, mouth and other details in the center, changing needle thread color as needed. (I use white thread in the bobbin at all times.) When you come to a large design area, first outline, and then fill in. Continue sewing from the center out, moving the fabric in the direction you want to stitch. When doing a design that is totally covered like this one, do the prominent parts in each section, such as the facial features, first. Then fill in the background before going on to the next section. The yellow thread surrounding the face, for example, was filled in after the facial features were outlined satisfactorily.

As you sew, snip stray thread ends left from changing the color of the thread. Thread does not have to be pulled through to the underside as it is anchored firmly. You may make a mistake or two in the evenness and direction of the stitches but it is usually not necessary to remove such mistakes as they go unnoticed in the context of a completed design. Of course, a major error or bunching of thread and stitches should be ripped out and re-done.

Needlecrafts
Folk art hanging

¢ ⊠ ⋏ ⚲

Ideas for free embroidery designs come from many sources and if you look closely, you will see design ideas everywhere you turn. Wrapping paper, greeting cards, coloring books and magazines often have designs you can trace. (It's a good idea to keep a file of ideas like these you can refer to when looking for a design.) Leaves, flowers and other living things are natural sources. The pear and leaves in the hanging below were inspired by a tree in our garden. The light-colored background fabric, chosen for contrast, is a linen-like cotton blend that is closely woven and easy to sew on.

1: The shirt is smoothed over a piece of cardboard so the fabric won't slip while you transfer the pattern. Holding the tracing paper and carbon paper in place with strips of masking tape is also helpful.

2: In free embroidery, your hands guide the fabric in the direction you want to sew, a circle in this case. You may have to go over the traced lines several times for the design to stand out.

3: The design is worked from the center out. After you finish the face, add blocks of blue and red for the surrounding circle. Outline a block first, then fill it in with rows of stitches.

This free-embroidery folk art hanging was done on a light background to emphasize the delicate lines and soft colors. Designs are derived from real-life objects, in the folk art tradition.

4: This detail illustrates how an outlined area can be partially filled in, allowing some background fabric to show through.

Thread tension

Most tension adjustments can be made by adjusting the needle thread (upper thread) tension rather than the bobbin thread (lower thread) tension.

If the upper thread tension is too loose (or the lower thread tension too tight), the thread will lie stretched out on the underside of the fabric, as above.

When the tension of the upper thread is too tight (or the lower thread too loose), the thread lies stretched on the top of the fabric.

If tensions are properly adjusted and in balance, the threads are drawn equally into the fabric and stitches look alike on both sides.

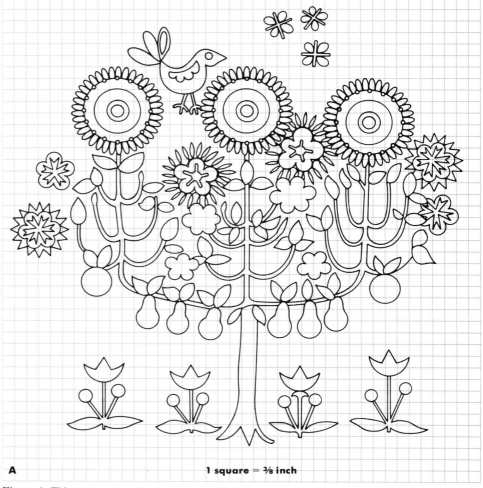

A   **1 square = ⅜ inch**

Figure A: This pattern is one-half actual size. To enlarge the pattern, draw a grid with squares measuring ⅜ inch, then copy the appropriate section of the pattern in each square, one square at a time.

Materials

To make the folk art hanging you will need the same materials used for the workshirt, page 1106. Use dressmaker's carbon paper that washes out and don't trace the design too heavily. The pattern (Figure A, above) is one half actual size, but can be enlarged to any size you choose. If you plan to frame the piece, allow a 2-inch margin on all sides.

Stitching the Hanging

The effectiveness of this design depends on the interplay of filled in and open areas, and shows that an object can be most attractive even if it is *not* totally filled in. To begin, enlarge and transfer the design to the right side of the background fabric. The most prominent parts of the design should be done first. I stitched the three main flowers first, then the bird, then the fruit. The last things stitched were the leaves. This sequence is recommended because the flowers, which dominate the design, might take on a different look as you sew them, suggesting a corresponding change in the look of the leaves.

The colors of the different motifs are reasonably realistic, but there is no rigid color scheme that must be followed. The direction of the stitches should follow the shape of the object so that stitches seem to flow. Each motif is outlined before any filling in is done. For an interesting variation, try outlining a section and not filling it in. This was done with the bird's eye. As you work, iron the fabric periodically to keep it smooth. Snip any loose thread ends.

Needlecrafts
Appliqued wall hanging

¢ ☒ ♣ ♫

Use a zigzag machine with a regular foot attachment to make this wall hanging with its machine-appliqued sunflower. The design makes an attractive hanging for a kitchen or child's room. It could also be used on a skirt or table cover.

To make the hanging, pieces of colored felt are machine-stitched onto a background material. But the applique process requires several steps before the actual stitching begins. First, the design is transferred to the wrong side of the fabric. Next, patches of felt, each about an inch larger than finished size, are basted to the right side of the fabric. The design is then stitched once on the back of the fabric with a tiny zigzag or straight stitch to anchor the felt patches in place. Finally, each section of the design is stitched on the right side with decorative stitches that cover the earlier stitches. This process keeps the work smooth and prevents puckering, and is recommended for all applique work.

Working the sunflower hanging will teach you some of the decorative stitches that can be used for machine-applique. (Stitches are shown in the Craftnotes below.) You can, of course, get effects that differ from those shown here by varying the choice of fabric and thread. Burlap or wool sewn with embroidery floss, yarn, or even metallic thread are alternate materials.

What You Need
In addition to a zigzag sewing machine you will need: a 9-by-18-inch piece of felt for the background; tracing paper; dressmaker's carbon paper and a dressmaker's toothed tracing wheel; a piece of fusible interfacing the same size as the felt background. (Fusible interfacing is a non-woven fabric used as a backing to give a finished piece more body. It is available by the yard in fabric shops and is attached by pressing with a steam iron.) You will also need felt patches in assorted colors— green, gold, orange, rust; thread in colors to match the felt (mercerized cotton thread is recommended for smoother stitches); green pearl-cotton or buttonhole twist thread for the stem; needle and thread for hand-basting; scissors; felt-tip pen; steam iron. To hang the finished applique you will need a frame, thin rod or dowel.

Nancy Weber started machine sewing at the age of 10 and has been sewing ever since. A home economist with the White Sewing Machine Company in Cleveland, Ohio, Nancy combines her hobby with her job. She demonstrates and teaches machine sewing at fairs, stores and schools.

This applique sunflower is made with felt, decoratively stitched with the satin stitch and irregular zigzag stitch (see Craftnotes, left). The stem is made straight-stitched with green pearl cotton thread.

MACHINE EMBROIDERY CRAFTNOTES

Basic stitches

Straight stitch: The needle moves up and down only in this basic sewing stitch—done in a continuous row.

Zigzag stitch: The needle swings from side to side. The width (side-to-side measurement) and length (spacing of stitches) can be adjusted for variations in effect.

Satin stitch: This is made with zigzag stitches that lie very close together, that is, have a near zero length. This stitch is basic for decorative effects.

Decorative stitches
These stitch patterns are built into the better zigzag machines. They can be approximated on other machines by varying widths, spacings, and tensions.

Irregular zigzag stitch: This is a series of first wide, then narrow zigzag stitches.

Triangle stitch: Stitch width increases then decreases to form a triangle.

Scallop stitch: This is a wide stitch followed by 10 narrow stitches in a slight curve.

Shell stitch: A series of stitches of various widths done in an oval-like pattern.

B   1 square = ½ inch

Figure B: Draw a grid with ½-inch squares and enlarge the pattern for the sunflower by drawing it on the larger grid one square at a time.

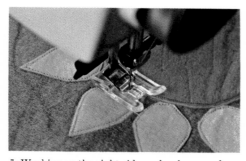

7: Working on the right side, a closely-spaced satin stitch is used to outline each gold petal. The stitch length is set at 0, so the fabric edges will not show through.

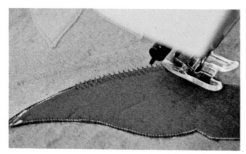

8: The leaf edges are outlined with an irregular zigzag stitch that catches both the leaf and background felt. A satin stitch can also be used.

Preparing the Design

The first step is to make a paper pattern by enlarging the sunflower in Figure B on ordinary tracing paper. Attach the interfacing following package directions before transferring the design. Then, use dressmaker's carbon paper and a tracing wheel to outline the pattern on the fusible interfacing. Put the carbon paper face down over the interfacing and place the pattern face down over the carbon. Go over the pattern lines with the tracing wheel. Since you are working on the wrong side and marks will not show through, go over the design with a felt-tip pen to darken the carbon lines. This makes it easier to stitch the lines exactly.

Basting and Preliminary Stitching

Working on the right side (front) of the material, position a large patch of green felt where each leaf will be and use one patch of gold felt large enough to cover the area where all the flower petals will be. Rust and orange felt for the flower's center will be basted on later. Each felt patch must be larger than the figure it will become in the finished applique as it is first sewn in place, then trimmed to shape. Decorative details are applied by stitching over the edges.

Baste the felt patches in place by hand (photograph 5). Working on the wrong side of the felt, go over the lines of the design with a tiny zigzag stitch or a straight stitch, following the lines drawn on the interfacing. Then cover the stitches just made with decorative stitches worked on the right side of the fabric. Outline the stem in a straight stitch using pearl cotton, a heavier-than-normal thread, in the bobbin. The pearl cotton adds texture to the design.

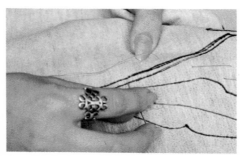

5: Hand-basting will keep patches of felt from slipping while you sew. After basting, the design is outlined on the wrong side of the fabric with a tiny zigzag or straight stitch.

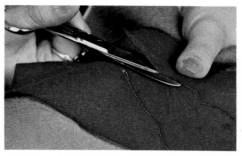

6: Patches of felt for each section are trimmed close to the preliminary stitches. Then decorative stitching can be worked over these stitches on the right side of the fabric.

Decorative Details

A closely spaced satin stitch is sewn around each gold petal and an irregular zigzag stitch outlines the leaves (see Craftnotes, page 1109). For the satin stitch, adjust the machine for a narrow (⅛-inch-wide) zigzag stitch. Set the stitch length regulator close to 0 so the fabric moves slowly and the stitches lie close to each other, and adjust the thread tension to get a smooth, close satin stitch. If your machine has a numbered tension, lower it 1 or 1½ numbers from normal position. Take a few practice stitches on a scrap piece of felt to make sure the stitch is even. If the thread breaks, the tension is still too tight.

To outline the petals, sew slowly and position the fabric so that the needle catches the petal and then goes off onto the background felt. To follow the petal curves, do not turn the fabric while sewing. Rather, take a few stitches and stop sewing; then leave the needle in the fabric and turn the fabric slightly. Repeat around the curve. In this way, the line you're following is always in front of the needle and you don't have to force the fabric to turn.

To detail the leaves, adjust the machine for an irregular zigzag stitch, that is, a series of wide and narrow zigzag stitches. If your machine does not have this stitch, use any decorative stitch at least ⅛ inch wide or use the satin stitch. The thread used here matches the felt. If you prefer a bold outline effect, use black or contrasting thread. Sew as you did the petals, making sure you cover the preliminary stitching and stitches are taken smoothly around curves.

Baste a large piece of orange felt and then one of rust felt where the center of the flower will be. Working on the wrong side of the fabric, go over the circle and checkerboard lines with a tiny zigzag stitch, just as you did the leaves and petals. Turn the fabric over and trim away the excess felt, cutting close to the stitching. Because you have an extra layer of felt, you will have to trim carefully.

For the checkerboard effect, squares of rust felt are cut out, so the orange felt can show through. Make sure you cut only the squares that are to be orange by penciling an X on these squares. Cut away the rust squares you have penciled, taking care not to cut into the orange felt.

Thread the machine with rust thread and, using the satin stitch used for the petals, stitch over the checkerboard lines. The stitch used on the outer edge of the circle is the triangle stitch shown in the Craftnotes, page 1109. It is found on many automatic zigzag machines. The satin stitch is a substitute.

The stem is sewn on the back of the hanging. A simple straight stitch is used—the unusual braided effect comes from using pearl cotton in the bobbin. Buttonhole twist can be substituted for the pearl cotton. The upper (needle) thread is regular sewing thread. To sew the stem, first loosen the bobbin tension so that the thread passes through gently. Set the machine for a long straight stitch. Outline the stem first, then fill it in with about six rows of stitches.

The hanging may be finished by cutting the outer edges with pinking shears, and stitching a hem on the top edge to hold a dowel. Or the hanging may be framed.

Nancy Weber shows the capabilities of a zigzag sewing machine by decorating the place mat set with satin, shell and scallop stitches.

Needlecrafts
Personalized place mat $ ⊠ ★ ⚗

The place mat set below combines a bold selection of thread and stitches created with an automatic zigzag machine. If your machine cannot duplicate all of the stitches, substitute any decorative stitches it can do.

Since place mats and napkins are washed often, choose a durable fabric such as cotton or linen (I used green chino). The directions here are for one mat, napkin and napkin holder, so when you estimate the fabric needed, multiply the amount given by the number of place settings you plan.

The fabric should be preshrunk. To do this, simply put the fabric in water, remove and let it dry. Also preshrink the thread to be used for the cord effect (see below). This will not be threaded in the machine; it is laid on top of the mat, just at the edge, and anchored with a decorative scallop stitch.

A bright place mat with contrasting stitching combines decorative stitches and cord for an attractive edging. The monogrammed napkin holder matches it.

ABCD EFGH IJKL MNOP QRST UVWX YZ

C

Figure C: This alphabet can be traced (or enlarged to any size if you prefer) for monogramming the napkin holder or the pillowcase (page 1115). Draw the letter on the fabric in pencil first.

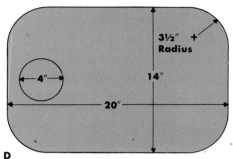

D

Figure D: This place mat is 14 by 20 inches but you can alter the size or shape. The napkin holder is a 4-inch coaster-size circle.

9: Hold the cord toward you as you stitch the scallop stitch, making sure this stitch just reaches the outer edge of the mat.

10: The inner row of shell stitches is positioned one presser foot away from the blue cord. Using the presser foot as a guide helps keep the outer and inner rows parallel.

Materials

The place mat is 14 by 20 inches; the napkin is 14 inches square and the napkin holder is a coaster-like circle, 4 inches in diameter. For each set you will need about ½ yard of fabric. The blue cord around the outer edge of the mat and napkin holder is made of four strands of pearl cotton, hereafter referred to as the cord. Pearl cotton is a rolled cotton thread with a shiny texture. Use No. 3 or No. 5 pearl cotton if you can get it; otherwise, any crochet thread or embroidery floss can be substituted. About 20 yards are needed for each set.

Other materials needed are: mercerized cotton thread, pink for the outer scallop stitch and blue for the inner rows of stitching and the monogram; several sheets of typing paper to back the stitching; and scissors.

How to Stitch

Cut out the place mat according to the dimensions in Figure D. Or use a place mat you already own for a pattern. Fabrics with a twill weave like chino cotton have a tendency to ravel; going over the raw edges with an overcast or zigzag stitch will prevent this. After stitching, pluck any stray threads that peek through. For the place mat, start by sewing on the cord. It is difficult to work with a piece long enough for the entire perimeter of the mat but use long pieces so thread ends will be butted in only a few places. To sew, lay a long piece of cord along the perimeter of the fabric. Leave a 2-inch tail unsewn where you begin so that when you put on the last section of cord, you will have room to fit the pieces together neatly.

The pink stitch used to anchor the blue cord is a scallop stitch (see Craftnotes, page 1109); a double strand of pink thread is used to make the thread appear heavier and more pronounced. If your machine does not have spindles for holding two spools of thread, place a bobbin wound with pink thread under the pink spool.

Set the machine for the scallop stitch. Use a regular foot or clear embroidery foot if your machine is equipped with one. To sew, place the blue cord directly under the machine's foot and guide the fabric so that the outer edge of the pink scallop stitch falls at the edge of the mat, forming a neat border (photograph 9). Continue sewing around the perimeter. When working on a curved corner section, sew a few stitches, then stop, leaving the needle in the fabric. Then turn the fabric and sew a few more stitches, and repeat around the corner.

The second stitch is a shell stitch, done in blue thread to match the cord. The stitch is worked ½ inch in from the inside edge of the pink-trimmed cord. Lining up the stitch one presser foot away from the cording makes a convenient guide (photograph 10). As you sew, watch the presser foot to keep the row of shell stitching parallel with the cord edging.

This stitch will be smoother and flatter if you place a sheet of typing paper under the fabric before beginning to sew. Excess paper is later peeled away—the part caught by the stitches will wash out.

The napkin is edged with the same scallop stitch as the mat. The edges of the napkin are first overcast as the mat edges were, then they are turned under ¼ inch and pressed. The scallop stitch is applied the same way it was for the mat.

Monogrammed Napkin Holder

Work on a large piece of material to make sewing the monogram easier. You may first want to back the fabric with regular or fusible interfacing so that it will be stiff (see page 1109 for information on fusible interfacing). Draw the letter you wish to monogram, then adjust the stitch length so that stitches are very close together.

Back the fabric with a piece of typing paper so that the stitches will lie flat. Then use a satin stitch for the vertical lines of the letter.

The curved lines of the letter are best done with the shell stitch (photograph 10). When sewing the shell stitch along a curve, let the machine complete a full stitch pattern before you turn the fabric.

After applying the monogram, cut the napkin holder into a circle, 4 inches in diameter. Overcast the edges as for the place mat and sew the scallop stitch over the 4-strand cord. Then sew the inner row of blue shell stitches as you did for the place mat. Attach the napkin holder to the mat with a few straight stitches on each side, placed close to the cord where they will not show.

Needlecrafts
Trapunto bag

A wide zigzag stitch sewn over lengths of jute gives this evening bag an embossed elegance. This style of needlework, where a design stands out in relief, is called trapunto and is actually a form of quilting, as the jute or cord is usually placed between rows of stitches. Yarn, cord, string or jute can be used for the raised design. The 10-by-14 ½-inch bag is made flat, much as you might make a pillow cover. Two pieces of fabric, with two layers of interfacing sandwiched between them, are stitched along three sides on the wrong side. The bag is then turned right side out and the remaining opening stitched closed. The finished bag measures 14½ by 10 inches unfolded. It is folded in half lengthwise when carried and a small pocket sewn to the lining is the only carrying space.

Materials
This bag is made of gray peau de soie, but polyester satin, satin or rayon fabric might also be used. About ½ yard is needed (2½ times the size of the bag), because an identical piece is used for the lining, and another piece, half the finished size, is used for the inside pocket. This amount also allows for a ½-inch seam on all sides. Besides fabric you will need: pink and gray thread; tracing paper; carbon paper; pencil; scissors; spool of jute or medium-weight twine; two layers of medium weight interfacing; straight pins; hand sewing needle; a covered snap, to close the bag.

Preparing to Sew
Cut three pieces of fabric, two 15½ inches long by 11 inches wide, for the outside piece and the lining, the third 9 by 7 inches for the pocket. Also cut two layers of interfacing, 15½ by 11 inches.

Since the design is simple, you might draw it freehand. If you wish to copy it exactly, enlarge the pattern shown in Figure E on a sheet of ordinary tracing paper. Transfer the design to the wrong side of the outside piece of fabric. To do this, place the carbon paper face down on the wrong side of the fabric and put the traced pattern face down on top of the carbon paper. Go over the design with a hard pencil or dressmaker's tracing wheel. The lines will show you where to lay the jute, and after it is sewn over with a wide zigzag stitch, the design will appear as a raised area on the right side of the fabric.

Johanna Bafaro is a designer/editor for Woman's Day *magazine, where she covers all aspects of home projects and hobbies. She studied at the New York School of Interior Design and has been consultant to the editor of the* Betty Crocker Cook Book of Entertaining Dinner Parties.

E   1 square = ½ inch

Figure E: Enlarge this design by drawing a grid of ½-inch squares, then transferring the pattern to the ½-inch grid one square at a time.

11: Lay the jute on the traced lines and slowly sew over it with a wide zigzag stitch. The thread tension is set tighter than normal to bring the fabric together around the jute.

This evening bag is decorated trapunto-style. A wide zigzag stitch encases lengths of jute on the wrong side of the fabric, creating a relief effect on the right side. The bag is one large piece folded in half.

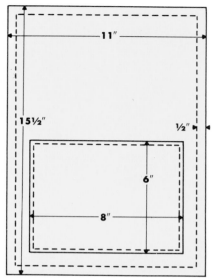

F

Figure F: The 9-by-7-inch pocket piece is turned under ½ inch all around to conceal the raw edges, then straight-stitched to the lining before the bag pieces are joined.

Pillow front is decorated with iron-on seam binding, which is then stitched over with decorative stitches, done in contrasting thread.

Decorative stitches can cover the edges of the iron-on seam binding or can be sewn in the middle of a strip.

Sewing

Set the thread tension tighter than for normal sewing and adjust the machine for a wide zigzag stitch—about ⅜ inch in length and ¼ inch in width. Practice sewing a small piece of jute on scrap fabric to make sure the tension is right.

Begin sewing the jute at an edge of the outside piece, following the traced lines, but do not start at a corner. You can turn a smoother corner if some of the jute is already sewn in place. Work with long pieces of jute and when cutting it, make it a few inches too long to avoid running short where two pieces meet.

A good way to anchor the ends of the jute pieces is to sew one or two straight stitches before and after the zigzag stitches. The ends should be butted rather than overlapped for a smooth look. After completing the trapunto design on the outside piece, attach the pocket to the lining (Figure F).

The bag is now ready to be assembled. Pin the two layers of interfacing to the back of the trapunto piece and baste in place along the outer edges. Next, pin the lining to the front of the bag holding the right sides together.

Using gray thread and a straight stitch, sew around three sides leaving a ½-inch seam. Leave enough of the bag's bottom edge open for you to turn it right side out.

Once this is done, slip stitch the opening closed. To use, fold the bag in half, carrying small items in the pocket. If you want to sew on a snap, sew it in the center of the bag's bottom edge where it will not show.

Needlecrafts
Ribbon pillow

This pillow's ribbon-like decorations do not come from ribbon at all, but from easy-to-use seam binding that is ironed on—not stitched to—the pillow. The decorative stitches added to the iron-on seam binding are those found on regular and automatic zigzag machines. Consult your instruction manual for specific stitch directions and if your machine cannot make all the stitches used here, substitute any that it will do. The pillow here is 12 inches square, but you can use decorative stitches with seam binding on any size pillow.

Polished cotton was used for both the pillow front and back. Remember to allow a ½-inch seam allowance on all sides. Also needed are: several packages of iron-on seam binding in various shades of brown; a package of seamed cotton cord piping tape for the pillow welting; thread in assorted contrasting colors; polyester stuffing or a 12-inch pillow form; scissors; pins; steam iron; hand sewing needle.

How to Assemble

Cut the fabric to the finished size, plus ½ inch all around for seam allowance. Next, cut strips of seam bindings in various lengths and arrange them on the fabric. (You may want to first draw lines on a piece of paper the same size as the pillow front and then measure the lines to see how long each strip should be.) Use the photograph at left as a guide or arrange the seam binding to your liking. To vary the ribbon effect, overlap the seam bindings so that they appear to be different widths as well as different lengths. Once you have the strips of seam binding arranged; iron them onto the fabric, following package directions. Apply the long vertical strip last, as it covers the ends of all the other strips.

Practice different decorative stitches on scrap pieces of fabric, and choose those that look best. Sew them along the seam where two pieces of binding meet and in the center of a binding strip. Use contrasting thread to highlight the stitches. When the decorative stitching is completed, press the pillow front well.

Cording is now attached to the pillow front ½ inch in from the fabric edge (at the seam allowance), so it will serve as a decorative edge when the pillow front and back are joined. Line up the cording so that the seam stitches are on top of the seam allowance. Sew on the cording along the line of stitches, using a zipper foot, and following package directions.

Join the pillow front and back. This is done by placing the right sides together and stitching around three sides of the pillow. Leave the bottom side open. Turn the pillow right side out, stuff, and hand sew the bottom.

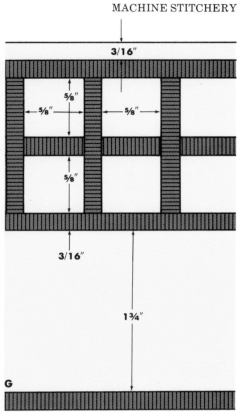

Figure G: This full-size section of the pattern is repeated for the pillowcase design. It can be traced or drawn freehand following the dimensions given.

A pattern done in satin stitch dresses up an ordinary pillowcase with a geometric design. The pillowcase is coordinated with a purchased sheet. The design might also be used on sheets and towels.

Needlecrafts
Embroidered pillowcase

If you have a favorite set of decorated sheets or a bedroom wallpaper pattern you particularly like, you can decorate a plain pillow case to match, as in the color photograph above, in under an hour. Machine embroidery can add interest to old pillowcases this way; it is also an inexpensive way to create a new bedroom set from plain sheets and pillowcases. Materials needed are a pillowcase, dark brown and rust thread for the pillowcase shown, pencil and scissors.

Design and Sew
This border design was adapted from a printed sheet, but any design might be used in similar fashion. The stitch used is the satin stitch (see Craftnotes, page 1109). The border design in Figure G is actual size and can be traced directly on a pillowcase. Copy it on the right side of the case, and when you sew over the pencil lines, make sure the stitches are close enough together to cover the pencil lines.

The tension should be normal, and the machine set for zigzag stitching. Experiment with stitch length (that shown here is 3/16 inch). Stitches are taken as close together as possible. The long rows of dark brown thread are sewn first, so they appear to be continuous.

You may wish to add a monogram to the pillowcase and this is also done with the satin stitch. Place a sheet of typing paper under the fabric when sewing to aid in smooth stitching. The monogrammed letters look best if they are fairly long and block-like since the pillowcase design is geometric; but feel free to vary your choice of stitch and any other design element to fit your taste and bedroom decor.

For related projects see the entries "Applique," "Crewelwork Sampler," "Embroidery," and "Sewing without a Pattern."

MACRAMÉ
All Tied Up In Knots

Sue Preston (left) and daughters Laura (center) and Rachel (right) are known in craft circles as The Prestons. They create, each in her own style, beautiful and functional pieces of macramé that have been exhibited at craft shows, galleries and shops. Sue Preston teaches macramé and is publicity director for an annual crafts show at Bear Mountain, New York. Laura, an illustrator, hopes to collaborate on children's books with her father. Rachel, a graduate of Duke University, divides her time between the Preston home in Blauvelt, New York, and her home in Durham, North Carolina.

Few crafts have attracted such a diverse following as macramé. Salty old sailors, proper Victorian ladies, and teen-agers have all taken to this ancient art of knotting with equal enthusiasm and often quite different results.

One of the marvelous things about macramé is exactly this versatility. Macramé can be whatever you want it to be—strictly functional, pure fantasy, or a little of both. It can take shape as a decorative trimming, as a textured fabric, or as a three-dimensional sculptural form; the knots can be tied with anything from tough, earthy-color ropes to peacock-hued sewing threads. You can add feathers or beads or leather to macramé, or you can simply add your imagination.

Another nice thing about macramé is that although it often looks complicated, it is really quite easy to learn. You do need lots of patience and an eye for detail, but the knotting itself is not difficult to master. Macramé consists of a few basic knots plus many fancy knots, but you needn't learn them all; you will be surprised by how much you can do with just a few of the basic knots.

Materials and Tools

Macramé knots are worked with cords that are flexible enough to be knotted, yet not so elastic that they lose their shape. Some suitable cords of varying thicknesses and weights are listed in the column at the right. They can be found around the house; in hardware stores, yarn and craft shops, housewares and upholstery departments, and mail-order catalogs; and at weaving suppliers, notions and stationery counters.

Cords that are generally not suitable include flat leather lacings that are hard to control, nylon cords that tend to slip, and knitting worsted yarns that are too fuzzy and stretchy for satisfactory knotting.

Most of the cords you will buy are white, off-white, or natural color; some can be dyed successfully at home with fabric dyes. For an even color, dye the cords before knotting and always test a sample before you start. To fix the color, add salt when you dye rayon, cotton or linen cord and add vinegar when you dye silk or wool. For an antique look in white cords, try steeping them in very strong tea or coffee. Remember that any dye will look darker when wet.

Your basic tools are your own two hands. You will also need a simple knotting board to work on—this can be a rectangle of rigid plastic foam, a light-color cork bulletin board, a polyurethane-foam pillow form, a piece of insulation board, or corrugated cardboard ½ to 1 inch thick. The board can be marked with a grid if you feel that such a guide is helpful.

Gather together your cords, the knotting board, scissors, a tape measure or yardstick, T-pins to hold the knots, rubber bands or yarn bobbins to keep the excess cords out of the way, liquid glue to prevent fraying, and you are all set.

Some suitable cords
Natural or dyed jute
Sisal
Seine twine
Butcher's twine
Clothesline
Cotton cable or shear cord
Polished cotton navy cord
Rayon twist or flag cord
Rattail rayon
Linen rug warp
Venetian-blind traverse cord
Upholstery welting
Pearl cotton
Crochet cotton
Non-stretch yarns
Dental floss
Cotton or silk sewing threads
String

A four-panel macramé screen serves as a movable space divider and gives a sense of privacy, yet it has an open, airy look. Two panels are made of square knots with a central diamond motif; the other two are a repeat of an open diamond pattern. For directions, turn to page 1124.

Reverse lark's head knot

Double the cord and bring the loop end up under the mounting cord and to the front. Bring the ends through the loop; tighten.

Square knot

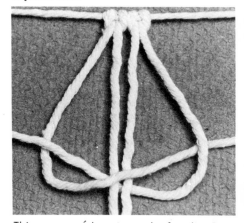

This macramé knot is not the familiar Boy Scout square knot; it is always worked with four cords. First, the right cord is brought under the two center cords and over the left cord; the left cord is placed over the center cords and under the right cord.

Next, the first half of the knot is tightened, then the left cord is brought under the center cords and over the right cord; the right cord goes over the center cords and under the left cord.

Finally, the second half of the knot is tightened. Each half is called a half knot; a chain of half knots makes a twist.

Alternating square knots

The first row is worked with all the cords. The second row skips the first two cords, works a square knot with the next four cords and continues across, ending with two unworked cords. The third row repeats the first row, starting at the extreme left and working with all the cords.

The granny knot

This, in macramé terms, is a square knot without the two center cords.

The bobble

Make a chain (a sennit) of square knots.

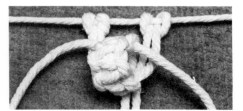

Then bring the two center cords up and back down through the top of the chain.

Horizontal double half hitch (cording)

First, the anchor cord is placed straight across the working cords. Each working cord is brought under and looped over the anchor cord.

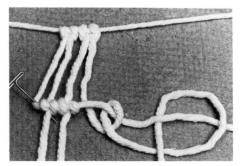

Next, the same working cord is brought over and looped under the anchor cord, to the right of the first half of the knot.

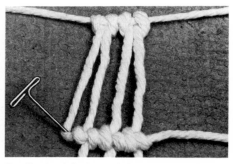

Finally, both halves of the knot are tightened over the anchor cord.

KNOTS

X of diagonal double half hitches

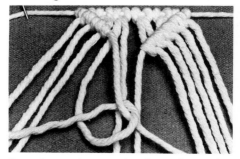

First, the cords on each side are knotted on the diagonal with a double half hitch. The outside cords are the carrying cords.

Next, the left carrying cord is double half hitched to the right carrying cord.

Then, two more rows of cording are worked below the first two. The row on the left stops at the center; the right-hand row continues across to the left edge.

Finally, on the bottom half of the X, the second row on the left becomes the first row on the right. The X is shown here with a diamond of alternating square knots and the beginning of a second X below.

The berry knot

First, make two square knots under the rows of diagonal cording.

Here the first row of the berry knot is shown. Cords on the right are carrying cords only; cords on the left are working cords only.

Here, four rows of cording for the berry knot are shown before they are tightened.

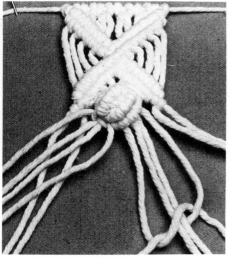

Finally, gather up the cording into a rounded shape and secure underneath with two square knots.

Alternate half hitch chain

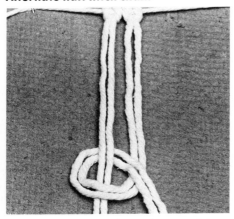

First, loop the two right cords around the two left cords.

Then loop the two left cords around the two right cords. Tighten the loops.

Father, mother and teen-agers can all wear a diamond-pattern belt like this with their jeans. The diamonds are alternating square knots outlined with diagonal double half hitches.

Another belt you can make combines square knots, diagonal double half hitches, berries (center), bobbles (top and bottom), and half knot twists.

Weaving, Braiding, Knotting
Adjustable belt

This diamond-pattern belt has a casual, tailored look that appeals to almost everyone. The buckle's hook fits between knots so eyelets are unnecessary.

Size: 36 inches long (adjustable) and 1¾ inches wide.

Materials: 4 ounces of linen rug warp. Buckle with a hook.

Knots: Reverse lark's head knot, alternating square knots, diagonal double half hitch, alternating half hitch chains (see Craftnotes, pages 1118 and 1119).

Belt: Cut 12 cords as follows: one cord 18 feet long, two cords 23 feet long, and nine cords 28 feet long. When estimating the length of the cords needed for any project, plan on each cord being about eight times as long as the finished length. Because the cords are doubled over the mounting cord, each end will be about four times the finished length. Some knots take more cord than others so it is a good idea to work a sample. Knot one pattern repeat to see how much cord is needed and multiply that amount by the number of repeats in the project. Always add a little for good measure; it is easier to trim the ends than to splice two cords near the end.

Center and pin the 18-foot-long cord horizontally on the knotting board with the center section about 1¾ inches long. This will be the mounting cord that holds the other cords and the two long ends will be cords No. 1 and No. 24 at the extreme sides (what will be the top and bottom edges of the belt).

Mount the nine 28-foot-long cords on the mounting cord, between the two ends, using reverse lark's head knots (Craftnotes, page 1118). You will have 18 working ends, each about 14 feet long. The two remaining cords, each 23 feet long, will be mounted between the two outside ends and the center group and will be numbered 2, 3, 22 and 23. Mount them with reverse lark's head knots, leaving uneven ends—the No. 2 and No. 23 ends should be 9 feet long, No. 3 and No. 22 should be 14 feet long. The four outermost ends, Nos. 1, 2, 23 and 24, will be the carrying cords for the diagonal double half hitches that form the Xs in the pattern.

Tie all the working cords in butterfly bundles to keep them from tangling. To tie a butterfly, wrap the cord around your thumb and little finger in a figure-eight, then secure it with a rubber band. Start at a comfortable distance from the mounting cord, rather than at the end of the cord, to make it easy to pull the cord out. In order to keep track of the carrying cords, you can use four rubber bands of different colors to hold the butterflies on cords 1, 2, 23 and 24.

Working with all 24 cords, work 3 inches of alternating square knots. The alternating rows will have six and five knots each. End with a row of six knots. This section of the belt will be attached to the buckle. There are several ways you can attach it; see photographs 1 and 2.

On the following five rows, work five square knots, then four, three, two, and lastly, one, forming a V-shape in the center of the belt.

1: A macramé belt can be worked directly onto a metal buckle or a leather strip, using that as the mounting cord. Heavy-duty snaps make a belt wearable with several different buckles.

2: Lacing is the simplest way to attach a macramé belt to a buckle. Pull one end through the buckle and fold it over, then lace a double length of cord through both layers and tie it with a granny knot.

Next, work a diagonal row of double half hitches (also called cording or clove hitches) down one side to the center of this V shape. Use the outermost cord as your carrying cord, the cord over which the knots are formed. Repeat the diagonal double half hitches down the other side, using the outermost cord on that side as the carrying cord. Double half hitch No. 1 onto No. 24. Repeat the two rows of diagonal double hitches, this time using the next cords, Nos. 2 and 23, as the carrying cords. Double half hitch No. 1 onto No. 23, then hitch No. 24 onto No. 2 and No. 2 onto No. 23. This completes the top of the X.

Now work the alternate half hitch chains that fill in the sides between the arms of the Xs. Pick up the four outside cords on one side and, with two cords worked as one, make a chain of eight half hitches. Using the next four cords, work a chain of four half hitches. Repeat the chains on the other side, starting at the outside and working toward the center. (The remaining cords on each side of the X will not be worked.)

You will now work the bottom half of the X in cording or diagonal double half hitches. With No. 2 as the carrying cord, double half hitch down to the right. Next, with No. 23 as the carrying cord, double half hitch down to the left, starting with the No. 24 cord. (The colored rubber bands will help you find the right cords here.) The bottom row on the upper left arm of the X will become the top row on the lower right arm and the bottom row of the upper right arm will become the top row on the lower left.

Work the two bottom rows of diagonal double half hitches with No. 1 as the carrying cord for the left side and No. 24 as the carrying cord for the right side.

Fill in the diamond with alternating square knots, starting with one knot under the crossing of the X, working to a full row of six knots at the center of the diamond, then back down to one knot at the bottom point.

Outline the diamond with cording as before. Repeat this diamond pattern with cording and alternate half hitch chains until the belt is about 6 inches from the finished length. After the bottom half of the last X, finish by making a section of alternating square knots ending in a V-shape point and add four more rows of cording.

Use a tapestry needle to pull the cords through the knots on the reverse side and cut them close. Dab white fabric glue over the ends to prevent fraying.

For a simpler X with arms that cross exactly in the center: Work the two rows of diagonal double half hitches on one side, first with the outside cord and then with the next cord; double half hitch the two carrying cords. Switch to the other side and work both rows, first with the outside cord and then with the next cord. Double half hitch the two carrying cords on that side and then join the two sides with a double half hitch of the two inner carrying cords. To work the bottom half of the X, count to the center and pick up the two center cords as the carrying cords. The cord on the left goes to the left, the cord on the right goes to the right. For the second row, pick up the cords next to the center cords and work as before.

1121

A dress yoke is an unusual way to show off your macramé skills. The yoke and matching sash are made with double half hitches.

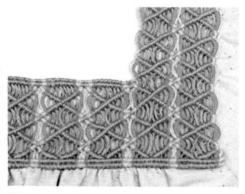

This is a detail of one corner of the yoke. The front and back yokes and the shoulder straps are worked in one continuous piece.

Dress yoke and sash

A muslin peasant dress becomes something special when you add a macramé yoke and sash done in a natural color spiced with yellow and orange.

Dress sizes: Small, medium or large. Directions are given for the large size; see Figures A and B for directions for converting to small or medium.

Materials: Dress takes about 3½ yards of cotton muslin and ½ yard of narrow elastic. If you wish to make a print dress with a macramé yoke of one color, you can use an Indian-print cotton bedspread or any lightweight fabric. Yoke and sash together take approximately 4 ounces of linen rug warp (natural) and 2 ounces each of yellow and orange pearl cotton.

Knots: Horizontal and diagonal double half hitches (see pages 1118 and 1119).

Cutting: For the yoke, cut the cords as follows:

Natural
16 cords 100 inches long
48 cords 28 inches long
2 cords 30 inches long
2 mounting cords 18 inches long
1 mounting cord long enough to tie around your board

Orange
8 cords 100 inches long
24 cords 28 inches long

Yellow
8 cords 100 inches long
24 cords 28 inches long

Mounting: Mount all 100-inch-long cords and half of the 28-inch-long cords of each color on one mounting cord which you have tied around and pinned to your knotting board (see Figure A). (Because the cotton cord is half as thick as the linen cord, you need two ends of cotton to equal one end of linen.)

For each side piece that starts in the front yoke, goes into a shoulder strap and ends in the back yoke, use 8 natural cords, 4 yellow cords and 4 orange cords, each 100 inches long. For the center of each yoke, use 24 natural cords, 12 yellow cords and 12 orange cords, each 28 inches long. Mount the side cords so that each end is 50 inches long; mount the center cords so that each end is 14 inches long, except for the linen carrying cords that are mounted unevenly as shown in Figure A. (The carrying cords are indicated by the dash lines.) Mount only the front yoke center to start; mount the center of the back yoke when the shoulder straps reach that point.

Introduce one of the 30-inch linen cords directly below the mounting cord and work two rows of horizontal double half hitches (cording) with this as the carrying cord. Work ends of the carrying cord through knots on the reverse side.

Work the rest of the front yoke in diagonal double half hitches, using Figure A as a guide for the direction of the carrying cords. When the long cords reach the edge, they turn back into the work and continue to zigzag throughout the entire piece. Let the cords curve between the rows of cording, rather than pull them tight; some will even overlap. In the beginning you might want to pin them to get the proper spacing, but with practice it will come easily.

When you reach the shoulder straps, mount an 18-inch-long cord to the carrying cords which reach the corners and work two rows of cording over this cord. Work ends through knots on the reverse side and cut close.

Figure A: The pattern is for the front yoke and half of the shoulder straps; flop the pattern over for the other half of the straps and the back yoke. The pattern shown, when enlarged on a half-inch grid, is for a large size. A small size would have four sections of natural cords in the center. A medium size would have five sections of natural cords in the center.

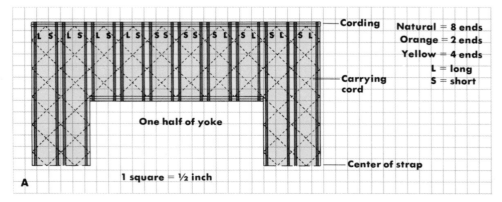

Cording
Carrying cord
One half of yoke
Center of strap
1 square = ½ inch
A

Natural = 8 ends
Orange = 2 ends
Yellow = 4 ends
L = long
S = short

Continue to work the shoulder straps until they are the desired length. The average total length of the yokes and straps is 15 inches. At the beginning of the back yoke, attach another 18-inch long cord to the carrying cords at the corners of the shoulder straps as you did at the finish of the front yoke. Again, work two rows of cording over this cord, then continue across the entire width of the piece with diagonal double half hitches. Finish with two more rows of cording worked over a newly-introduced 30-inch cord. Work ends through knots on the reverse side.

If you make a one-color yoke, you can vary the macramé design by putting beads, berry knots or bobble knots inside the diamonds.

The Dress

To make the dress itself, enlarge the patterns in Figure B, adjusting the length to suit you. Place the sleeve pattern on a lengthwise fold and cut two. Place the pattern for the body of the dress on a fold and cut it out; cut two, since the front and back are identical.

Sew two rows of gathering stitches at the top of the dress front and dress back and at the top of the sleeves, ½ inch and ⅝ inch from the edges.

Sew the side seams of the dress and the sleeve seams with double seams such as those on blue jeans. To do this, first sew the seam with the right side of the fabric out, then turn so that the wrong side is out and the seam is inside. Stitch the length of the seam again, enclosing the raw edges of the seam inside. Open the fabric, press the seam flat, and top-stitch two rows about ½ inch apart on the right side over the double seam.

Next, gather the sleeves and with the right sides together, pin the sides of the sleeves to the curved armhole sections of the dress. Sew, being sure that the gathering stitches are inside the seam allowance. The center sections of the sleeves will not be sewn to the dress; they will be joined to the shoulder straps of the yoke. To finish these seams neatly, trim the seam allowance of the sleeve just above the gathering stitches, turn the edge of the dress seam allowance under and stitch over the seam, encasing the edges. Or, bind the edges with double-fold bias tape.

Make shallow hems on the sleeves, leaving a small opening on each, and insert narrow elastic to fit comfortably around your wrists.

At this point, try the dress on and have a friend pin the yoke in place, wrong side of the yoke on the right side of the fabric. Put the bottom rows of cording over the rows of gathering stitches at the top of the dress and cover the gathers on the sleeves with the edges of the shoulder straps. Hand-sew the yoke to the dress with strong, invisible stitches. Trim the seams that still show on the inside and cover with bias tape.

The dress as shown can be washed by hand in cold water. If other fabrics and cords are combined, keep them compatible in their care requirements.

The Sash

The sash that matches the yoke is worked much the same as one shoulder strap. Cut a linen mounting cord about 12 inches long. Cut 8 cords each of yellow and orange, each about 18 feet long. (When working with the colored cords, use two cords as one, just as you did for the yoke.) Cut 16 cords of natural linen, each about 24 feet long.

Make overhand knots at the ends of the mounting cord and pin it to your knotting board. An overhand knot is a simple knot you use all the time. Bring the top end of the cord down and make a loop; bring the end through the loop and tighten. Using the overhand knot and leaving 7 inches for fringe, mount the working cords in the center of the mounting cord, following the pattern for the strap in Figure A. There will be 8 cords in each natural section.

Work two rows of cording or horizontal double half hitches, using the two yellow cords at one side together as the carrying cord. Work in diagonal double half hitches to form the X-and-diamond pattern for the desired length of the sash— about 5 feet. End with two rows of cording (add a 12-inch linen cord inside the second row to match the mounting cord at the other end) and leave 7 inches for fringe. Untie the overhand knots at the ends of the mounting cord and let the ends become part of the fringe.

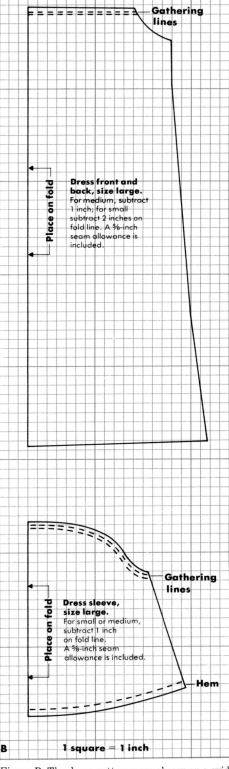

Figure B: The dress patterns are shown on a grid in which one square equals 1 inch. Make a grid of 1-inch squares on tracing paper. On this larger grid, mark off the same number of squares as shown on the pattern grid and transfer the outline of the pattern, one square at a time. You will find it easy to copy the pattern in small segments.

1123

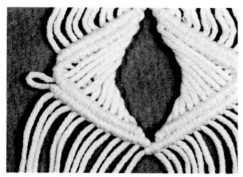

3: Loops on the outside edges of each panel, spaced about 4½ inches apart, will be used to attach the panels to the frame of the screen.

4: To create the open diamond pattern with diagonal double half hitches, the cord being knotted is brought underneath the other working cords before it is hitched to the carrying cord.

5: The last two carrying cords of the open diamond are hitched in the center of the pattern to bring the two sides together.

Weaving, Braiding, Knotting
Room-divider screen

Your patience will be well rewarded when a screen like the one pictured on page 1116 takes its place in your living room and inspires compliments from your guests.

Size: Screen as shown has four panels of macramé, each about 17 by 64½ inches. The design can be adapted to fit any screen frame (I found this one at a flea market).

Materials: Sixteen 140-yard boxes of No. 50 cotton cable cord; staples or brads; four-panel hinged screen frame or the materials to build one.

Knots: Alternating square knots, diagonal double half hitch (see Craftnotes).

A test swatch: It is most important to keep the tension of the knots loose enough so the macramé will fit the screen frame. Work 3 inches of alternating square knots with 12 ends each 16 inches long. If your knotting tension is average, you will have about 4 inches left. If you have more or less, adjust the amount of cord needed. Also, measure the width of your test swatch (12 ends across). If you need to add cords to fit the width of the screen, always add them in multiples of four.

Square Knot Panels

For each square knot panel (first and third in the photograph on page 1116) cut 46 cords, each 48 feet long. Cut a mounting cord to fit across the top of the screen. (You can work right on the screen frame, on a dowel that will be inserted into the screen, or on a large sheet of insulation board or cork.) Mount the 46 cords with reverse lark's head knots so that there are 92 ends, each 24 feet long.

Work one row of cording (horizontal double half hitches) at the top of the panel. Work alternating square knots for 4½ inches, ending with a row of 23 knots. Here, and every 4½ inches, leave a loop on each side as shown in photograph 3. Simply put a T-pin at the outside edge and loop the outer cord around the pin. This loop will be attached to the side of the screen frame when the panel is completed.

On the next row, start the diamond pattern by working 22 knots, 11 on each side, and *not* working the four cords in the exact center of the row. Continue decreasing the number of knots until you have a row with 7 knots on each side and 36 unworked cords in the center. This will be the widest part of the diamond. On the next row, work 8 knots on each side, and continue increasing the number of knots until the bottom half of the diamond is completed. The diamonds will be about 4½ inches long with 4½ inches of square knots between, depending on the tension of your work.

When you reach the bottom of the panel, work two rows of cording and pull any loose ends through the last row. Gather the centers of both sides of the diamonds with a short cord and tie in back with granny knots (see Craftnotes, page 1118). Use staples or brads to attach the panel to the frame, through the loops on the sides and through the rows of cording at the top and bottom. Cover the edges with strips of wood molding, about ¼ inch wide, if the back of the screen will be seen.

Open Diamond Panels

Each second and fourth panel has alternating rows of four diamonds and three diamonds; each diamond has 24 ends, 12 on each side. Therefore, you will need to cut 48 cords, each about 42 feet long.

Mount the cords with reverse lark's head knots and work one row of cording at the top, as you did for the square knot panels. The diamond pattern is worked in diagonal double half hitches and each diamond is about 4½ inches long. Start each diamond with 12 ends on each side. Work 2 rows of diagonal half hitches on each side, using the four inner cords as carrying cords (first 12 and 13, then 11 and 14). At the end of the second row, double half hitch the first carrying cord on each side to the second carrying cord on that same side (12 onto 11 and 13 onto 14). On the bottom half of the diamond, the cord being knotted is brought *underneath* the other working cords (photograph 4). Start the bottom half with the last-used carrying cords first (11 on the left, 14 on the right) and start knotting from the center out to the sides. (On the left, the order will be 10, 9, 8, and so on.) When the open diamond is completed, hitch the last two carrying cords, 12 and 13, in the center of the pattern (photograph 5). Make attachment loops and finish with cording.

Weaving, Braiding, Knotting
Willow tree sculpture

These weeping willows are pure whimsy; three colors of jute and the square knot are all you need to make your own macramé sculpture (see Craftnotes, page 1118).

Size: The base is about 9½ inches long (without fringe) and 5 inches wide. The tallest tree is 8 inches high.

Materials: Three 4-ounce cones of jute, one each of natural, green and brown.

Base: Cut 12 cords of natural jute, each 5 feet long. Mount them on a mounting cord with reverse lark's head knots so that there are 24 ends, each 2½ feet long. Work in alternating square knots (6 knots and 5 knots per row) for 6 rows. On the next row, begin adding cords for the natural-color tree as shown in Figure C, page 1126. The numbers indicate the number of ends (2 ends to a cord). To add one cord, simply include it in the center of the square knot. To add 2 cords, add the second cord between the knot being formed and the one above. The extra cords should be

Deborah Susswein has a flair for the unusual that comes across in her macramé sculptures. Debbie is a member of "A Show of Hands," a craft cooperative in New York City, where her work has been exhibited in a one-woman show. She plans to work in the field of art therapy, helping both children and adults.

A macramé sculpture of weeping willow trees has a fall of fringe and a lawn of green jute woven into the square-knot base. As shown in the three photographs below, it would be a perfect hideaway if you were only two inches tall.

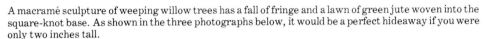

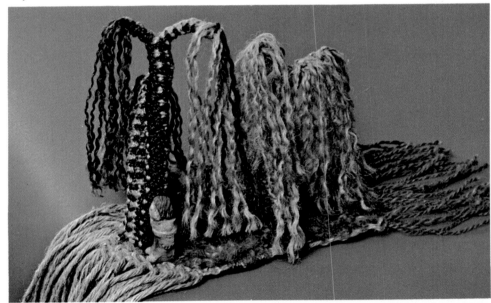

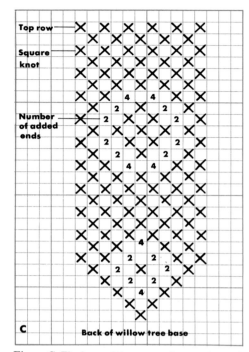

Figure C: The base of the tree sculpture pictured on page 1125 is made of alternating square knots (indicated by the Xs). Ends are added in the numbers indicated and these extra cords are knotted in a spiral to form the tree trunks. The pattern shows one way to place and shape the trees; feel free to make them as individual as you like.

6: The pointed end of the base ends in fringe. The dark spots are the brown cords added to the natural-color base.

5 feet long. Continue working the base, adding extra cords as indicated. For the two-tone tree in front, stagger the colors any way you like for the light-and-dark effect. On the third row of this tree, start decreasing the number of knots in the base to form the V-shaped point. When the base is completed, the leftover cords will form the fall of fringe. (Photograph 6, this page, shows the back of the base.)

Trees: To form the hollow tubular trunks, work square knots in a spiral with the cords you added to the base. Continue the spiral, always using the next four cords for the next knot, regardless of their colors. Where you want a fork in the trees, divide the cords and work in two separate spirals. Leave long ends and unravel them to make the weeping willow branches.

Lawn: Cut short ends of green jute and weave through the knots in a random pattern for the grass. Remove the mounting cord and knot medium-long lengths of green jute to the loops for the grassy fringe.

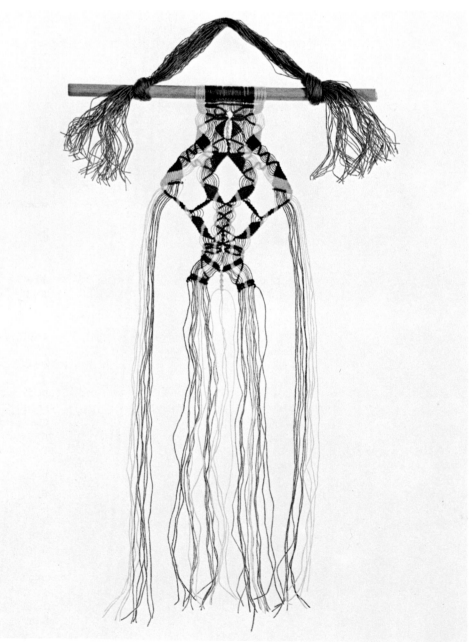

Micromé is macramé in miniature, worked with cotton sewing threads. This hanging is only 7½ inches long to the bottom of the fringe.

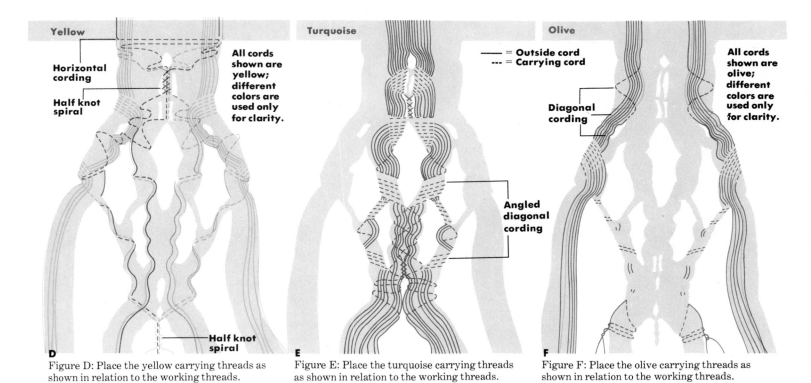

Yellow

Horizontal cording

Half knot spiral

All cords shown are yellow; different colors are used only for clarity.

Half knot spiral

Turquoise

— = Outside cord
--- = Carrying cord

Angled diagonal cording

Olive

Diagonal cording

All cords shown are olive; different colors are used only for clarity.

D
Figure D: Place the yellow carrying threads as shown in relation to the working threads.

E
Figure E: Place the turquoise carrying threads as shown in relation to the working threads.

F
Figure F: Place the olive carrying threads as shown in relation to the working threads.

Weaving, Braiding, Knotting
Micromé hanging

¢ 🎲 🧍 🎨

Micromé is my word for macramé done on a very small scale with sewing threads. It takes nimble fingers and lots of patience, but the finished project is a small gem to be treasured.

Size: From the dowel to the tip of the fringe is 7½ inches.

Materials: Three 125-yard spools of cotton sewing thread in yellow, turquoise and olive; a wooden dowel, ¼ inch in diameter and 4 inches long.

Knots: Diagonal and horizontal double half hitches, half knot chains (see Craftnotes, pages 1118 and 1119).

Hanging: Cut 25 threads—9 turquoise, 8 olive and 8 yellow, each about 14 feet long. Tape the dowel to the knotting board and mount the threads in the center of the dowel in this order: 4 yellow, 4 olive, 9 turquoise, 4 olive, 4 yellow. There will be 50 ends. Because you are working with thin threads that tangle easily, butterfly bundles are impractical. Instead, wind each end around the center of a small piece of folded paper, and thread it through a small slit at one end (Figure G).

Work two rows of horizontal double half hitches with the end yellow thread on the left as the carrying thread. Continue to work in horizontal and diagonal double half hitches, following Figures D, E and F for the placement of the carrying threads. Be sure to keep the knots tight. You may use fine needles or silk pins in place of T-pins to hold the work in progress. The yellow and turquoise chains, or sennits, of half knots twist to the right so you tie only the second half of a square knot (right thread under, left thread over the two center threads).

Follow the color photograph on the opposite page for the overall color arrangement, but if Figures D, E and F are not followed, the overall color pattern will change. Trim the ends, tie a thick bundle of leftover turquoise threads about 7 inches long to the dowel with overhand knots, and hang the micromé in front of a light to show it to best advantage.

For related entries, see "Lace," "Rope Sculpture," "Sculpture," "Sprang Weaving" and "Weaving."

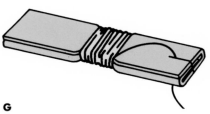

G
Figure G: Tiny paper bobbins keep the ends of the threads untangled as you work micromé.

MAGIC
Modern Wizardry

Magic has fascinated people throughout the ages. From the time of the Pharaohs of ancient Egypt there are records of wonders performed by Dedi, a magician summoned by Cheops, builder of the Great Pyramid. Dedi was able to slice off a bird's head and then make the bird whole again, a feat that won him the king's favor. Magic's appeal was not only to royalty, however. In India, early conjurers were street magicians, attracting huge crowds to witness their knife swallowing wonders and feats with cups and balls.

Historically, magic was closely allied with religious superstition and magicians were thought to have mysterious powers. Today's magicians do seem to display such powers, but their purpose is solely to entertain as they mystify, confuse and amuse. Since magic's appeal is mystery, once secrets are revealed the fun is over. Some of the tricks shown in this entry are not explained—so as not to violate professional magicians' trade secrets. When you do learn a trick, however, bear in mind that if you tell how it is accomplished, you will spoil the element of surprise and wonder that makes magic so much fun.

The tricks on the following pages demonstrate some of magic's basic effects. An effect is what the audience sees. For example, a *restoration* occurs when an object that has been destroyed is restored. The napkin trick, beginning on the next page, demonstrates such a restoration. Other effects include the *vanish*, making an object disappear or seem invisible; the *production*, making an object appear apparently from nowhere; the *transformation*, causing one object to change into another; the *transposition*, making two objects change places; the *escape*, freeing a person or thing that was securely bound in one place; the *levitation*, making objects rise or float in space without visible means of support; and the *penetration*, making a solid object pass through another solid, seeming to defy laws of science.

How to Present Magic

The tricks described here are examples of close-up magic, tricks that can be done within a few feet of the audience. Household objects are used so you do not have to buy ready-made magic tricks. The key to successful magic lies not in apparatus but in *misdirection*, directing the spectator's attention away from the key move or action of the trick. When performing, direct your eyes where you want the audience to look, and they will follow your lead. Misdirection is also accomplished with the hands. Throw a coin up in the air, look up, and point with one hand. No one is likely to see the hanky-panky you may be doing with the other hand.

The illusion will be more successful if you incorporate these guidelines into your performance: Let your spectators know that they are going to be astonished. Tell them in general what you will do, what you are doing and what you have done. But don't let the audience know what is about to happen in any great detail. Your patter, what you say while you are doing the trick, should be worded in general terms and practiced often. This does not mean that you have to memorize a script, but practice your descriptions of movements often enough so that you can be natural in your speech and offer simple explanations for what you are doing. Examples of appropriate patter accompany the tricks in this entry.

When presenting the trick (you must practice long and hard before performing), every movement you make should have a simple and logical explanation. Tricks should be accomplished by the simplest means.

When performing, even for an audience of one, never repeat a trick or use the same method during one performance. If the spectator knows what to expect, the trick will fail. Watch where you stand, and the angles from which spectators view the trick, particularly the coin vanish, page 1136, and the water-in-the-hat, page 1139. If you feel you are not completely safe from detection, do not do the trick.

"Funny, there was a rabbit in there a minute ago," muses George Schindler, a magician who demonstrates a few tricks on the following pages. Abracadabra, presto-change-o, you can be a magician too.

George Schindler, left, is past president of the New York Chapter of the Society of American Magicians. A comedy magician and ventriloquist, he performs in theaters, nightclubs and on TV. George has written books on comedy and magic and produced magic shows. He is an owner of the School for Magicians in New York.

Frank Garcia, right, a professional magician for 30 years, is best known as an authority on cardsharps. Called "the man with the million dollar hands," because of his famous card manipulations, he has lectured and performed all over the world. He is the author of a number of books on magic and gambling and is an owner of the School for Magicians.

Manipulating cups and balls is an ancient magic feat. These handmade Hindu cups have knobbed tops, permitting dexterous handling.

Before You Begin

For all the following tricks, suggested patter (what you say) is in quotes. Photographs that show the secrets— actions the audience does *not* see—are labeled "behind the scenes."

Torn and Restored Napkin

After a paper napkin is torn into tiny pieces, the magician mysteriously restores it to its original form. The secret: two paper napkins, but the audience sees only one. (This trick is also effectively done with tissue paper.) This should be done at least 6 feet away from the audience.

Preparation

Crumple a paper napkin into a ball and place it on your table before performing the trick. The napkin that will be torn is placed over the crumpled ball to hide it from view as shown below.

1: Behind the Scenes: Hiding the ball.

2: Behind the Scenes: When you lift the napkin at the beginning of the trick, the crumpled ball is picked up and hidden in your right hand, behind the napkin.

3: "Ladies and gentlemen, I'm going to use a paper napkin for this demonstration."

4: "I'll need a few pieces." Tear the napkin down the center, in half and in half again.

5: Continue tearing the napkin. Keep talking as you do this. The crumpled ball remains concealed in your right hand, out of audience view.

6: Behind the Scenes: This is the best way to conceal the napkin, in the crook of your fourth and fifth fingers. Your other fingers are then free to tear the napkin.

7: The torn napkin is crumpled into a ball. Explain this and continue talking as you press both hands together. At this point an important switch occurs, unseen by the audience.

8: Behind the Scenes: As you press your hands together on the crumpled ball, the concealed napkin is rolled to your left and the torn one placed in your right hand.

9: Place the torn ball in your pocket and leave it there, while saying, "We'll just add a sprinkle of magic dust." Bring out your hand to sprinkle imaginary dust on the napkin.

10: Blow gently on the napkin and begin to open it slowly. Avoid tearing it as you open the ball.

11: "Voila! The napkin is whole again."

A Delicate Balance

In the demonstration of this trick the photographs tell most of the story. You will need a small glass and a playing card to do the trick.

12: "Ladies and gentlemen . . . a playing card and an empty glass."

13: "And now for an exhibition of skill. Hold your breath as I try to balance the glass on the edge of the playing card."

14: The glass apparently balances on the edge of the card. Note the position of the hand.

15: Behind the Scenes: The secret—your tricky thumb is really balancing the glass.

Cut and Restored Rope

This classic trick illustrates a restoration. A rope is apparently cut into two pieces, then magically restored to a single length. All you need is a 4-foot length of soft rope and scissors.

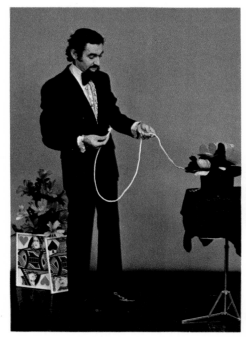

16: "Here's what you can do with a leftover piece of rope," says George Schindler.

A

Figure A: A square knot is tied by bringing the right end over the left, then the left over the right. The cut must be to the right (where the scissors are) of the square knot.

17: "I'll tie a simple knot in the center of the rope" (see Figure A). Bring the lower end of the rope to a point near the center, but actually tie a square knot.

18: "Watch carefully as I cut the rope in the center." Cut to the right of the square knot (Figure A), and trim the short end of the rope. After the rope has been cut as shown here, you supposedly have two pieces of rope but really have one long piece and a false knot. The cutting merely snipped off a small piece from one end of the rope.

19: "Two pieces of rope held by a knot . . . and now some hanky-panky . . ." Blow toward the knot and pull the ends of the rope apart with a snap.

20: The false knot flies into the air as the rope snaps. The rope is now seen to be in one piece. You will surely be asked, "How did you do it?" One answer: "Very effectively."

Color Changing Wand

This is a good opening trick that can be performed anywhere, any time. You will have to make a magic wand but after all, what magician doesn't have a wand? Besides, you'll then have a wand to use for other tricks. The wand in this trick is a *feke*, a magician's word for gimmick, and it is easily made from a wooden dowel. This is an example of a transformation because it involves a color change.

Preparation

To make the feke wand you need: a wooden dowel 13 inches long and ½ inch in diameter. Dowels can be bought at any lumberyard. The length is not critical but 13 inches is easy to handle. The wand will later be wrapped with construction paper two inches smaller; thus, a standard-size 8½-by-11-inch sheet of construction paper will fit a 13-inch dowel perfectly.

Paint the dowel a bright color, in this case red; then paint an inch of white at each tip. Glossy enamel paint is recommended. When the paint is dry, cut a strip from an 8½-by-11-inch sheet of green construction paper wide enough for the paper to cover just the colored section of the wand, leaving the white tips exposed (photograph 21). Next, wrap the paper around the wand forming a tube. With clear tape or rubber cement, secure the tube so that it fits snugly around the wand (photograph 22), but not so tight it will keep the dowel from sliding out. You now have a green wand. In addition to the wand, you need a sheet of newspaper, preferably tabloid size, which is easy to roll.

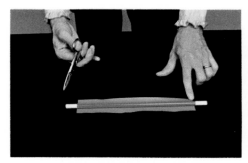

21: Behind the Scenes: A piece of colored construction paper, 2 inches shorter than the dowel, is cut to fit around the colored part of the dowel.

22: Behind the Scenes: Tape the construction paper around the dowel so that the wand appears to be the color of the paper.

Presentation

Pick up the wand in one hand and the sheet of newspaper in the other.

23: "For this demonstration we will use a sheet of newspaper and a green wand." Stress the word green; the effect will be more astounding later on.

24: Position the wand as you start to roll so that a white tip is visible beyond the newspaper's edge. "I am going to hide the wand in the newspaper."

25: Roll the newspaper several times around the wand so the wand is covered (not too tightly). Every so often push the wand, keeping one of the hite tips in audience view at all times. Now, blow gently on the newspaper. "Abracadabra." (Use any magic words.)

26: "Now I simply remove the wand from the paper. Watch the miracle as it magically changes from green to red." Be sure to grip the center of the paper firmly so that the green tube slides off and stays inside the newspaper.

27: Present the red wand. Remember to crumple the newspaper immediately and throw it away.

Sleight-of-Hand

"The hand is quicker than the eye," one often hears after someone is fooled by a sleight-of-hand performer. Quick movements aren't always the key to card tricks, coin tricks and vanishing and reappearing balls, however. Speed is important, but it is the mind that is fooled, not the eye. Sleight-of-hand feats are accomplished by misdirection (distracting the audience away from the key movement) and skillful manipulations. The effects on these two pages by Frank Garcia are modern classics demonstrating various sleights without giving away the trade secrets.

Multiplying Ball Trick

Originally done with billiard balls, this trick is now performed with golf balls. Many hours, or even years, of practice are needed before a magician can cause the balls to appear and reappear skillfully. Here we see a single ball which multiplies to two, then four, and finally eight balls from thin air. Entire books have been written on this trick with its many variations.

Cups and Balls

A drawing depicting this trick was found on the wall of an Egyptian temple, so it was always thought to have originated there; but now there is further evidence to suggest that this most ancient of tricks was devised in China using sea shells at an even earlier date. Today, Canadian Dai Vernon is considered to be twentieth-century master of cups and balls.

In the following sequence, Frank Garcia demonstrates a classic cup-and-ball feat. A ball is placed under each cup. The balls then vanish, one by one, and finally reappear in the center cup.

Salt Vanish

This is a modern classic originally presented by vaudeville magicians. The trick is accomplished with sleight-of-hand and is a feature of Frank Garcia's stage act.

29: The salt is then poured into the left hand.

28: First, the magician mysteriously produces a salt shaker from nowhere. He puts the cap in his pocket.

30: The salt mysteriously vanishes from the magician's hand.

31: Salt reappears and seems to pour endlessly from the *right* hand.

Coin Vanish

This is a trick that can be done at a dinner table. It baffles everyone who sees it, yet the secret is simple. Your audience can be only a few feet away as you perform the trick: a glass is placed over a coin and "presto," the coin disappears. The method is based on the "black art" principle. Black against black will not be seen, nor will white against white.

Preparation

Here's how it is done. The open end of a glass is secretly covered with a piece of white paper, (Figure B below). White adhesive-backed vinyl, available by the yard, is recommended because it peels off easily when required. The trick is ideally done on a white surface of the same white vinyl so that the whites match exactly. Then, when the glass covers the coin you see white on white with no variation in color.

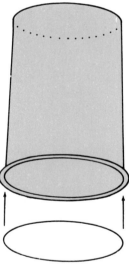

B
Figure B: Invert the glass on the sticky side of the vinyl. Cut off excess so that the vinyl is flush with rim of the glass.

32: Rest the inverted glass on a white surface. Have a paper napkin handy. Borrow a coin from a spectator and place it on the white paper.

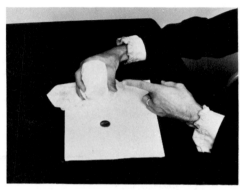

33: Cover the glass with the napkin so that the napkin molds to the glass as shown. Explain what you are doing. "Let's cover the coin to see if you can remember if it's heads or tails." Lift the glass still covered with the napkin and place both on top of the coin.

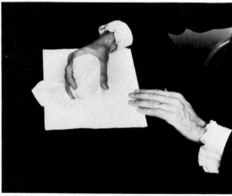

34: Be sure to center the glass over the coin or the trick won't work. "Is it heads up or tails up?"

35: Lift only the napkin, taking care not to crush or crumple it. "Wrong, it's gone!" (The coin is actually hidden by the vinyl.)

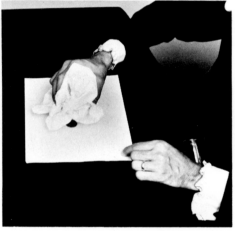

36: "Let's see if we can make it reappear. Do you know any magic words?" Cover the glass with the napkin again. "One, two, three." Lift the glass off the coin. Astonishingly, it has reappeared.

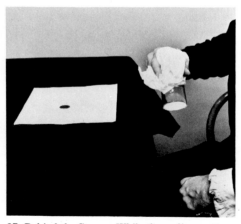

37: Behind the Scenes: While the audience attention is on the coin, bring the glass and napkin to the edge of the table. Drop the glass in your lap, but continue to hold the napkin (which holds the shape of the glass) as if the glass were still there.

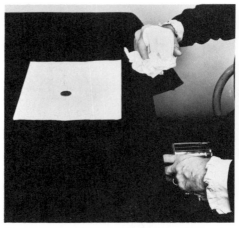

38: As your hand pretends to hold the glass under the napkin, suggest to the audience, "Now we'll make the coin change value."

39: Place the "glass" (actually just the napkin) back over the coin. Dramatically, smash it flat with your left hand. The "glass" is gone.

40: Reach under the table with your right hand and peel off the white paper and drop it to the floor. "Sometimes the trick backfires and the glass goes through the table."

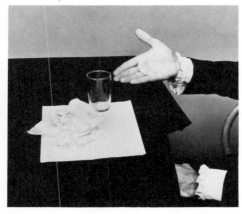

41: Bring the glass from under the table and present it to your astonished audience.

Paper Bag Mysteries

There are hundreds of tricks one can do with a paper bag or two, especially bags with false pockets. In this trick, a handkerchief seems to have traveled invisibly through thin air from one bag to another. The same bag can be used to make a handkerchief vanish or to produce a stream of colorful ribbons or handkerchiefs.

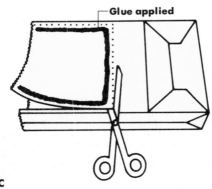

Glue applied

C

Figure C: Cut out a section from the side of a small grocery bag, slightly smaller than its width and about half its length. This section will be pasted inside an identical bag.

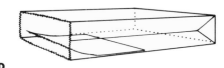

D

Figure D: Dab rubber cement around three edges of the pocket and glue it in place inside the bag. The top of the bag and the top of the cut section should be flush.

Preparation

Before doing this trick you need to prepare two bags with false pockets. The size of the bag is not that important but a No. 6 grocery bag works well. Figures C and D below show how to prepare a bag with a false pocket; you should prepare two such bags. A false pocket is made by cutting a section from an identical bag and pasting it inside the bag used for the trick. This trick uses two bags with false pockets so you need four No. 6 grocery bags to prepare the trick. You also need scissors, a small amount of rubber cement, and two identical handkerchiefs.

42: Behind the Scenes: After the false pocket is glued in place, it is large enough to hide a small handkerchief. (Silk is best if available.)

43: Behind the Scenes: Before your performance, one handkerchief is inserted into the false pocket of one of the bags. An identical handkerchief and second prepared bag are on the table as well.

44: "A small bag with nothing inside." Take care to keep your fingers over the pocket where the handkerchief is hidden when you display the bag to spectators.

45: Pick up the green handkerchief and stuff it into the pocket of the *other* bag, making it appear that you are putting it into the center of the bag. "Keep your eye on the bag with the green handkerchief."

46: Looking toward the first bag, supposedly empty, have everyone call out a few magic words. (Make up your own.)

47: Slowly extract the green handkerchief from the false pocket. "We have just caused the handkerchief to fly around the room and into the empty bag."

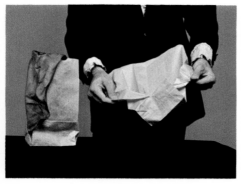

48: Just to prove to the audience that the handkerchief has really moved from one bag to another, tear the other bag apart (holding the false pocket tightly closed, of course).

Variation

This trick can be performed as a "vanish" with one bag. Take a silk handkerchief and stuff it into the false pocket while you pretend to push it into the bag, distracting your audience with patter. Now tear the bag apart, being careful to tear only the outer bag, not the false pocket. The handkerchief is gone!

Water in the Hat

This trick is fun at a party and one you can prepare quickly at home or in a friend's house. You will need two medium-sized paper cups, the sturdy kind with a lip at the top, a pitcher of water, and a hat that will hold a cup so that it does not show above the brim.

Preparation

Figure E, below, shows how to prepare the paper cups. With a razor, cut the bottom out of one cup. Cut the top lip off the second cup. The bottomless cup will then fit inside the lipless cup. This done, the "feke" now looks like one, not two, cups.

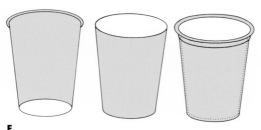

E
Figure E: A cup without a bottom (left) is fit into a lipless cup (middle) to make a "feke" cup (right).

Presentation

Explain that you recently started doing magic and you just learned a new trick. Ask to borrow a hat from someone in the audience, but be prepared with your own in case no one is wearing one. The effect depends upon how well you appear to be making mistakes.

49: The hat, water and fitted cups are placed on your table. Be sure to keep the hat *above* the eye level of your spectators.

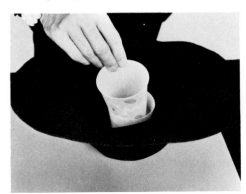

50: Place the double cup in the hat. "The idea is to pour water into the cup so that it looks like it's going into the hat." Behind the Scenes: Remove the cup (the inner section only, as shown by placing the index finger inside the cup and the thumb outside. Pull up with the index finger and down with the thumb). Show the cup then replace it, as if absentmindedly, on the table instead of back in the hat. The lipless cup remains in the hat. (So you see, that's how you create the illusion.)

51: Pick up a pitcher of water and begin to pour some into the cup in the hat. "You see, it looks like it's going into the hat, but it actually goes into the cup" (referring to the cup on the table). This usually gets a laugh.

52: Do a double-take. "Oops, wrong way. I forgot to put the cup in the hat."

53: Now, take the bottomless cup and fit it into the cup in the hat.

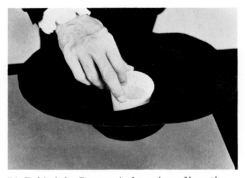

54: Behind the Scenes: A close view of how the two cups fit to look like one.

55: "Was this a very expensive hat, sir?" After your laugh explain, "I'm new at this. But I can fix it." Take the double cup out of the hat and pour the water back into the pitcher.

56: Show the hat empty and dry.

MAPS AND PATHFINDING
Finding Your Way

Right now, you know where you are. You are sitting comfortably in a chair in your living room, perhaps. All is well. The purpose of this article is to keep you that way, to help you carry your easy-chair security around with you wherever you roam. In times past, when wilderness prevailed, people were far more preoccupied with trying to maintain their bearings. Nowadays it is possible to spend a lifetime without ever experiencing a shadow of a doubt about where one is. Apart from the rudimentary navigation involved in making our way around town, we may even forget entirely about questions of orientation. Nevertheless, wilderness areas do exist—and they seem to beckon more as their size diminishes—so everyone needs to know a little about the best means of finding his way, of keeping track of himself, in the woods or in any other unfamiliar terrain.

Those who periodically approach the unknown—even the most venturesome of spirits—maintain a lifeline in the form of memory tricks to restore them eventually to the known world. In many primitive regions, native guides are famed for their uncanny powers of orientation. Their senses do become keenly honed from living in the wilds. But much of their expertise must be credited to their trained powers of observation and memory and their familiarity with broad expanses of land. They carry mental maps around with them that they update as they go.

As a culture develops and expands, mental maps no longer suffice, and real maps become necessary. To this day, wandering peoples such as Polynesians, Eskimos and Bedouins carve maps of their world on wood or bone, or draw them on the ground with sticks and shells. Drawn maps date back to 600 B.C. in Greece, with probable antecedents in Babylon and Egypt.

Crude compasses appeared in China around 2500 B.C. and were among the articles brought back to Europe by Marco Polo in the thirteenth century.

Once you have mastered the use of maps and compasses, there is little likelihood that you will ever lose your bearings. Instructions for making and using them are given below, followed by a discussion of more primitive means of orientation.

Roger "Strider" Coco is one of the new breed of mountain men. At home in the wilderness (and Elmhurst, New York), he's a skilled hunter, trapper and prospector. When he's not out leading mountain packing expeditions in the American and Canadian west, he draws maps for Walking News, Inc., and maintains trails and shelters for the New York/New Jersey Trail Conference.

Putting yourself on the map

The single best way to get and keep your bearings is to use an accurate map. You can make it work for you like an aerial view of the area you are in. You can put yourself on the map, spotting yourself from the air as it were, and thus see what lies beyond your limited horizons. Maps produced by the U.S. Geological Survey are highly recommended. They are reliable because they are precisely detailed (most are made from aerial photographs), and many of the more popular ones are revised frequently. They indicate mountains, valleys, water, the general slope of the land and other physical features. Consulting one can save a lot of unnecessary climbing and descending. For a price list of inexpensive geological survey maps of the area where you live or region you intend to visit, write Distribution Section, U.S. Geological Survey, 1200 South Eads Street, Arlington, Virginia 22202 (locations east of the Mississippi River), or Distribution Section, U.S. Geological Survey, Federal Center Building 41, Denver, Colorado 80225 (locations west of the Mississippi). Many foreign governments also publish maps of this type. In Canada, write Map Distribution Office, Department of Mines and Technical Surveys, Ottawa, Ontario, and in Mexico, Direccion de Geografia y Meteorologia, Tacusaya, Distrito Federal. Hiking clubs, local governments, geographic societies, and commercial map publishers are likely sources of other good maps. But some maps will let you

The call of virgin wilds like this one in New Brunswick, Canada, grows louder with the spread of civilization. But how to get around amid all those trees and streams? This entry will help you refresh your knowledge of basic pathfinding skills.

Symbol	
Land area	
Water area	
Area sometimes under water	
Marshy area	
Hard surface highway, heavy duty	
Hard surface highway, medium duty	
Improved dirt road	
Unimproved dirt road (jeep trail)	
Trail	
Bridge	
Ford	
Railroad	
Building	
School	
Church	
Cemetery	
Telephone, telegraph, pipeline	
Power transmission line	
Open pit or quarry	
Spring	
Well	
Summit	
Seasonal stream	
Perennial stream	
Contour line	

A

Figure A: The symbols above are commonly found on hikers' maps and represent a wide variety of both man-made objects and natural features.

1142

down just when you need them most—in the least accessible regions. Taking the accuracy of a map for granted can be as much of a folly as assuming something is true because it appears in print. If you can, ask local residents to verify the accuracy of maps you have or ask them to sketch a map of their immediate countryside. Gas-station maps and commercial touring atlases are usually fairly accurate for highway travel, but they are often inaccurate and too small in scale for use off the pavement path.

Reading a Topographical Map

The map opposite is an actual-size reproduction of a section of a geological survey map. It has a scale or 1:24,000. This means that 1 inch on the map represents 24,000 inches, or 2,000 feet, on the ground. As with most maps, north is at the top. This map is distinguished by a wealth of information it gives about topography—the earth's contours. Land areas are shown in green, water areas in blue. Marshlands are represented by blue tufts of grass on a green background. The brown lines are contour lines, indicating elevation; the elevation of all points on a given contour line will be the same. Thin lines show intervals of 20 feet of altitude; thick ones occur at multiples of 100 feet above sea level. Thus four light lines would be found between each pair of dark lines where the terrain sloped continuously. Numbers on the dark lines represent their elevation in feet above sea level; the direction of a slope can be determined by noting whether the sequence of numbers ascends or descends. The steepness of a slope is indicated by the relative density of contour lines; lines close together show a steep slope or cliff, and lines at wide intervals indicate gentle slopes. The elevation in feet of lake surfaces and mountain peaks is shown numerically. The names of important physical features are given; buildings, roads and other man-made objects are shown symbolically. Figures in the lower right-hand corner and along the sides of the map give the longitude and latitude of the area shown. (Figure A shows commonly used map symbols, and Figure B shows a perspective view of a landscape with a topographical map of the same area.)

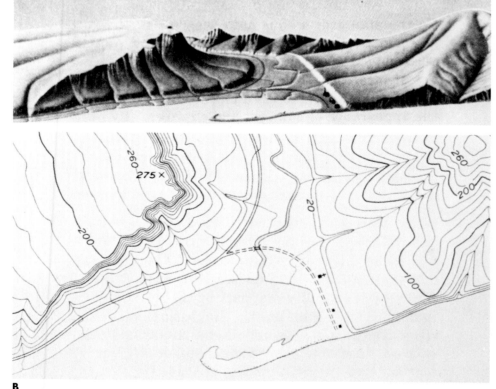

B

Figure B: The topographical map of an imaginary landscape, above, faithfully shows the land forms and other features depicted at top in an artist's perspective sketch of the same landscape. The difference between steep and gentle slopes is shown by the relative frequency of contour lines.

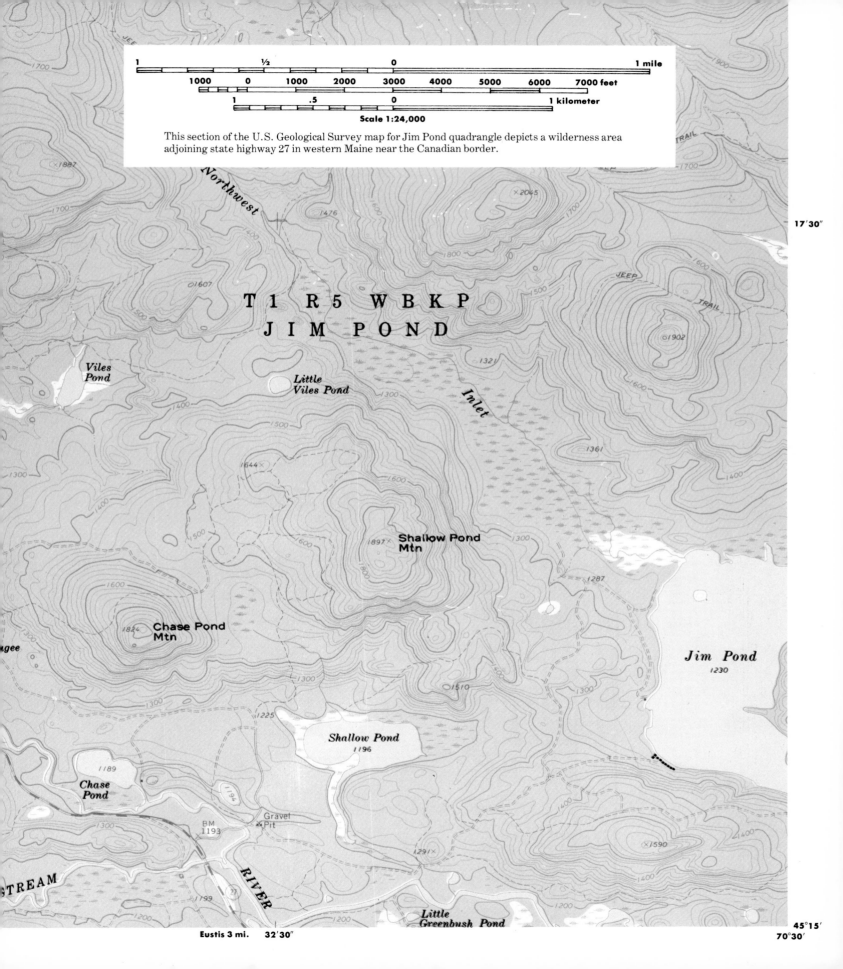

Scale 1:24,000

This section of the U.S. Geological Survey map for Jim Pond quadrangle depicts a wilderness area adjoining state highway 27 in western Maine near the Canadian border.

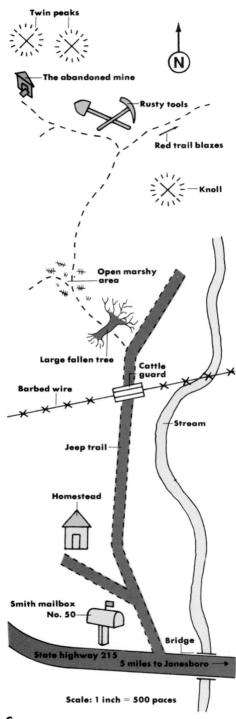

C

Figure C: This freehand map shows the way from state highway 215 to an abandoned mine. It incorporates many of the details that make a map useful: identification of north, a good scale, road access, physical features, man-made objects, trail junctions and intermediate landmarks.

Using a Topographical Map

To illustrate how a map such as the one on page 1143 might be used, imagine that a man wise in the ways of the woods has been fishing without success on the north end of Viles Pond (left of center) and decides to head for Jim Pond, where fishing is reported to be better. He could take a familiar roundabout way by using the dirt road that skirts Chase Pond Mountain to the west and south and leads to the gravel pit where the Jim Pond turnoff begins. Or he could use this map to find his own path through the woods—and get a chance to try out two rarely visited ponds along the way. He takes the trail that leads east from Viles Pond. He plans to leave the trail where it veers to the northeast and head through the woods from there to Little Viles Pond. By measuring the length of this section of trail against the scale shown at the top of the map, he estimates that he will have to leave the trail after about 1,500 feet, for him a 10-minute walk. Having walked this long, he notices that the trail does indeed veer off to the left, so he heads into the woods on the line that the trail would have followed if it had continued straight. The two thin brown lines on the map between this point and Little Viles Pond tell him that he will have to walk gradually uphill, as they represent ascending contours 1,360 and 1,380 feet above sea level from west to east. The dark brown lines to the left and right of his course each mark the 1,400-foot contour and tell him that he will need to stay within a gentle depression to stay on course. Looking at the actual landscape, on his right he can see two peaks. The map identifies them as Chase Pond Mountain and the slightly higher Shallow Pond Mountain. Straight ahead rise two higher but unnamed peaks. The one to the south lies directly on his course—the map shows it to be in line with his path to Little Viles Pond. Walking within all these guidelines, he arrives at Little Viles Pond in about 10 minutes. After fishing awhile, he decides to move on. From this point a straight-line hike to Jim Pond would take him up and over the steep eastern slope of Shallow Pond Mountain. He avoids the unnecessary climb by skirting to the east of the mountain. Traveling east toward the original target peak, his path starts downhill toward a marshy stream. So he veers to the right to stay on level ground, keeping the marsh on his left and the steeper slope of Shallow Pond Mountain on his right. He visualizes a path on the map between the 1,300- and 1,400-foot contour lines that go east and south from the vicinity of Little Viles Pond. After walking for some time, he notices that he has passed the peak of Shallow Pond Mountain, and the steep slope on his right has begun to level off. He climbs a low tree and sees the blue water of Jim Pond about a mile ahead, and about halfway to it the much smaller outline of a tiny unnamed pond west of Jim Pond. He works his way down to the little pond, and after fishing it for a while, heads east until he hits the jeep trail that leads to his destination. This method of staying on a track by using the land forms shown on contour maps can be used independently or with the help of a compass (page 1146).

The practice of traveling short distances across wilderness areas without regard to established trails, as in the example just given, is known as bushwhacking. Although it is a satisfying test of agility and ingenuity, it is not recommended as a general practice. Bushwacking should be attempted only by an experienced woodsman for a special purpose—fishing, hunting, trapping, photographing, prospecting or cave exploring.

Making a Map

At some point you may want to make a map yourself to keep track of your whereabouts or to give a friend directions. The geological survey map was prepared with sophisticated equipment. But you can make a usable map with pencil and paper alone (Figure C). Begin by indicating north (or any other direction) on one side. Then establish some reasonable scale, such as 1 inch equals 100, 500, or 1,000 paces. It will be helpful to remember that on flat and open terrain, an average walker covers about 100 paces a minute. Knowing how fast you walk will save you the trouble of counting every step. Indicate the access to the mapped area— highway, jeep trail, foot trail, river or other familiar landmarks. Include the approximate locations of any features, natural or man-made, that will reassure the user of the map that he is traveling the right way. It is not necessary to draw every little bend in the trail, but every trail junction should be clearly indicated. If a trail is blazed with a particular marking or color (page 1151), this should also be shown.

CRAFTNOTE: THE EARTH'S CIRCLES

Many pathfinding skills are derived from elementary principles of navigation, which in turn come from geometry. Two systems of notation indicate parts of (and points on) circles of the earth: compass directions, as applied to a real or imagined horizon, and the circles of longitude and latitude, as marked on globes and maps. Both are based on the same set of measurements but they differ in their applications.

For convenience, any circle can be divided into four quarters with a cross running through the circle's center. If the

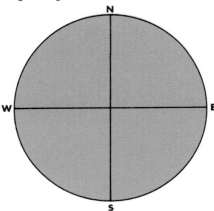

horizon is viewed as a circle, this cross can indicate the cardinal directions: north, east, south and west. To locate points between cardinal directions

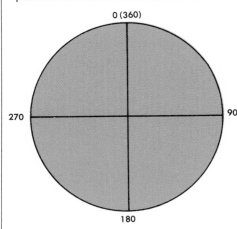

geometers have divided the circle into 360 arcs called degrees. These can be visualized as the gaps between 360 equally spaced spokes radiating from the circle's center. This number, 360, is convenient to use, being divisible by many numbers: 2, 3, 4, 5, 6, 8, 9, 10, 12, 15, 18, 20, etc. One degree can be subdivided into 60 smaller units called minutes, and one minute into 60 seconds.

In navigation, north is the starting (and finishing) point of the circle of compass directions and is designated as 0 or 360 degrees. The sequence of numbers runs clockwise, so east is 90 degrees, south is 180 degrees and west is 270 degrees. Since 90 degrees refers to a bearing that runs exactly to the east, 45 degrees would indicate a bearing halfway between north and east, called northeast, and so on.

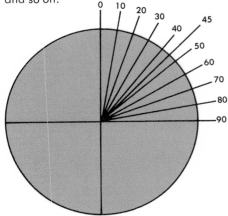

When we move from a horizon that is two-dimensional to a three-dimensional globe, this simple system is no longer adequate. To divide up the earth's surface, a grid system has been devised, based on an imaginary line running through the interior of the earth from pole to pole sliced in half at right angles through the middle of the earth. The intersection of this slice with the earth's surface is the equator; designated as 0 degrees, it is the primary east-west mapping line. Other east-west lines running parallel to it, called parallels of latitude, are designated by the number of degrees of a circle equal to their distance, north and south of the equator. All the parallels lie between 0 and 90 degrees north (the North Pole) or 0 and 90 degrees south (the South Pole). The

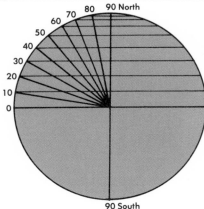

equator itself is then divided, like any other circle, into 360 degrees, and these points are connected to the poles by meridians of longitude. (The width of 1 degree of longitude is about 69 miles at the equator, decreasing to zero at the poles. The width of 1 degree of latitude is about 69 miles everywhere.) The meridian of Greenwich, England, has been

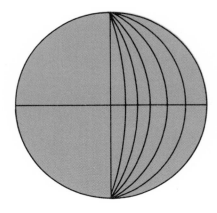

established as the starting point of the longitude circle and is designated as 0 degrees. Longitude is measured 180 degrees east or west of Greenwich, the two together making the full earth's circumference. With the resulting gridwork of meridians and parallels any place on the earth's surface can be measured and recorded. A point described as 30 degrees N., 60 degrees W. is located on the 30th parallel north of the equator and on the 60th meridian west of Greenwich—a point near New Orleans, Louisiana.

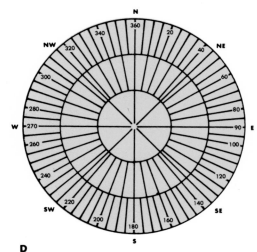

D

Figure D: A navigational protractor divides a circle into 360 degrees, numbered clockwise from the top (representing north). Some compasses have one built in.

A compass with a mirror at a 45-degree angle, a sighting device (gap at top) and a built-in movable protractor can be used to project an exact horizontal bearing onto a vertical landmark.

Making and using a compass

A compass is simply a balanced strip of magnetized metal free to swing in any direction. You can make one by stroking a needle in one direction (from eye to point is safest) with a piece of silk and floating it in a still liquid, such as a small puddle or a glass of water. To keep it from sinking, oil it lightly (by running it—carefully—through your hair if no other means is available). Then lower it gently onto the water with loosely looped strands of thread or blades of grass. Once it is afloat remove these supports. The needle will turn until it comes to rest in a north-south direction. If you have stroked the needle from eye to point, the eye will point north.

A home-made compass is inconvenient because it has to be remagnetized frequently and because each reading requires a delicate manipulation. Commercial compasses are easier to use because "north" is clearly marked and the arrow is suspended on a point and protected by a case. Some compasses may have a needle that glows in the dark, a clip for fastening to clothing, a mirror and sighting apparatus to project a bearing onto a vertical landmark, or a housing that can be rotated to indicate the exact number of degrees your bearing varies from north. If you buy a compass, also buy a spare in case—as often happens—you doubt the accuracy of a reading. Even good compasses sometimes demagnetize or jam. Keep the compasses away from each other and from other metals. If there is a discrepancy in the two, favor the one whose needle oscillates more freely.

To use a compass, hold it still and level until the needle comes to rest. Then double-check by turning it over a few times (gently) and taking a second reading. Make sure the indicator is swinging freely. The pointer will indicate north, but if the compass does not have a housing that rotates, other directions must be filled in mentally. Points other than the cardinal directions can be estimated to within a few degrees by comparing the compass reading with a protractor (Figure D). Most compasses with movable housings have protractor calibrations marked on them.

Determining the direction of landmarks with a compass is useful whenever you come to high ground or a clearing that exposes a distant horizon. A careful reading of a map will tell you what you are looking at, and the compass reading will indicate its direction. Later, when your landmark is obscured from view, you will still be able to head directly toward it. (However, in using the compass with a map, you will have to compensate for the fact that magnetic north and true north are not identical, as explained below.)

You may want to test your ability with a compass on familiar ground. In a large open area such as a city park, place a coin (or, if you are not a gambler, some other small object) at your feet. Take a compass reading and walk 100 paces in a straight line in any direction. Then take a new reading and alter your course by adding or subtracting 120 degrees from your original bearing. If, for example, you started by traveling due south (180 degrees), take a new bearing at either 300 or 60 degrees

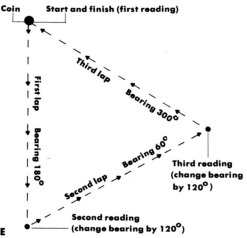

E

Figure E: To test your skill with a compass, walk off a triangle with equal sides of any number of paces, changing course by 120 degrees of the compass at each turn. Place a coin on the ground at your starting point and see if you can return to the coin by following your compass bearings alone.

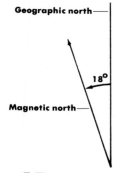

F

Figure F: The compass-error diagram for the map on page 1143 indicates that a magnetic north compass reading taken within the area shown on the map will lie 18 degrees to the left (west) of geographic north—on which the map is based.

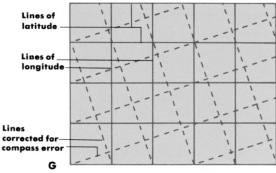

G

Figure G: To adjust a map for field use, redraw its lines of latitude and longitude, as shown in dashed lines, to reflect the fact that magnetic north and geographic north differ; here, an 18-degree adjustment toward the west is shown.

(Figure E). Resume your walk on this new bearing and travel the same number of paces. Finally, alter your course once more by 120 degrees in the same direction and walk off the same number of paces. If you have used your compass skillfully, you will be standing close enough to your starting point to find your coin easily.

When traveling with map and compass, a distinction must be made between the geographic north pole (on which maps are based) and the magnetic north pole (which controls compasses). The magnetic north pole is a point in northern Canada about 1,400 miles from the geographic north pole. In most places on earth, a compass reading of north will come close to true north but will not exactly coincide with it, and in the northern corners of the U.S. (not including Alaska) the error may be as much as 25 degrees. At points on a line that passes through Hudson Bay, the western Great Lakes, and the western Carolinas, the compass will point directly at the North Pole. Geological survey maps include a marginal diagram giving the correction needed to make compass reading and map agree. The diagram for the Jim Pond map is shown in Figure F. It shows that magnetic north is 18 degrees west of true north. If you were traveling with this map and a compass, you could either add 18 degrees to every compass reading you take or place an overlay grid on the map tilted 18 degrees counterclockwise so map and compass agree.

Getting Back

There are two special ways to use a compass that will be valuable when you are camping. In the first instance, if you locate your camp next to a long and easily followed guide such as a river, you can travel away from camp in the morning free from care if you note your direction of travel and keep approximately to it. But if you travel north in the morning, for example, do not make the mistake of simply traveling south on the return trip (Figure H). That would get you back to the river, but then you would not know whether camp lies upstream or down. To avoid guesswork, make your return trip several degrees to one side of the outbound path (Figure I). Then, when you hit the river, you will know without doubt which way to go. If you slanted off to the left on the return trip (east), then turn right (west) at the river, and camp lies just ahead.

The same idea can be used in returning to an existing dead-end trail (Figure J). Here, however, you also need to note the time you left the trail. If you leave camp at 5 A.M., say, reach the end of an existing north-south trail at 8 A.M., and walk north from the end of that trail for two more hours, to expect to rejoin the trail by simply walking south for two hours would be risky indeed. Instead, to avoid guesswork, walk south-southeast for three hours. The extra hour will guarantee that you have pulled alongside the existing trail. Then walk west to pick up the trail (Figure J).

A watch is useful in the wilds because it is easier to measure distance in time than in miles. You don't need to know how many miles you have walked. But you can be sure that if you return over similar terrain at about the same pace, a like amount of time will bring you close to your starting point.

A watch can also be used as a compass if the sun is casting a shadow and if you have the watch set to local standard (not daylight savings) time. Hold the watch

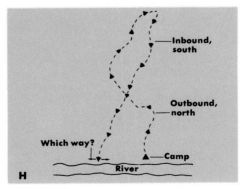

Figure H: If you return to a camp on a river by traveling generally south after a northerly outbound walk, you will not know in which direction camp lies when you reach the river.

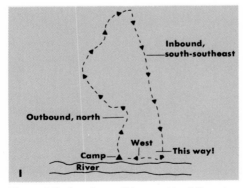

Figure I: By keeping well to one side of the outbound path on the return trip, you will have no doubt as to which way to turn when you arrive at the river. (Camp lies just ahead.)

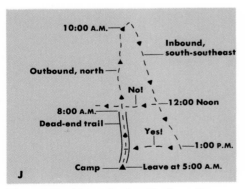

Figure J: To pick up a dead-end trail, use the same technique of keeping to one side, but lengthen your return walk to make sure you are alongside the trail you are trying to find.

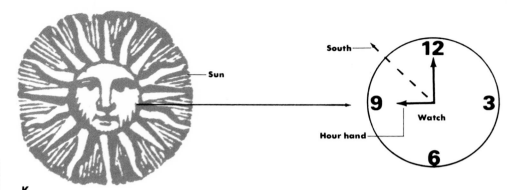

K

Figure K: You can use your watch—assuming it is set accurately on standard time—as a makeshift compass. Hold it horizontally and point the hour hand at the sun (or align it with a shadow cast by the sun). South will lie midway between the hour hand and twelve.

Date	Variation from true east at sunrise and true west at sunset at the equator
January 1	23 degrees South
February 1	18 degrees South
March 1	8 degrees South
April 1	4 degrees North
May 1	14 degrees North
June 1	22 degrees North
July 1	23 degrees North
August 1	18 degrees North
September 1	9 degrees North
October 1	3 degrees South
November 1	14 degrees South
December 1	22 degrees South

face horizontally with the hour hand pointing at the sun. This can best be done by holding a twig vertically at the edge of the dial so it casts a shadow directly along the hour hand. South—give or take a few degrees—will lie midway between the hour hand and the number 12. If you were to do this at 9 A.M., a line from the center of the watch to a point midway between 9 and 12 would point south (Figure K).

Survival Skills
Natural guides

Most pathfinding problems are solved with map and compass. It would be foolish not to use these aids when they are available. But if you have reason to doubt their accuracy, you can orient yourself with a careful reading of sun or stars—in favorable conditions, it should be noted. Other natural aids such as vegetation, winds and watersheds are general indicators but less reliable.

The Sun

The sun is the most widely used indicator of direction. We know the sun rises in the east and sets in the west, of course, but a large error can result if this is taken too literally. The sun rises exactly in the east and sets exactly in the west on only two days of the year, the vernal and autumnal equinoxes (around March 21 and September 23). At other times, it varies from these points by as much as 23½ degrees at the equator. At other points of the globe, the variation is even greater. In addition, the sun's back-and-forth movement is not constant, but slows as it approaches the year's solstices (about December 22 and June 21) and speeds up as it moves through the equinoxes. The table shown at the left gives the fluctuations from true east at sunrise and true west at sunset for different times at the equator. The accuracy of the table decreases gradually away from the equator, but the figures given are correct to within a few degrees at 50 degrees latitude (southern Canada). The error increases sharply nearer the North Pole.

Determining a direction by the point of sunrise or sunset is further complicated by the fact that an ideal horizon—such as an expanse of ocean or flat, bare ground—is rare. The sun moves at right angles to the horizon only twice a year in the tropics; at other times and in other places it rises and sets at a highly variable angle to the horizon, fluctuating a full 90 degrees depending on latitude and time of year. Because even a distant range of low hills obscures the sea-level horizon, the angular movement of the sun can cause a considerable error, as much as 10 or 15 degrees (Figure L). Where high mountains block the view, greater inaccuracies will occur.

Much simpler is to note the sun's location at true noon. North of the Tropic of Capricorn (23½ degrees north of the equator) the sun will always be exactly south at noon. (Local time, especially daylight savings time, may vary from true noon by as much as 90 minutes. For this reason, a watch set by local solar time is a great convenience in the woods.)

It is sometimes hard to get an accurate reading of the sun; clouds may make it impossible to know just where the sun is, though shadows are cast even on an overcast day. In regions and seasons in which the sun approaches the overhead

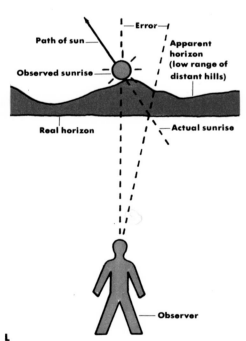

L

Figure L: Anyone watching the sun rise over terrain that is not level sees the sun appear at some distance to one side of its actual point of rising, since the sun's ascent is not vertical.

The rising sun in a far country may warm your heart, but it is unlikely that it will appear exactly in the east, as the text explains.

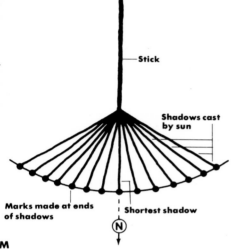

M

Figure M: To establish a north-south line, put a vertical stick in the ground before noon and mark the end of its shadow every 15 minutes, as long as the successive readings shorten. When they begin to lengthen, the mark closest to the stick will be directly north of the stick.

point, it is not easy to relate its position to a point on the horizon. In cases such as these, you can read the sun indirectly from the shadow cast by a vertical stick. The shadow will, of course, point north at true noon.

If you do not know the time, you can still take your bearings by putting a stick in the ground well before noon. Mark the end of its shadow every 15 minutes or so. The shortest shadow will occur at true noon, and the mark closest to the stick and the stick itself will establish a true north-south line (Figure M).

Once you are oriented, you will not have to stop for new readings—so long as you can travel in a straight line. If you carry a protractor such as the one in Figure D—or even a makeshift version—you can move in a direction other than one of the cardinal points. An additional reading at sunrise or sunset will tentatively verify your direction until a new reading is possible the following noon.

The Stars

Finding directions by the stars is simple and reliable, though it can be done only at night when the sky is clear. Night orientation provides a good double-check of calculations made during the day. It is usually easy to locate the North Star, the absolute and invariable indicator of true north. While all the other stars move across the heavens nightly and appear or disappear seasonally, only the North Star seems to stand motionless, the pivotal point around which the other stars seem to rotate. (It lies so close to the center of stars rotating above us that its movement is imperceptible except in a time-lapse photograph.) You can locate this bright star by following an imaginary line through the two stars that form the outer edge of the Big Dipper (Figure N). If you have trouble finding the Big Dipper, look for Cassiopeia, the W-shaped constellation that is always on the opposite side of the North Star and about the same distance away (Figure N).

Vegetation

When the sun is hidden, the old adage that moss grows thickest on the shadiest part of a tree can be helpful, but it can also be misleading too. Normally the shadiest part of a tree will be the north side in the northern hemisphere—but only if the tree happens to be growing in the open, where full sunlight can reach it throughout the day. A tree growing north of a high cliff may actually have moss on the south side. Furthermore, some growths resembling moss thrive on the sunniest part of the tree. So, unless you can distinguish them, this method is worse than useless.

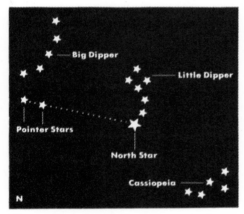

Figure N: To locate the North Star, extend an imaginary line from the pointer stars of the Big Dipper (the two outer stars of its cup). If the Big Dipper eludes you, look for it opposite W-shaped Cassiopeia, an equal distance on the other side of the North Star.

But the relationship of growth to light can help in other ways. Trees and other vegetation tend to grow more profusely on a slope that faces south, more sparsely on one facing north. Tree rings, visible in a stump, tend to be wider on the sunny side. Do not jump to any conclusion on the basis of only one or two observations. A good guess is possible only after making several, perhaps as many as a dozen, and then disregarding the more doubtful cases.

Trees frequently bend—and fall—in the direction of strong prevailing winds. If a region's wind pattern is known, a series of fallen trees can be used to get approximate bearings.

Wind

Reading the wind is possible too, though chancy. Wind does not blow in random directions; every region has its own prevailing patterns. If this pattern is known, it can provide a useful way of getting a quick approximate orientation. If, for example, the region you are in is one where the wind usually blows from the west, it would be easy to keep track of the direction by noticing the breeze from time to time. But since the direction of prevailing winds is usually only an average, this method is inexact in most places.

Indirect results of prevailing winds may be more helpful. Treefall is generally in the direction of strong prevailing winds, and both sand dunes and snow banks tend to be narrower and lower in the direction the prevailing wind comes from, higher and wider to leeward. Such indicators are usually more reliable than the wind itself because they tend to cancel temporary fluctuations.

Watercourses

The fact that water flows downhill, though useless as an indicator of direction, should not be overlooked. Smaller streams merge to form larger ones that eventually form rivers large enough to support farms and towns. So in general, the downstream direction is the way to civilization. There is always a chance, of course, that a strange stream may flow into an isolated lake or disappear into the ground. But such occurrences are relatively rare.

To cross a stream in the woods, look for a place where it is wide, because the shallowest water is almost always found in a wide bed. Let your feet get wet rather than risking a crossing on a slippery log or unsteady stones; if you must wade, remove clothing to keep it dry. Avoid steep banks because they are likely to continue steep below the water's surface.

Any time you come across an old wall or fence, a deserted mine or farmhouse, or an overgrown road or path, you will be in contact with civilization for you will almost always be able to see how those particular remnants were once reached from more permanent settlements.

Associated with streams are game trails. These natural paths—identifiable by animal tracks—bypass swampy bogs in wet country and lead to water in dry country. They are generally unrelated to compass direction but they are a help in walking through thickly overgrown land, in finding a gradual descent from high ground, and generally in avoiding natural obstacles.

Trails

From ancient times, trails have been marked in ways that should be known by all hikers. The almost universal symbol for a marked trail in the woods is the blaze—a half-moon shape cut from the bark of a tree. To blaze a trail, the woodsman picks trees that stand out in some way from others (as by unusual size or shape) and drives his hatchet first downwards into the bark at an almost vertical angle, then horizontally at the bottom of the first gash to remove a small chip (Figure O). Blazes are spaced at intervals depending on terrain and vegetation. Sometimes blazes 25 yards apart are difficult to follow; at other times they can be much farther apart. A general rule is that from a point midway between the two blazed trees, both should be visible, but closer placement avoids the need to search for the next blaze, and thus permits a faster rate of travel.

Many woodsmen blaze both sides of a tree, one blaze at eye level and the other lower. The lower blaze indicates the direction of the trail at that point. To make trails easier to follow, blazes are sometimes placed off-center on a tree. Thus, if you are following a straight trail marked by blazes centered on tree trunks and come upon a blaze placed left of center—perhaps with a corresponding off-center blaze on the back of the tree—it is probably a signal that the trail curves off to the right.

Some woodsmen oppose the use of hatchet blazes, especially in heavily traveled regions, and use alternate types of blazes such as paint dabs, cairns (neat, small piles of rocks), even metallic or plastic markers nailed to trees.

Getting Back on Course

If you should lose a blazed trail, do not settle for guesswork. The first step—assuming you can't work your way back to the last blaze you saw—is to establish a new starting point. Choose a landmark that is widely visible and use it as a pivot point for methodically searching in a spiral path. If no such landmark is available, pick any point and travel away from it and back to it in straight lines. Mark your exploratory paths with blazes or other signs that will help you to return to the starting point. At the moment when you first feel unsure of the trail, you probably are not very far from it.

It is sometimes hard to follow an old blazed trail. Trees fall or are scarred by fire; new growth hides old markings. In these conditions, look carefully at blazes to make sure they are man-made. Marks left by peeling bark and gnawing animals sometimes look like blazes. (In snow country, bark may be chewed well above ground level in winter.) A true blaze will be flat, will often be accompanied by a matching blaze on the other side of the tree and will usually bear the telltale grooves of the double hatchet blow at the bottom.

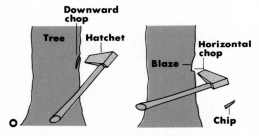

Figure O: A tree blaze is made by driving a hatchet down into the bark at a nearly vertical angle, then disengaging a chip of wood with a horizontal chop at the base of the first cut.

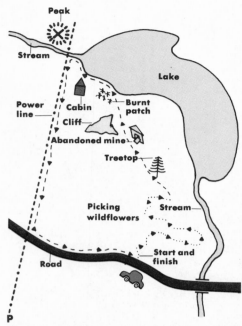

Figure P: This imaginary map shows an area surrounded by linear landmarks. A traveler can easily find his way by sighting on objects that will let him walk a straight line in any direction until he meets the perimeter, which will eventually lead him back to his starting point. Aimless wandering is avoided by homing successively on sighted objects two or three at a time (such as, in this case, the treetop, abandoned mine, cliff, burnt patch, cabin and peak).

Looking Back

When going through unfamiliar territory, look behind you occasionally to see what a rock or tree looks like from the opposite direction. This obvious—but often overlooked—trick will be a big help on your return journey.

Walking a Straight Line

If you are in an area that you know from experience or reliable maps to be circumscribed by roads or other easily identifiable boundaries, such as a river or a lakeshore (Figure P), you're as safe as you would be in your own backyard. Imagine you've parked your car at the roadside and gone into the woods to pick wildflowers. After a while you decide to return to your car. Which way to go? You know from the map that you can find your way back simply by walking in a straight line in any direction until you reach a perimeter marker that will lead you back to your starting point. To walk a straight line—not easy because there is a natural tendency to walk in a circle—you pick three landmarks (tree, rock outcropping and hilltop, for example), all directly in line. When you reach the nearest one, you select a fourth landmark beyond the third, proceed to the second, and so on. With practice, you would be able to walk in a straight line with only two landmarks in sight. This simple technique is invaluable in a real wilderness and worth practicing in the relative safety of, say, a city park.

For related projects, see "Bicycles," "Canoeing," "Gold Panning," "Kayaks," "Piloting," "Survival Skills" and "Shelters and Tents."

If you lose a blazed trail, choose a widely visible landmark close to you such as the bent tree-trunk this hiker is facing and use it as a pivot point for methodically searching in widening spirals around the landmark.